ICSA Study Text

International Finance and Administration Qualifications

Investment

ICSA Study Text

International Finance and Administration Qualifications

Investment

John Fadden and Peter Watterston

icsa

The Governance Institute

First published 2015
Published by ICSA Publishing Ltd
Saffron House
6–10 Kirby Street
London EC1N 8TS

Typeset by Paul Barrett Book Production, Cambridge
Printed in Great Britain by Lightning Source, Milton Keynes, Buckinghamshire

British Cataloguing in Publication Data
A catalogue record for this book is available from the British Library.

ISBN 9781 86072 735 1

Contents

Foreword

This study book is part of the investment in your success and demonstrates our commitment to help you achieve your qualifications.

It is specially produced for Intertrust and for your use.

Good luck with your studies.

HR, Learning & Development

How to use this study text

ICSA study texts developed to support ICSA's Level 4 International Finance and Administration Qualifications follow a standard format and include a range of navigational, self-testing and illustrative features to help you get the most out of the support materials.

Each text is divided into three main sections:

- introductory material
- the text itself
- additional reference information.

The sections below show you how to find your way around the text and make the most of its features.

Introductory material

The introductory section of each text includes a full contents list and the aims and learning outcomes for the modules in question.

Where relevant, the introductory section will also include a list of acronyms and abbreviations or a list of legal cases for reference.

The text itself

Each part opens with a list of the chapters to follow, an overview of what will be covered and learning outcomes for the part.

Every chapter opens with a list of the topics covered and an introduction specific to that chapter. Chapters are structured to allow students to break the content down into manageable sections for study. Each chapter ends with a summary of key content to reinforce understanding.

Features

The text is enhanced by a range of illustrative and self-testing features to assist understanding and to help you prepare for the examination. Each feature is presented in a standard format, so that you will become familiar with how to use them in your study.

These features are identified by a series of icons as shown below.

The texts also include tables, figures and other illustrations as relevant.

Reference material

The text ends with a range of additional guidance and reference material, including a glossary of key terms, a directory of web resources and a comprehensive index.

Stop and think

Test yourself

Worked examples

Making it work

Case law

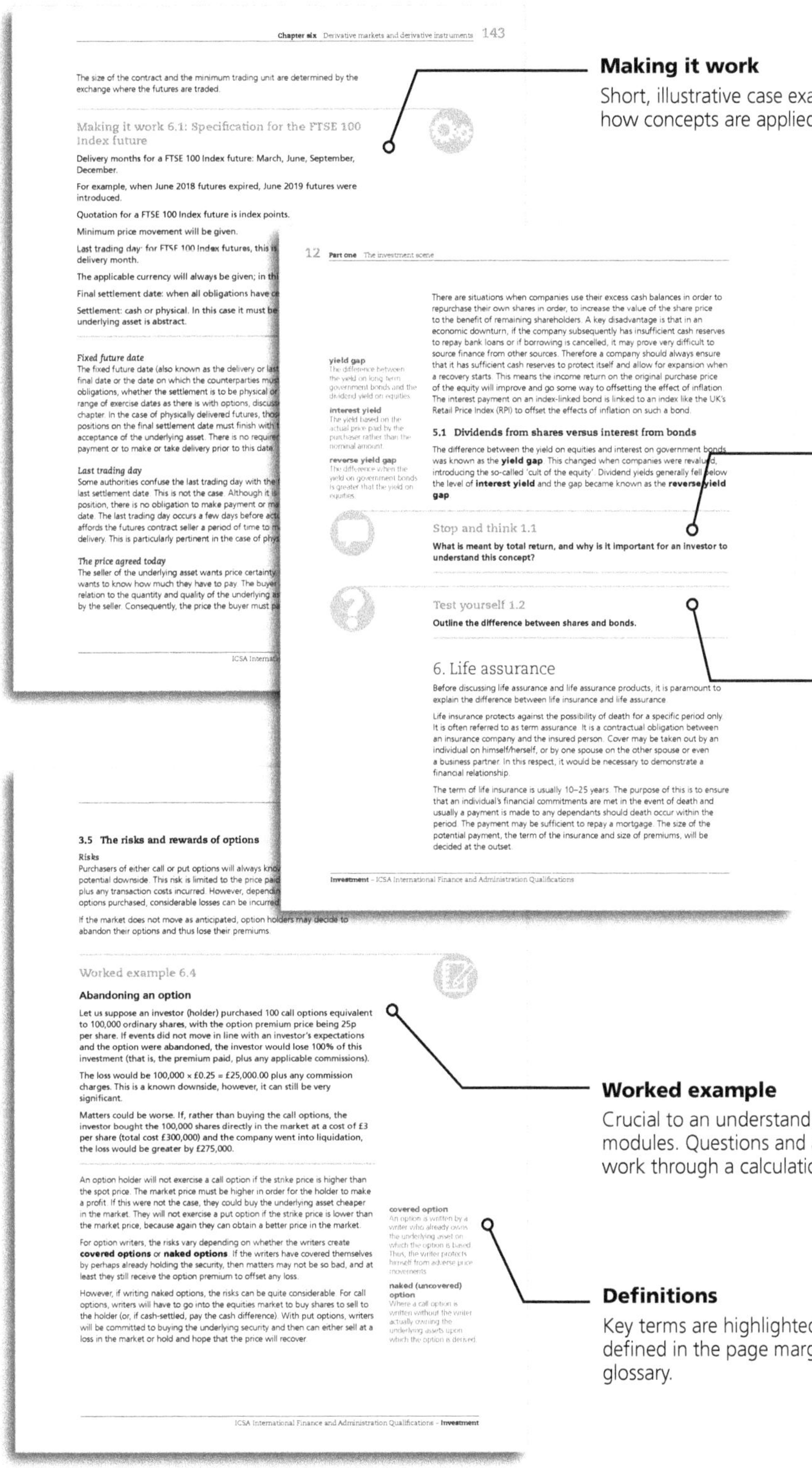

Making it work

Short, illustrative case examples which look at how concepts are applied in practice.

Stop and think

Stop and think boxes encourage you to reflect on how your own experiences or common business scenarios relate to the topic under discussion.

Test yourself

Short, revision-style questions to help you re-cap on key information and core concepts.

Worked example

Crucial to an understanding of finance-base modules. Questions and answers allow you to work through a calculation as part of your study.

Definitions

Key terms are highlighted in bold on first use and defined in the page margins and the end of book glossary.

The Investment modules

Aims

These modules provide an introduction to the types of investment product available in offshore finance centres and how they work. This includes an overview of key investment products such as shares, collective investments, fixed-interest products and derivatives.

Learning outcomes

After successful completion of these modules, you will:

- Understand savings and investment products and how they are managed
- Understand economic statistics relevant to investment
- Know about business cycles
- Understand supply and demand theory and the conditions required for a perfect market
- Know about different company structures in the UK
- Understand how companies finance their overall operations and growth
- Know about securities markets
- Understand sources of information available to assess the value of share prices
- Understand the role, operation and regulation of stock markets and trading platforms
- Understand the derivatives market and derivative instruments
- Know about money markets and money market instruments
- Understand principles of foreign exchange
- Know about fixed-interest securities
- Understand the characteristics of different types of bonds
- Understand the risks involved in investing in bonds
- Understand the features of collective investment schemes.

A note on calculation in the Investment modules

The Investment study text contains examples of investment calculations in Chapters 3, 4, 6, 7 and 8. Questions may be set in the exams, particularly in Sections A and B of the paper, which reflect the type of calculations shown here. Calculations are less likely to appear in Section C of the paper, which contains longer essay-style questions.

The level of rigour of calculation questions in exams will be set at Level 4, reflecting the standard demonstrated within this text. Questions set in the exam may be variants of worked examples already included within the text. Questions may also be set where ratios/formulae have already been provided.

The subject matter relating to any calculations or ratios used within the study text may be examined, so you are strongly recommended to study the text in its entirety, particularly the worked examples within the chapters.

Past papers and practice questions

Students can access sample papers for these modules by logging into the 'My ICSA' area of www.icsa.org.uk.

Acronyms and abbreviations

ADR	American Depository Receipts
AGM	annual general meeting
AIF	alternative investment fund
AIFM	alternative investment fund manager
AIFMD	Alternative Investment Fund Managers Directive
AIM	Alternative Investment Market
ASX	Australian Securities Exchange – now NYSE MKT LLC
AUD	Australian dollar
BCN	broker crossing network
BATS Chi-X	BATS Chi-X Europe – multilateral trading facility
BATS	BATS Global Markets Inc – US equity market operator
BP	British Petroleum
CAC 40	Cotation Assistée en Continu 40
CBOE	Chicago Board Options Exchange
CBOT	Chicago Board of Trade
CCF	Irish Common Contractual Fund
CCP	central counterparty
CD	certificate of deposit
CDS	credit default swap
CEO	chief executive officer
CFD	contract for difference
CGNCR	Central Government Net Cash Requirement
CGT	capital gains tax
CHF	Swiss franc
CIS	collective investment scheme
CME	Chicago Mercantile Exchange
CP	commercial paper
CPD	continuing professional development
CPI	Consumer Price Index
CSD	central securities depository
DAPS	discount add, premium subtract
DAX 30	Deutscher Aktienindex 30
DB	defined benefit (pensions)
DC	defined contribution (pensions)
dis	discount
DJIA	Dow Jones Industrial Average

DMO	Debt Management Office
Dow	Dow Jones Industrial Average
DTCC	Depository Trust and Clearing Corporation
DY	dividend yield
EC	European Commission
ECB	European Central Bank
EEA	European Economic Area
EGM	extraordinary general meeting
EMH	efficient market hypothesis
EMSR	Equity Market Share Reporter
EPS	earnings per share
ESMA	European Securities and Markets Authority
ETF	Exchange-traded fund
EU	European Union
FAV	formula asset value
FCA	Financial Conduct Authority
FCP	Fond commun de placement
FE, Forex, FX	foreign exchange
FEC	forward exchange contract
FIX	Financial Information eXchange (protocol)
FOS	Financial Ombudsman Service
FSE	Frankfurt Stock Exchange
FWB	Frankfurter Wertpapierbörse (Frankfurt Stock Exchange)
GBP	British pound
GDP	Gross Domestic Product
GEMM	gilt-edged market make
GNP	Gross National Product
GRY	gross redemption yield
HKEx	Hong Kong Exchanges and Clearing Limited
HMRC	Her Majesty's Revenue & Customs
HNWI	high net worth individual
ICE	Intercontinental Exchange
ICMA	International Capital Market Association
ICVC	investment company with variable capital
IDB	inter-dealer broker
IFA	independent financial advisor
IG	index-linked gilt
IPO	initial public offering
IRD	interest rate differential
IRP	interest rate parity
ISA	individual savings account
ITC	investment trust company
JPX	Japan Exchange Group
JPY	Japanese yen
KII	Key Investor Information
LIBOR	London Interbank Offered Rate
LIFFE	London International Financial Futures and Options Exchange – now part of IntercontinentalExchange

LP	listing particular
LSE	London Stock Exchange
M&A	mergers and acquisitions
MiFID	Markets in Financial Instruments Directive
MMI	money-market instrument
MTF	Multilateral Trading Facility
NASD	National Association of Securities Dealers
NASDAQ	National Association of Securities Dealers Automated Quotation
NAV	net asset value
NR	no rating
NYMEX	New York Mercantile Exchange
NYSE	New York Stock Exchange
NZD	New Zealand dollar
NYSE MKT LLC	Equity capital market for small cap companies – formerly AMEX
OECD	Organisation for Economic Co-operation and Development
OEIC	open-ended investment company
OMX-AB	Swedo-Finnish exchange group – part of NASDAQ OMX
ONS	Office for National Statistics
OTC	over-the-counter
OTF	organised trading facility
P/E ratio or PER	price/earnings ratio
P&L	profit and loss
PAOF	Post Auction Option Facility
PE	private equity
plc	public limited company
pm	premium
PRA	Prudential Regulatory Authority
PSBR	Public Sector Borrowing Requirement
PSNCR	Public Sector Net Cash Requirement
QE	quantitative easing
RDR	Retail Distribution Review
REIT	Real Estate Investment Trust
RIE	recognised investment exchange
RNS	Regulatory News Service
RPI	Retail Price Index
RSI	Retail Sales Index
S&P	Standard & Poor's
SCT	Split Capital Trust
SEAQ	Stock Exchange Automated Quotation System
SEC	(US) Securities and Exchange Commission
SETS	Stock Exchange Electronic Trading System
SFO	Serious Fraud Office
SGX	Singapore Exchange Limited
SI	systematic internaliser
SICAV	Société d'Investissement à Capital Variable
SIX	SIX Swiss Exchange
SMEs	small and medium enterprises

SOCIE	statement of changes in equity
SSE	Shanghai Stock Exchange
SSP	Single Shared Platform
STRIPS	Separate Trading of Registered Interest and Principal of Securities
TARGET2	Trans-European Automated Real-time Gross Settlement Express Transfer System
T-Bill	Treasury Bill
TER	total expense ratio
THB	Thai baht
TR	Thomson Reuters
TS2	TARGET2-Securities
TSE	Tokyo Stock Exchange
UCIS	unregulated collective investment scheme
UCITS	Undertakings for Collective Investment in Transferable Securities
UHNWI	ultra high net worth individual
UKLA	United Kingdom Listing Authority
USD	United States dollar
UT	unit trust
VAT	value added tax
VCT	Venture Capital Trust
WIP	work in progress
XD	ex-dividend
ZAR	South African rand
ZDP	zero dividend preference share

Part one

Chapter 1
Savings and investment

Chapter 2
The investment scene

The investment scene

Overview

Should one save or invest? This Part looks in Chapter 1 at the differences between savings and investment, considers speculative products and examines the investment market in light of the 2007–08 credit crisis and the resulting global recession.

Chapter 2 then provides an introduction to economic statistics and measurements used to make informed investment decisions, followed by supply and demand theory as applied to markets.

Learning outcomes

By the end of this Part, you will:

- understand savings, investment, speculative products and how they are managed;

- understand economic statistics relevant to investment which will aid; investment decisions;
- know about business cycles; and
- understand supply and demand theory and the conditions required for a perfect market.

Chapter one
Savings and investment

List of topics

1. Reasons for investing
2. Cash savings
3. Fixed interest securities
4. Equities
5. Equities versus bonds
6. Life assurance
7. Pensions
8. Property
9. Other investment options
10. Intermediation, maturity mismatch and maturity transformation
11. The 2007 credit crisis

Introduction

This chapter provides an introduction to the more detailed chapters that follow. However, before progressing through the investment study text, it is essential first to understand the difference between savings, investment, speculation and gambling. The chapter also introduces the main types of investment.

Savings

Savings is money put aside (saved) for a specific purpose or purposes, usually out of excess income. People may save for any number of reasons, such as for a home, a new car or holidays, or just 'for a rainy day'.

There is not usually an intention to obtain large returns; rather the money is put aside for a specific purpose. This is often a near-term or relatively near-term purchase.

This money may be deposited in any number of low-yielding bank or building society savings accounts. The saver is more concerned with security of capital in order to make their purchase in due course.

However, savings do not have to be placed in any form of bank account; the saver may decide to keep them in the form of cash at home. Savers may not be interest-focused or concerned with the fact that inflation may erode their money's real value. Children in particular tend to save rather than invest, and saving is the best way of using money if you do not have much capital or are financially less knowledgeable. Savers tend to be very risk-averse.

Savings products include:

- bank and building society savings accounts; and
- NS and I premium bonds.

Investment

Investment is very different from saving. Investors will not tend to keep money in the form of cash, and instead will put money into something with the hope of returns in excess of inflation. Investors require returns in terms of increased capital and/or income. Unlike savers, they are not prepared to have the value of their capital eroded by inflation. They usually have more disposable income than savers and use this to generate additional returns, in terms of either income or capital appreciation or both. Consequently, they use different and more sophisticated products to achieve these aims.

Investment products include ordinary shares, corporate bonds, property, and alternative investments such as art, wine or vintage cars. While investors require returns, they still want varying degrees of security for their investments. It is also important to note that some investments, such as ordinary shares, could be viewed from different perspectives. Some may see them as investments with potential for both regular dividend and capital growth. However, others may regard the same investments as merely speculative or indeed gambling. There has been a significant number of examples in recent years where ordinary share investors have lost everything, including Northern Rock, Bradford and Bingley, and Railtrack. Under normal circumstances, these particular ordinary shares would have been considered relatively safe investments. However, they were ultimately no more than speculative/gambling products, as all investors' money was lost.

With investment products there is an expectation of a return or profit: an investor wants more out than they have put in. By contrast, a saver will receive only what they put in, more or less. If it is more, the amount needs to be viewed in relation to the level of inflation.

It should also be borne in mind that the act of investing involves putting money in to something in order to achieve returns. However, there is a cost to this, in that an investor is losing control over his/her money as it is being put into another product with a certain degree of risk. Some investments are defined as being near cash products but they are not cash and they cannot be used to fulfil the functions of cash. Generally, money is being loaned to an organisation in order that an investor can get out more than was invested.

Two key principles of investment are as follows:

1. Diversification: 'do not put all your eggs in one basket', meaning do not put all your money in one asset class, such as ordinary shares or, worse still, a single stock. A diversified portfolio will include property, equities, corporate bonds and gilts. Well-diversified portfolios will be spread over a number of geographical regions.
2. Liquidity: it is absolutely imperative that investors retain enough spare capital to meet near-term requirements to avoid having to sell any investments in a depressed or falling market.

Speculation

This is very different from investment as investors strongly anticipate a return. Speculators, on the other hand, tend to use financial instruments where there is an increased risk of some loss, total loss or even losses representing multiples of their initial outlay. The financial instruments that speculators tend to use are higher-risk equities and derivative instruments. In relation to derivative instruments which include options, futures and covered warrants. It must be borne in mind that there is no ownership of any underlying asset and losses may be many multiples of the original outlay. However, the rewards may be equally large.

Gambling

Gambling means taking often considerable chances with the hope of high/immediate returns.

For some instruments or financial products discussed within this study text, it is difficult to discern whether they involve speculation or gambling. Contracts for difference (CFDs) perhaps falls into this grey area.

Gambling is often described as an all-or-nothing situation, but this is not strictly true. For example, if a gambler were to place £10 to win on a horse priced at 10/1 and the horse won, the gambler would receive £110 (£100 plus the original stake). If the horse came second, the gambler would receive nothing and would lose the original stake of £10. However, if that gambler placed a stake of £10 each way on the same horse, the outlay would be £20 and if the horse were to come second or third, the gambler would perhaps receive 10/1 divided by 4 = £25 plus the £10 stake. In this instance, the gambler would receive £35 for his £20 stake.

In roulette, if a gambler were to put money on any single number he or she would receive 36 times an original stake if that number came up. If it did not, the entire stake would be lost. However, if the same gambler placed a stake on evens chances red or black/high or low and the ball landed on zero, 50% of the original stake would be returned.

This illustrates that gambling is not always all or nothing; sometimes a percentage is returned. However, gambling is not recommended. The something back often represents only a fraction of the original stake.

It is often stated that with higher returns there is a higher risk. This is true, but the converse is often cited: with increased risk there will be increased returns. This is absolutely not the case, as increased risk can result in partial or total loss.

If an investor does not understand the financial product they are intending to invest in, they should seek the advice of an independent financial adviser before making any financial commitment.

It is not necessarily the financial instrument itself that is an investment or speculative product; instead it could be viewed from the perspective of the purchaser, whether an individual or institution. For example, an individual may purchase 100,000 ordinary shares and hold them for five years, hoping to receive regular income in the form of dividends and capital appreciation over that period. A speculator, such as a day trader, may buy the same 100,000 shares in the morning and sell them in the afternoon.

1. Reasons for investing

There are many reasons why governments, companies, trusts and individuals invest.

Unless individuals come from wealthy families, have a large lottery win or receive a large inheritance, they are likely to have to earn enough money to support themselves and their family throughout their working life and beyond. They will want to purchase a home or homes, and pay for the education of any children that they have. Individuals will work to earn money to make purchases and also to provide for their retirement. In this respect, they may well need to invest money in order to be able to support their lifestyle. The desire to invest is a part of everyone's life, whether direct or indirect, and in order to help people achieve their investment aims and objectives, there are multitudinous investment products with varying degrees of risk.

investment
Placing money in a financial product or alternative investment to make a profit.

Today the creation of wealth through **investment** is part of everyday life in most countries. Large and increasing populations with longer life expectancies have made the need for good investment returns a priority.

The specific reasons may include:

dividend
An income distribution made by a company to its shareholders, normally paid twice a year.

inflation
A rise in the general price level of goods and services, leading to a reduction in the purchasing power of money. Often measured over a 12-month period.

- to make profit – ordinary share returns can be achieved in two ways: capital gains from rises in the share price and also income returns in the form of **dividends**. Placing money into company shares may also contribute to the growth prospects of the company, enabling it to expand. It is wise to search for companies with good growth prospects, as these should provide greater returns. Investors in bonds receive coupon payments and would receive a higher yield if they purchased junk bonds rather than investment-grade bonds, but there is greater associated risk with the former;
- to keep pace with or beat **inflation** – if money is not placed into a product that at least keeps pace with inflation, in real terms, there will be a loss of purchasing power with the uninvested money. Some authorities state that investors are losing money. This is not true – it is the purchasing

power of money which is diminishing. Investing should as a minimum mitigate or hopefully counteract the erosive effects of inflation;

- to make provision for retirement – individuals will need to achieve some form of return for their retirement. It is doubtful whether saving alone would achieve this, and consequently investment should be made into some form of pension scheme, such as defined benefit, defined contribution or self-invested personal pension (SIPP). There are significant tax advantages for contributions made into a pension scheme, with any taxation being deferred until retirement combined with tax-free growth until retirement;
- to attain their own financial goals with the right spread of investment; and
- to obtain financial independence and security.

The array of investment products has never been greater. However, although some of these are very straightforward, more products are being introduced with varying degrees of complexity and risk. An investor may invest directly by purchasing equities, bonds and property, and whatever product they put their money into, they will need to understand the associated risks. It will be necessary to calculate the expected returns in respect of both income and capital returns. If investing indirectly (perhaps through an investment trust or a REIT), they must decide whether they require capital growth or income return; if they are aiming for the latter, they must consider the effects of inflation. Others may prefer capital appreciation rather than income, thus reducing income tax liabilities. However, investment returns may be subject to capital gains tax, although there is an annual exempt amount (AEA). For the year 2018/2019, this was £11,700 for individuals in the UK, with a potential maximum rate of taxation of 20%. Another issue is how long an investment should be held, whether in isolation or as a component of a portfolio. This is really dependent on a number of factors, including the aims and objectives of an individual or fund manager and the tolerable level of risk.

1.1 The regulation of investment

Because investment decisions necessarily require such judgments, the growth in investment products has been mirrored by the development of rules – both law and regulation – that provide a framework for how investments are managed and traded.

Investment regulation has to strike a balance between facilitating business and preventing malpractice or fraud. The Certificate in International Finance and Administration (CIFA) core modules and study text cover how investment markets are regulated, identifying the main regulatory bodies internationally and outlining key regulatory codes and legislation, including the law relating to insider dealing and anti-money laundering. It is important to be familiar with this regulatory framework in order to understand the dynamics of the investment market.

It is essential not only to keep abreast with new laws and regulations in the domestic market and in those jurisdictions where investments are held or planned to be held which pertain to investment, but also to be aware of the relevant authorities and regulators within the investment environment. For example, in the UK, the Financial Conduct Authority has the responsibility for the financial conduct of over 58,000 financial services firms and financial markets, while the Prudential Regulation Authority (PRA) has responsibility for 18,000 of these.

These authorities will try to ensure that financial markets are not only honest and fair, but also effective. They try to ensure that markets work well for not only individuals and businesses but also the economy as a whole. The PRA regulates 18,000 banks, insurance companies, building societies and major investment firms. Its general objective is to promote the safety and soundness of the firms that it regulates.

The pensions regulator has a wide range of powers that it can implement to protect workplace pensions. These will enable it to deal effectively with risks associated with workplace pension schemes and members' savings. However, the regulator aims to prevent issues from occurring in the first instance, through a risk-based approach. The regulator tries to anticipate potential problems through education, enablement or enforcement.

In 2018, under Basel III, the liquidity coverage ratio will be made mandatory. This standard aims to ensure that a bank has an unencumbered stock of high-quality liquid assets (HQLA) comprising of cash or near-cash assets that can be converted into cash at little or no loss of value in private markets in order to meet its liquidity needs for a 30-day liquidity stress scenario. At a minimum, this stock of unencumbered HQLA should enable a bank to survive until the end of these 30 days, by which time it is assumed that appropriate corrective action will have been undertaken by management.

1.2 Taxation

The two main types of taxation in relation to the investment environment are income tax and capital gains tax.

Income tax is levied on income including share dividends and bond coupons. However, there are exemptions and products where no income tax is payable. Consideration must also be given to corporation tax if companies rather than individuals are investing.

Capital gains tax is levied on capital gains – that is, the difference between the purchase price and selling price of an asset. There are annual allowances and the rate of tax can be considerably lower than income tax. There are also indirect taxes including VAT. Different tax regulations will apply to an individual depending on their residence and domicile. The principles and implications of tax law and regulation are covered in more detail in the CIFA International Business Environment module.

1.3 The pace of change

The investment world is a fast-paced one where new products and trends constantly emerge and evolve to meet market needs. In turn, laws and regulations are also dynamic. While this text is concerned primarily with the principles behind the main investment options, it is also necessary to keep up to date with what is happening in the investment community by using the web resources identified in the directory of web resources (page 310).

2. Cash savings

As discussed earlier in this chapter, saving usually involves depositing surplus cash into an account that earns interest. The amount of interest earned depends on the level of **interest rates** and the amount deposited. This interest can be withdrawn on a regular basis, so that nothing Is added to the original amount. If interest is not withdrawn, then the amount grows not only by the interest earned on the original amount, but also on the added interest that has become part of the savings. This is known as compound interest and although it may appear small when an account is opened, over a large time period (e.g. 20 years), it can grow to a large amount. However, inflation has a negative effect on the buying power of the amount saved, and this should be considered whenever cash is held on deposit. The effect of inflation will be explained in Chapter 2.

interest rate
Charge made for a loan/paid on a deposit, usually expressed in terms of percentage per year. Interest rates tend to be higher the larger the amount invested.

2.1 Deposit accounts

There are many different types of deposit accounts available from **building societies** (or their equivalent) and banks. In the simplest terms these deposit takers – the banks and building societies – receive spare cash from people and pay interest on it. They then lend this money to borrowers who have to pay a higher charge to the deposit takers for the amount they borrow, thereby allowing the deposit takers to earn a fee based on the difference between these two rates. As of 2018, returns on deposit accounts may be less than 1%, whereas interest charged on loans may be as much as 20% annually.

building societies
Mutual associations largely dedicated to home-mortgage finance. They are broadly similar to savings and loans associations in the US. Since the Building Societies Act 1986, various (but not all) societies converted to banks, and offer services such as current accounts.

3. Fixed interest securities

Fixed-interest or fixed-income securities usually pay an annual fixed rate of interest, known as a coupon, that does not vary with any external factor, such as an increase or decrease in external market interest rates (LIBOR). The coupon values are known from the outset (the time of purchase) and are generally for the same amount being paid at regular intervals, usually semi-annually.

There are a number of notable exceptions to the coupon payments, such as zero-coupon bonds; although these are classed as fixed interest securities, they do not actually pay any coupons or fixed interest at all. The most important of all fixed-interest securities are bonds. These include government bonds (whether domestic or overseas), corporate bonds and eurobonds. The nature of the bond market tends to be of a longer-term nature when compared and contrasted with the shorter-term nature of money market instruments. From the perspective of the bond issuer, they will not need to repay the principal for many years hence. This does not preclude bonds from being actively traded in the secondary market.

The main group of fixed-interest securities are bonds, which include:

- government bonds (domestic or overseas);
- UK government bonds (gilts);
- corporate bonds;
- eurobonds; and
- debentures.

gilts
UK government bonds.

capital return
What is returned to the investor at the end of the predetermined investment period or when the asset is sold.

floating charge
This is secured against a range of assets determined by the company which crystallises in the event of a default.

fixed charge
This means that identifiable assets are used to secure the bond and can be sold to repay the debenture bondholders in the event of a default.

asset
Something of value (to its owner). However, if sold, the price obtained will only be the amount a buyer is willing to pay for the asset.

UK government bonds are known as **gilts**. If a bond has a repayment date, there will be a predetermined level of capital repayment on the repayment date in addition to a regular income received over the period that the bond is held.

If a bond is sold before the repayment date, the **capital return** will be determined by the prevailing market interest rates, and may be more or less than the original purchase amount.

Corporate bonds are issued by companies and the rate of return is usually greater than the return available on a government bond at the time of purchase, but there is a greater risk. However, in the UK, most corporate bonds repay the promised amount at the repayment date and therefore they can be safer than investing in shares.

A debenture is a secure type of corporate bond linked to either a fixed or **floating charge**. A **fixed charge** means that identifiable **assets** are used to secure the bond and can be sold to repay the debenture bondholders in the event of a default. A floating charge is secured against a range of assets determined by the company, and this arises in the event of a default. The debenture holder receives regular interest payments over the life of the debenture.

Test yourself 1.1

a) explain the differences between savings, investment speculation and gambling.

b) What are the main types of fixed interest investments?

4. Equities

Equities are the most common form of stock in the UK. They are fixed units of the share capital of a company and are the most important component of a company's capital structure. The funds raised from issuing equities are used not only to finance expansion but also to reduce debt.

Ordinary shares (or equities) derive their name because the ordinary shareholders own the equity of the company. Consequently the stakeholders are entitled, after prior charges such as preference share dividends and bank interest, to all distributed profit.

If liquidation should occur, the ordinary shareholders will be entitled to any residual assets, but only after all other creditors have been satisfied.

Ordinary shares are also referred to as voting shares. Although there may be some classes of ordinary share that have no voting rights, each ordinary share represents an equal share in the company. These may be designated as either A or B shares.

Each ordinary share of the company will have the same nominal value; consequently all shareholders are on an equal footing which is directly proportional to their total holding.

Having been issued initially in the **primary market**, ordinary shares may subsequently be traded freely in the **secondary market** (the market for second-hand securities), enabling investors to make a profit, break even or limit their loss.

primary market
Where bonds or equities are issued for the first time. In the gilts market this would be the issuance by the DMO through its auctions.

secondary market
The market for second-hand securities. Securities are bought and sold between investors rather than the original issuer. The securities must have been issued in the primary market first.

The ordinary shareholders will provide capital in exchange for their shares. From the company's perspective, this will be its issued share capital, and forms the equity capital of the company.

Each individual share will possess an equal right to share in the distributed profits of the company. If, for example, a company has issued 1,000 ordinary shares, each share will be entitled to receive 1/1000 of the distributed profits – this is different from 1/1000 of the overall profits. Preference shareholders (if there are any) must receive their fixed dividends before ordinary shareholders receive their dividends, and some of the profits will usually be retained for future growth.

5. Equities versus bonds

The choice whether to invest in bonds or equities depends not only on personal preference, but also on aversion to risk.

In relation to equities, there should be dividend payments the level of which will be dependent on the company's profitability. Dividends are paid from after-tax profits. In good years, dividend payments may be excellent. However, in poor years, there may be no dividend at all – payments are made solely at the discretion of the directors. If the shareholders want a return of capital, they will have to sell in the secondary market to other shareholders, usually via a stockbroker.

In relation to bonds, there is a contractual obligation for the company itself to return the capital back to the investor at maturity date, but not before. If an investor wants a return of capital, the bond may be sold in the secondary market at a profit or loss. There is also an obligation for the bond issuer to pay a fixed coupon payment, based on the nominal amount, to the bond holder. Whether the company makes huge profits or incurs huge losses, the bondholder is only entitled to the fixed coupon payment. If a bondholder does sell in the secondary market, the new owner is entitled to the return of capital at maturity and coupon payments. However, it would be necessary to ascertain whether or not the bond was purchased ex or cum dividend.

There are situations when companies use their excess cash balances in order to repurchase their own shares in order, to increase the value of the share price to the benefit of remaining shareholders. A key disadvantage is that in an economic downturn, if the company subsequently has insufficient cash reserves to repay bank loans or if borrowing is cancelled, it may prove very difficult to source finance from other sources. Therefore a company should always ensure that it has sufficient cash reserves to protect itself and allow for expansion when a recovery starts. This means the income return on the original purchase price of the equity will improve and go some way to offsetting the effect of inflation. The interest payment on an index-linked bond is linked to an index like the UK's Retail Price Index (RPI) to offset the effects of inflation on such a bond.

yield gap
The difference between the yield on long-term government bonds and the dividend yield on equities.

interest yield
The yield based on the actual price paid by the purchaser rather than the nominal amount.

reverse yield gap
The difference when the yield on government bonds is greater than the yield on equities.

5.1 Dividends from shares versus interest from bonds

The difference between the yield on equities and interest on government bonds was known as the **yield gap**. This changed when companies were revalued, introducing the so-called 'cult of the equity'. Dividend yields generally fell below the level of **interest yield** and the gap became known as the **reverse yield gap**.

Stop and think 1.1

What is meant by total return, and why is it important for an investor to understand this concept?

Test yourself 1.2

Outline the difference between shares and bonds.

6. Life assurance

Before discussing life assurance and life assurance products, it is paramount to explain the difference between life insurance and life assurance.

Life insurance protects against the possibility of death for a specific period only. It is often referred to as term assurance. It is a contractual obligation between an insurance company and the insured person. Cover may be taken out by an individual on himself/herself, or by one spouse on the other spouse or even a business partner. In this respect, it would be necessary to demonstrate a financial relationship.

The term of life insurance is usually 10–25 years. The purpose of this is to ensure that an individual's financial commitments are met in the event of death and usually a payment is made to any dependants should death occur within the period. The payment may be sufficient to repay a mortgage. The size of the potential payment, the term of the insurance and size of premiums, will be decided at the outset.

Life insurance may be taken out when any dependants are young, and the end of the term may coincide with a child's 18th or 21st birthday, or the conclusion of university studies.

The most important feature is that life insurance protects against something that might happen, not something that will happen. Thus if an insured person arranges cover for exactly 15 years and makes the premiums up to and including this end point, but no death ensues during the period, no payout will be made. If the same individual dies after the term, again there will be no payout. There is no residual value. For a payment to be made by an insurance company, two conditions must be fulfilled: death, and this death occurring within the term of insurance.

Life insurance premiums depend on a number of factors including:

- age;
- sex;
- health history;
- amount of cover;
- duration of cover;
- number of insured persons; and
- smoker/non-smoker.

Generally, the younger and healthier the insured is, the lower the premium will be. This will determine the amount of premiums to be paid. Life insurance is cheaper than life assurance.

With life assurance, In contrast with life insurance, a payout is guaranteed, whether to the assured person or to somebody else. As with insurance policies, people with dependants should make sure that in the event of their death, there will be financial security for those dependants. Unlike life insurance, life assurance has no fixed term and there is an element of investment.

There is an assurance of a payment, and the insured does not have to die to trigger this. However, if the individual does die, a guaranteed payment, possibly with bonuses, will be paid. The size of the payout will depend on the sum assured, the performance of the assurance company and the number of years that the policy has been in force. If the individual survives to the end of the policy, there will be a payout. This may include various annual bonuses plus a terminal bonus.

It is also possible to sell an assurance policy either back to the assurance company or to a specialist broker, provided that sufficient value has been accrued. It is not possible to resell an insurance policy, as there is no accrued value.

6.1 Types of life assurance policy

Whole-life policies

This type of life assurance policy pays out whenever the person who is the subject of the policy dies. There is therefore no fixed term; as long as the premiums are paid, a payment will be assured and made upon death. Assurance premiums are more expensive than life insurance premiums. The positive aspects of whole-life policies are in respect of the with-profits policies, where any profits made are distributed and allocated to the policyholders in the form of bonuses. Once allocated, they cannot subsequently be taken back. Policyholders may choose a range of options, including:

- fixed sum assured (non-profit or without profit) – a specific amount paid out upon death;
- with-profits – linked to growth of markets; and
- unit-linked – these are linked to the investment funds of the life assurance company, so the value of the policy can go down as well as up.

endowment policy
A life insurance contract, also known as an assurance contract, which pays a lump sum on maturity (after a specific term of years) or death.

Endowment policies

Endowment policies are actually savings products incorporating life assurance. They are longer-term investments and are often taken out in parallel with a mortgage and are for a defined period. At the end of an endowment period, the insurance company will make a lump sump payment which is hopefully more than sufficient to clear the mortgage liability. In the event of the death of the assured prior to the end of the term, the sum assured will be paid out. There are variants of endowments that are very similar to whole-life policies – with-profits and unit-linked – and the principles are the same. The proceeds of a maturing endowment policy are free of tax.

Because of the unclear nature of insurance companies' products, faith in these types of investment has diminished in recent years, especially in the UK. However, many people still buy these products. There are a number of areas where criticism has been levied, including:

1. cost – whole-life policies often attract criticism because of the price differential between them and life insurance policies;
2. suitability – a policy whether insurance or assurance is not suitable for everybody. Individuals have differing circumstances, and policies should reflect this. Choices need to be evaluated by prospective policyholders prior to making commitments. However, such policies may be ideal for young families concerned about providing financial for their family;
3. smoothing of returns (where an unusually high return in one year is spread over several years);
4. the interrelationship between products; and
5. underlying investment returns.

Other types of product associated with insurance companies are guaranteed income or growth bonds and annuities.

7. Pensions

The area of pensions is an extremely important area of the investment world; it is, and will continue to be, challenging. It will be very interesting to see how this area continues to evolve.

In 2015, the then Chancellor of the Exchequer, George Osborne introduced so-called pensions freedom which afforded retirees more control over their retirement savings/pensions. The retirees/pensioners were able to have full control over their pension pot including in the extreme to take out and use the entire fund as they wished, subject of course to taxation. This pension freedom has already caused a lot of issues including pensioners being cheated out of the entire funds by unscrupulous scammers.

A pension is a fund comprised of savings put aside throughout the course of a working life. The purpose is to support a retiree in later life. It is to be hoped that the money received will be adequate to support their desired lifestyle in retirement. However, this might not be the case if the retiree has made inadequate provision. The amount that can be contributed to a personal pension throughout a career is determined by government legislation because of the tax breaks available.

Most countries require that employers provide an additional pension scheme for employees, especially if it is considered that the state scheme may be inadequate in future years. Company schemes are often described as occupational schemes. There are two types.

7.1 Defined benefit pensions

In the United Kingdom it was standard practice for an employee to participate in a defined benefit pension (final scheme) scheme. In this situation, the retiree would receive a defined annual pension from their normal retirement date. This date was usually when the retiree attained 60 or 65 but it is now as low as 55 before pensions can be accessed. The amount of the defined benefit was dependant on a number of factors including the amount of final salary, number of years' service. For example, if an individual earned an annual salary of £50,000 and worked for 30 years for the company they may expect a pension of £50,000 x 30/60 = £25,000 annual pension. This would usually be linked to an index to protect against the effects of inflation.

Defined benefit schemes are being phased out as they are unsustainable from the perspective of an employer. There are also various options open to employers where they are still operative. They can phase them out completely, or close entry to new employees.

Despite this, many millions of people in the United Kingdom still have these defined benefit schemes, and at retirement they would be able to take 25% of their value as a cash free lump sum while taking the remaining 75% as a monthly salary. There are other options that are outside the scope of the syllabus. Defined benefit schemes are still prevalent in the public sector and civil service.

In relation to a defined benefit pension, the onus of ensuring that the retiree receives their defined benefit is the responsibility of the employer and in those circumstances where an actuary has identified a shortfall in the pension fund the employer may have to fund the shortfall.

There will be a pension contract between the employer and employee with most of the pension contributions being made by the employer but additional voluntary contributions (AVCs) can be made by the employee.

If an individual has worked for 40 years, they may have a number of different pensions of different types from a range of employers consequently they may have a defined benefit, defined contribution, SIPP and state pension, while others may be solely dependent on the state pension.

7.2 Defined contribution (DC) pension schemes

Defined contribution (DC) pension schemes from defined benefit schemes differ in that the employer will make a defined contribution for example 10% of annual salary into a pension fund in the name of the employee. The pension provider will usually be selected by the employer. The pension contribution is usually made monthly and may be placed into a range of funds. The employee has the responsibility for ensuring that there is enough in the fund to be able to fund a desired lifestyle at retirement, either by making additional contributions which will have various tax benefits or by managing the pension pot by switching from fund to fund. Contributions in to an employer's defined contribution scheme may be made as follows:

- entirely by the employer;
- in varying percentages by the employer and employee; or
- later on, entirely by the employee.

This will be explained in the pensions contract between employer and employee.

The investment returns achievable both during the time the funds are invested in the pension scheme and at the employee's retirement will also affect the amount they can receive in retirement.

7.3 The state pension

Most countries will provide some form of state pension to fund retirees in later life. These pensions are mostly funded by the working population, but could still could be partially funded by the individual retirees if they continue to be basic rate or higher rate tax payers in retirement. However, following the credit crisis of 2007/2008, coupled with the fact that people are said to be living longer, the UK state pension age was raised from 65 to between 66 and 68. It is probable that this will be increased further to 70–75, and will eventually be phased out depending on its degree of sustainability.

Due consideration should also be given to the fact that the state pension may be subject to income tax if the retirees other income takes he or she over the relevant threshold. Additionally as the state pension is spent, it will be subject to indirect taxes including VAT.

Personal pension savings are a feature in many countries because they relieve governments of the commitment to provide completely for pensioners in their later years.

Most countries provide some kind of state pension(s). The funding of these varies and if they are dependent on the contributions of the working population, they may create a financial strain on a country if the **ratio** of retirees to working population is too high. Japan is an example of a country with this sort of ratio, whereas the Scandinavian countries have made provision for a more robust state pension scheme for future retirees.

ratio
The quantitative relationship between two numbers which indicates the number of times one number either contains or alternatively is contained by the other number.

7.4 Personal pension schemes

Personal pension schemes or self-invested personal pensions (SIPPS) are pension contracts taken out by individuals. Those taking out such schemes do not necessarily have to be employees, they may be sole traders or self-employed – they may be employees transferring out funds from an employer's DC scheme after they have ceased to work for that employer. SIPPs are becoming increasingly popular especially as they provide a vast array of managed funds often achieving significant returns. These pension providers tend now to be specialist pension companies rather than traditional insurance companies. As is the case with defined contribution schemes the amount a retiree will receive will depend on the performance of the fund into which the funds have been invested. Some personal pensions allow employer contributions.

The topic of pensions is a complex issue and it is important for an employee to compare the benefits of a company scheme, if there is one, with those of a personal scheme. Some points that an employee should consider are:

- the level of an employer's contribution;
- stability of employment – possibility of relocation due to Brexit;
- financial security of employer's scheme;
- nature of benefits – for example, spouse benefits;
- assessment of investment prospects; wide range of funds in which to invest; and
- early retirement provisions.

In relation to the financial security of employers schemes this is generally in relation to defined pension schemes where a shortfall has been identified; however, if the employer cannot financially or is unwilling to fund the shortfall. This will become an increasingly large problem as more employers fail to fund the shortfall or ask employees to take a reduction in the defined benefit on which they had been depending.

Recent examples include:

- British Home Stores (BHS) Pension fund;
- Carillion pension fund; and
- Tata Steel UK.

Test yourself 1.3

Why is it important for people to invest in a pension scheme?

8. Property

Money that is invested in 'bricks and mortar' is known as property investments.

For most people, the purchase of a home will be their largest financial transaction. Although its prime function is as a place to reside, it may actually be a most valuable investment particularly if it is bought at the bottom and sold at the top and if located in a fashionable area of London such as Marylebone or Kensington and Chelsea, where properties could be purchased relatively cheaply even in the early 2000s. Most of the money required to purchase a home will be borrowed by way of a legal mortgage, which represents a legal charge on the property. They are usually spread over 20–25 years and interest payments may be fixed or variable. Fixed rate mortgages are preferred when interest rates are low. There is also the buy-to-let market.

mortgage loan
A loan provided by a financial institution such as a bank secured against a property or other real estate.

The most common types of **mortgage loan** are as follows.

Interest only

An interest-only loan is one where only the mortgage interest is paid for a set number of years. During this period, no capital repayment is made. However, at the conclusion of the period the mortgagee is responsible for either re-financing the terms of the loan or paying off the entire mortgage completely. This type of loan is appropriate for those individuals with variable income or someone who knows they will receive a considerable amount of money by the time the mortgage is due to be repaid.

Deferred interest

Deferred interest mortgages are where the interest has been accrued, not paid. A portion of the early years' interest is added to later years. In this circumstance, mortgage payments will cover the payment arrears. Deferred interest will accrue when the mortgage repayment is insufficient to cover the outstanding interest. This type of mortgage may be appropriate for those anticipating a large increase in salary within a few years.

Repayment mortgage

A fixed rate mortgage loan is one where the monthly payment is guaranteed to remain the same throughout the duration of the loan period. Terms commonly range from 10 to 30 years. In the early years, most of the payments will go towards paying the interest; in the later years, the principal amount will be cleared.

Pension mortgage

A pension mortgage loan is an interest-only mortgage, however, with the establishment of a separate plan in the form of a personal pension which will benefit from tax relief and tax-free profits within the plan. When the pension is paid the retiree is entitled to a 25% tax-free lump sum, which is used to pay of the outstanding mortgage. It should be noted that the mortgage debt will not reduce for the duration of the loan and there is no guarantee that the lump sum payment will be sufficient to discharge the mortgage liability. The lump sum must be used for this purpose and no other.

Non-status

Non-status or self-certification mortgages are for those who have difficulty in being able to prove their income, such as the self-employed. These mortgages are not as common as they were, and those who might have applied for non-status mortgages in the past now tend to apply for more traditional types.

Other property investments, such as 'buy to let', have been popular in recent years. As long as the rental income covers all outgoings and an amount can be put aside for repairs and modernisation, a 'buy to let' may, over time, turn out to be a good investment.

It is also possible to invest indirectly in property by using property funds including closed-ended funds such as REITs. A long-term investment in property offers security, as value and income tend to keep up with inflation. However, there are periods when both commercial and residential property fall in value and therefore become difficult to sell if required. It can also prove difficult to withdraw an investment made in an **open-ended fund** of property if the manager is unable to find buyers for the property investments held by the fund because of market conditions and the fund has insufficient cash to repay investors. This does not apply to **closed-ended funds** of property.

open-ended fund
A collective investment scheme that can issue and redeem shares at any time (unless stock market conditions prevent this happening). An investor will generally purchase or sell shares (redeem) in the fund directly from the fund manager rather than existing shareholders.

closed-ended fund
A collective investment scheme with a limited number of shares quoted on a stock market. They are limited companies.

Exchange-traded funds
Listed funds that usually track an index comprising the underlying stock that makes up the index or use derivatives to achieve the same returns as the index. They are used to track the value of assets generally, including commodities such as gold.

9. Other investment options

9.1 Commodities

Commodities, including minerals, precious metals (including palladium and gold) and crops, are a more specialised form of investment. Investing in commodities can be done through either a commodities exchange or a fund. **Exchange-traded funds** (ETFs) are a useful way of investing into commodities and will be discussed in Chapter 9.

9.2 Alternative investments

Alternative investments, such as art, antiques, fine wines and woodlands, attract interest from investors, especially in times of economic growth. These investments require specialist knowledge to ensure that the investor obtains a good return. Alternative investments also require a long period, in most cases, to make an investment worthwhile. Some of the more successful alternative investment returns have been made by members of the same family over several generations. Other problems to consider with alternative investments include difficulty in selling, especially during an economic downturn, and maintenance costs of the item(s), for example, the cost of providing insurance cover.

- Fine wines – Red Bordeaux – at the time of writing, Château Lafite Rothschild 1982 sells for over £2,000 for a single bottle.

- Watches – a Patek Philippe pocket watch sold for $24 million in 2014 and a stainless steel Rolex wrist watch once owned by the actor Paul Newman sold for $17.8 million in October 2017.
- Art – in May 2017, a painting by the American Artist Jean-Michel Basquiat was sold in New York for $110 million.

9.3 Crypto-currencies

What are crypto-currencies?

Crypto-currencies, of which there are now many, are digital currencies. Although like traditional so-called hard currencies such as the US dollar and Swiss franc they perform the medium of exchange function, they are unregulated by any jurisdiction. They also lack tangibility, unlike traditional paper money, and have no central bank control. The five mainstream crypto-currencies are:

1. Bitcoin
2. Ethereum
3. Bitcoin cash
4. Ripple
5. Litecoin.

For the purpose of the ICSA examination, the focus will be on one crypto-currency: Bitcoin, which was created in January 2009, ostensibly by Satoshi Nakamoto which would appear at first sight to be a plausible name for a Japanese male. It is, however, probably a pseudonym for a single or group of coders or encryptors who may or may not be Japanese. This is yet to be determined.

Bitcoin technology

Bitcoin employs technology known as blockchain, which is in effect a decentralised digital public ledger that records peer-to-peer transactions. Apparently it cannot mutate.

- Bitcoin is created by a process called 'mining'.
- Transactions are grouped together into blocks.
- These blocks are created by solving mathematical puzzles.
- When the puzzles have been solved and new blocks created, they are added to the public chain and become publicly visible.
- Puzzle solvers are rewarded with Bitcoin, and supply increases.

Circulation

As of June 2018, there are 16.7 million Bitcoins in circulation (many of these are missing or locked in electronic wallets on inaccessible PCs). However, only 21 million Bitcoins have been minted; consequently the supply is finite. The outstanding Bitcoins have yet to be issued, as this only occurs using the complex technology referred to previously. This lack of availability will naturally add to demand.

Crypto-currencies as an investment

Crypto-currency prices fluctuate widely and are not appropriate for all investors. Trading is not supervised or overseen by any EU or other jurisdictional regulatory framework. Therefore, capital is at risk.

Not only can crypto-currencies be bought on regulated exchanges the CBOE (10 December 2017) has allowed trading in bitcoin derivatives. This could be very dangerous from an investment perspective as the price of bitcoin is extremely volatile – the value of 1 bitcoin in June 2017 was only $771, however, in June 2018 it was trading at $7,619 for just 1 bitcoin, and reached a peak in excess of $20,000. Some authorities suggest that this will be the next big financial disaster since the dot.com bubble burst in 2000.

Risks associated with investing in crypto-currencies

- One needs to be extremely cautious when trading bitcoins directly as the price volatility is phenomenal. Whether this is a speculative product or gambling product has not fully become apparent; however, while there are those individuals/institutions who have made fortunes there are also many others who have lost fortunes depending upon when they bought or sold. If a purchaser entered at the bottom of the market he/she may have made millions; conversely if they bought at the top millions may have been lost.
- Trading futures in crypto-currencies, whether opening long or short positions, is even more speculative than trading traditional futures because of the leverage combined with volatility. This is the case particularly if short positions are opened.
- Volatility is colossal, and may be 40–50% in a single trading period.
- There are only 24,985 Bitcoin in circulation – a limited supply.
- The number of institutions prepared to accept Bitcoin is limited, although in early 2018 there was a case of a house being purchased with Bitcoin.
- All transactions are recorded and become publicly viewable.
- Although the Bitcoin blockchain has never been hacked, cyber criminals have stolen millions in terms of value from digital online wallets and also from crypto exchanges trading Bitcoin.
- Crypto-currencies are currently not widely usable – this may change.
- The medium of exchange function is dubious.
- Is it currency or a commodity? It is certainly not a savings product.
- It is mostly used by speculators.
- It is hard to ascertain when it is at the top or the bottom of market.
- Crypto-currencies are not held by institutions, meaning a risk of regulation. This is because institutions can only invest in regulated securities, and Bitcoin is not one.

Bitcoin transactions and ownership are effectively private, as although the blockchain's ledger is public and contains a record of every transaction ever made, owners are identified by digital credentials ('keys') and not by name or other identifying factors. Owners may store and safeguard their keys using a variety of methods.

Disadvantages include the following:

- As of June 2018, crypto-currencies are unregulated, but there has been evidence that some governments wish to introduce some form of control – after all, it is the central banks of countries that control their own currencies.
- Introduction of regulation – Indonesia threatened this but to date this has not been introduced.
- Somebody may decipher the code.
- Investors may lack an understanding of crypto-currencies generally or they may lack IT skills.
- They are restricted to IT-knowledgeable people.
- There is the potential to destabilise economies, particularly those of poorer or less stable countries.
- They may be used for money laundering and other criminal activities.
- If being bought or sold, they still have value in terms of hard currencies $ or £ – people still quantify profits or losses in terms of a hard currency.
- Many crypto-currencies will end up worthless.
- The loss of a password means loss of access to your digital wallet. If the price crashes, you then cannot sell, nor if the price rises.

Advantages include the following:

- The technology can be used by financial institutions.
- Where there is instability in more than one country, a universally acceptable currency may be popular not just for individuals but also for governments.
- Bitcoin has never been hacked, or compromised.

Test yourself 1.4

a) What are the most common types of mortgage?

b) Name some alternative types of investment.

intermediation
The process of moving funds between savers and borrowers in return for interest paid by a borrower to an intermediary, such as a bank, who in turn pays interest at a lower level to the saver.

liquidity
The flow of cash from depositors to banks and from banks to borrowers.

10. Intermediation, maturity mismatch and maturity transformation

One of the principal functions of banks and building societies is **intermediation**, whereby institutions receive deposits from those with excess **liquidity** and lend to those who need or wish to borrow.

Liquidity is where cash flows into banks from depositors, other lenders or markets, and the bank in turn lends the cash to borrowers. Typically, savers wish to retain a good degree of liquidity, and thus want to deposit with access to their money either at short term or even straight away, whereas borrowers quite often need or wish to borrow over the longer term. Therefore, a situation arises known as **maturity mismatch**, which is a discrepancy between maturities. Consequently, in addition to engaging in intermediation, banks and building societies need to engage in **maturity transformation** (also known as term transfer), which means that these institutions need to 'borrow short and lend long'.

maturity mismatch
When a bank or institution has substantial long-term assets like fixed-rate mortgages but short-term liabilities such as deposits. This can be measured by a duration gap which calculates risk due to changes in interest rates.

maturity transformation
An acceptance by an institution of short-term deposits which are lent out on a different basis – usually long term.

Banks provide many loans at short term (and overdrafts are, theoretically at least, repayable on demand), whereas maturity transformation can be even more pronounced in the case of building societies (and former building societies) because most of their lending is for financing the purchases of houses and apartments.

Unless banks and building societies are managed prudently, there is a considerable risk of them becoming illiquid given that depositors may withdraw their funds faster than borrowers repay their loans. Additionally, such institutions can be vulnerable to rising rates; for example, a mortgage lender taking floating-rate short-term deposits but lending in the long term at fixed rates.

11. The 2007 credit crisis

This crisis originated from the build-up of large savings in Asia over many years; these savings kept world interest rates and inflation rates low. They provided liquidity to Western banking systems, especially the US and UK mortgage and housing markets. The credit crisis from 2007 onwards arose because banks and other institutions lent money to many real-estate (property) purchasers who did not have sufficient earnings to support repayment of the loans given to them.

These loans (mortgages) were added together ('parcelled up') and sold as a 'safe property' package to institutions seeking an income stream.

The package was **securitised** (made into a tradable investment), and sold to investors, who miscalculated the risk value of the package. Unfortunately, when borrowers began to default on their loans, the 'low' risk, which had supposedly been offset through the credit defaults swaps market (a supposed insurance against default), was found to be inadequately covered by the **counterparty** to the swap arrangement.

securitise
Make a package of loans into a tradable investment.

counterparty
A party to a contract.

Confidence quickly fell with the collapsing real-estate market, and the packages of loans bought by banks round the world ceased to have the value expected. They were given the name 'toxic assets'.

The enormous sums of money involved caused a liquidity crisis. The banks and financial institutions that bought these 'investments' found that they did not have sufficient assets to back their everyday banking business as required under Basel II (one of a group of recommendations on banking laws and regulations). They therefore had no choice but to ask for government backing or go bankrupt.

Government backing was not forthcoming in all cases. For example, the firm of Lehman Brothers was allowed to collapse. In contrast, the insurance giant AIG was rescued. AIG had failed to provide sufficient liquid funds to cover the counterparty risk it had undertaken. The US government had little choice but to support AIG, because the consequences of a default for AIG would have been disastrous.

The crisis caused a lack of confidence in the world banking system. Liquidity dried up, and governments had to step in to fund the banking system to prevent complete economic collapse. Without liquidity, the trading of goods and services ceases to function.

The UK also found itself with several building societies and other mortgage lenders lacking sufficient assets to survive when their short-term loans could not be renewed and depositors withdrew their money. One of the reasons that certain building societies (and banks that had formerly been building societies) in the UK found themselves in difficulty was because they 'borrowed short and lent long' to a level greater than their loan-book could support, which is not how a sound society or bank should conduct its business.

Borrowing on a short-term basis from the money market and lending on a long-term basis to a house or flat purchaser is, as discussed earlier, known as maturity transformation. This only works if there is a beneficial difference between interest rates paid to the market and charged by the bank or building society to the borrower, and, crucially, if short-term market loans can be renewed at maturity (known as 'rolling over' the loan).

11.1 The response to the crisis

New laws, regulations and supervisory arrangements are still being proposed by the USA and the European Union (EU) to ensure that events such as those discussed earlier will be less likely to occur again.

It is expected that some types of investment discussed in the following chapters may not be allowed in future. However, it is important to understand them, as they may be reintroduced in the future under a different name.

At the Group of 20 (G20) meeting in June 2010, the major economies reaffirmed their commitment to regulation of over-the-counter (OTC) **derivatives** by making OTC trades use regulated exchanges or other trading platforms to ensure **clearing houses** process the transactions. This is now being implemented in Europe and the USA.

derivatives
Financial instruments, the prices of which are based on (derived from) the prices of different classes of underlying asset. Derivatives may be traded on exchanges, as in the cases of futures, or alternatively may be OTC products, as is the case with interest rate swaps.

clearing houses
Places or institutions where mutual claims and accounts are settled, as between banks.

Stop and think 1.2

Do you understand how the 'credit crisis' arose? What lessons have been learned from the crisis? Could it happen again?

Test yourself 1.5

What is meant by:

i) intermediation

ii) maturity mismatch

iii) maturity transformation?

Chapter summary

- Saving normally involves placing money on deposit whereas an investment entails higher risk to the capital through the purchase of either fixed interest stock such as bonds or equities which are quoted and traded on stock markets or other facilities, as discussed in later chapters.
- The return from a deposit is known as the interest received and can be paid to the depositor either monthly, quarterly, half-yearly or yearly, depending on the terms of the agreement and the amount placed on deposit.
- Equities are usually known as shares in the UK. Shareholders are the owners of a company and therefore run the risk of losing their investment if a company fails. Many companies pay dividends to their shareholders and if the company grows over the years, the value of the company's shares will rise.
- Life assurance is sometimes linked to a savings scheme to provide a return as well as life cover.
- Pensions are a very important form of investment for all individuals as the cost of providing for retirement rises as life expectancy increases.
- Other forms of investment include property, commodities and alternative investments such as woodlands, art, fine wines, watches, vintage cars.
- Crypto-currencies are a new electronic medium of exchange and have inherent risks.
- One of the principal functions of banks and building societies is intermediation, where they receive deposits from those with excess liquidity and lend to those who need or wish to borrow.
- Understanding the reasons for, and effects of, the 2007 credit crisis and resulting global recession provides important context for students embarking on the study of investment markets.

Test yourself answers

Test yourself 1.1

a) Saving is about putting money aside, usually in an account that earns interest, for use in later months or perhaps years, e.g. for large bills or holidays. Thus savings is for a purpose, not for a return. An investment, on the other hand, is normally about investing money into a bond or share for a period usually counted in years. It also includes investing in valuable items such as houses, paintings, wine, gold and art.

b) The main types of fixed-interest investments are:

- government bonds (gilts); and
- corporate bonds issued by companies.

Test yourself 1.2

Essentially, the difference between shares and bonds is that investing in shares involves buying partial ownership in a company, whereas bonds involve making a loan to a company. A company does not have to return share capital to shareholders but it does have to return a bonds principal amount at maturity and is obliged to make coupon payments throughout the duration of the loan. Shareholder dividend payments are at the discretion of the directors and may be suspended.

Test yourself 1.3

A pension is a saving put aside from money earned over a working life for the saver to live on in retirement. Pension holders hope that the money received from a pension will be adequate to support their lifestyle in retirement.

Personal pension savings are a feature in many countries because they relieve governments of the commitment to provide completely for pensioners in their later years.

Test yourself 1.4

a) The most common mortgage loans are:

- interest only, where the borrower makes separate arrangements to repay the capital;
- deferred interest, where a portion of the early years' interest is added to later years;
- repayment, where an equal monthly payment is made over the life of the mortgage;
- endowment, where interest is paid to the lender and the proceeds from an endowment policy is hopefully sufficient to repay the capital;
- pension, where interest is paid to the lender and part of the pension repays the capital; and
- non-status for the self-employed and relatively small loan amounts.

b) Alternative types of investment can include:

- antiques;
- art;
- fine wines;
- vintage cars;
- woodlands; and
- antique watches.

Test yourself 1.5

i) Intermediation involves institutions receiving deposits from those with excess liquidity and lending to those who need or wish to borrow.

ii) Maturity mismatch occurs when a bank or financial institution has substantial long-term assets such as fixed-rate mortgages, but short-term liabilities such as deposits. In other words, there is a mismatch between their liabilities and assets.

iii) Maturity transformation occurs when banks and financial institutions borrow money in the form of short-term deposits but lend long term.

Chapter two
The investment scene

List of topics

1. The role of economic statistics
2. Measurement of economic activity
3. Inflation, deflation and hyperinflation
4. The business cycle
5. Supply and demand
6. The perfect market theory

Introduction

This chapter will enable students to gain a thorough understanding of those economic statistics which are pertinent to the investment scene. The performance of markets depends on the performance of a country's economy, which is relevant as larger companies around the world raise capital through stock markets. This in turn leads to the successful expansion of a country's economy. The chapter gives an overview of the economic statistics and measurements used to make informed investment decisions and provides an overview of some of the most important areas of economics including the business cycle, supply and demand theory, and quantitative easing.

1. The role of economic statistics

The assessment of the likely performance of an economy and the companies operating within that economy is an important starting point prior to making an investment. The measures and indices covered in the first part of this chapter enable the assessment of the background of the country or countries in which a company operates. Most governments try to achieve an environment of real economic growth with relatively low inflation and unemployment within a **business cycle**. They aim to bring this about through monetary policy (control of interest rates and supply of money to the economy) and fiscal policy (level of government spending and taxation in an economy).

business cycle
The period of time over which an economy moves from an expansion phase to a contraction phase and back again. Also known as the economic cycle.

2. Measurement of economic activity

2.1 Gross domestic product (GDP)

The GDP figure or economic growth figure is of paramount importance as it is a key indicator of the overall strength of an economy reflecting the general standard of living of a country's residents. It is the main measure of economic strength and used to show whether a country's economy is expanding or contracting. It is used by governments to shape economic strategy and to assess the affordability of public spending.

The GDP figure (calculation) is itself comprised of a number of individual totals, which together show a country's total output or production in monetary terms and is based on the total value of goods sold during a period. The figure is usually measured over a given period; in the UK, this is quarterly.

GDP growth rate is the key indicator of either an increase or decrease in the percentage of economic output in monthly, quarterly or annual periods. A rising GDP would give rise to an expanding economy, whereas a falling GDP would tend to suggest a contracting economy.

This responsibility for calculation of the GDP rests with the Office for National Statistics (ONS). In order to elicit this information, the ONS will conduct a survey of many thousands of firms across many sectors.

There are two variants of GDP:

1. Nominal GDP – this is a measurement of the total value of final goods produced by an economy during a given period. The definition of a final good is one that is sold to an end user. Consequently, raw materials sold to manufacture final goods would not be considered to be final goods and thus would not be included in the GDP calculation.
2. Real GDP – the starting point is the nominal GDP figure, however, it is adjusted to take into account inflation or deflation. It does not follow, therefore, that an increased GDP means that an economy's gross production or output has increased. The increased figure may be as a consequence of inflationary pressures on raw materials, for instance. The method used to calculate real GDP is to take a base year as a standard and compare the quantity of goods sold in the current year with that of the base year and calculate the difference. This will show not only the quantity but also the output changes over the period. So whether prices rise or fall, it does not necessarily mean that GDP has risen or fallen. There must actually be an increase in domestic output adjusted for inflation.

The calculation of GDP

All individual totals comprising the overall GDP figure are gross, whether in the nominal or real variants, and no deduction is made for depreciation. Excluding inflation or deflation, it generally follows that one if quarter's figure is a higher than the previous quarter's figure, the economy is expanding. If one quarter's figure is lower than the previous month's figure, the economy is contracting.

A number of different formulae are used to calculate GDP. In this study text, the expenditure method (also known as aggregate demand) is the formula that will be used. This method is based on the money actually spent by various groups.

The expenditure formula is:

$$GDP = C+I+G+(X-M)$$

where:

- **C** = consumption or all private consumer spending within a particular country's economy, including food, rent and durable goods, non-durable goods and services. This excludes new houses;
- **I** = sum of a country's investment spent on capital equipment, inventories and housing;
- **G** = total of government expenditure on final goods and services including salaries of government employees, road construction and military machines, however, excluding social security spending;
- **X** = exports of goods and services; and
- **M** = imports of goods and services.

Disadvantages of GDP include the following:

- It does not reflect the so-called black economy which may be substantial in some countries. This black economy includes many illicit activities such as drug-dealing. Consequently, not including figures relating to the activities would not therefore provide an accurate interpretation of GDP.
- Using the UK as an example, earnings in the UK by an overseas company and remitted back to foreign investors is not included in GDP.
- Money spent on care for the elderly is not included in GDP.

However, with the help of what is known as 'Big Data' in the future, the calculation of GDP may better reflect trends in an economy.

Stop and think 2.1

Is GDP the best way to measure growth in an economy? What other measures can be used to calculate an economy's economic performance?

2.2 Gross national product (GNP)

Gross national product, like GDP, is a method of measuring a country's output of final goods. It is the value of all goods and services produced by a country's residents and companies, irrespective of where they are produced. Thus GNP includes investments made by UK residents and businesses both inside and outside the UK. In essence, it includes all of the products manufactured by domestic companies regardless of where they are manufactured. It can be calculated on a country basis or alternatively a country per capita basis, which would be GNP divided by its total population. This allows comparison of GNP of countries of differing sizes.

GNP excludes any income earned in the UK by foreign residents or businesses, and does not include products manufactured in the UK by overseas firms. GDP is a key indicator of the health of a country's economy as it measures production within a country irrespective of who makes that money. By contrast, GNP measures a country's income rather than its production.

2.3 Balance of payments

A balance of payment is a record of all of a country's international financial transactions made by its residents with other countries. It is effectively a record of the value of goods exported, less the value of goods imported, usually over a specific given time. In the UK, this is quarterly. It is the value of transactions that is being referred to, not the number of transactions. This record is made in the domestic currency.

If the balance of payments is in surplus, the value of a country's exports is greater than the value of its imports. By contrast, if the value of a country's imports is greater than its exports, there would be a balance of trade deficit. If the value of exports and the value of imports were equal, then the balance of payments would be balanced or in equilibrium. This would be highly unlikely. Again, BOP is a measure of how successful a country has been in selling its goods and services to other countries in comparison to other countries selling to it. If a country has a balance of payments surplus, it generally means that a country's economy is in doing well and that country will be able to lend money to other countries. Therefore, it can pay for all of its exports and still have surplus money.

The movement of transactions is divided into the current account and the capital account:

- The current account (balance of trade) measures international trade, the net income on investments and direct payments. It is comprised entirely of short-term transactions.
- Visible trade relates to the export and import of tangible items including, for example, raw materials, such as cocoa for chocolate manufacture, or oil. The balance of trade in relation to tangible items is referred to the visible balance and such items are referred to visible items.
- Invisible trade – trade in non-tangible items. Examples would include the City of London earnings, insurance, tourism, insurance, and compensation of employees giving rise to the current account balance.

The capital account is usually the smallest component of the balance of payments. It includes any transactions that do not effect economic output, notably income, production or savings – for example, items may include copyrights and trademarks. The transactions contained within the capital account are generally long-term transactions.

2.4 Level of employment

In addition to the measures discussed within the chapter, including GDP and inflation, a country's unemployment rate is a very significant factor. It is one of the macro-economic measures used to determine how well a country's economy is performing.

The stock market follows unemployment figures closely; therefore, in times of high unemployment stock markets will tend to be depressed, whereas in times of near-full employment stocks will tend to rise. This is a natural corollary, as the unemployed will have less money to spend on investment products. There is some discussion as to when a level of full employment is reached. It is generally thought to be about 3–4% of the workforce.

Level of employment and impact on a country's economic activity

The level of employment or unemployment can have a significant effect on a country's economy, whether positive or adverse. The two aspects are inextricably linked.

High levels of unemployment lead to a slow-down in economic growth. Employment itself is very dependent on economic activity. When economic activity is high, there will be an increased demand for goods and services and thus a demand for those individuals who manufacture those goods and provide those services.

In addition to the social costs of unemployment, there will be significant economic costs. These will include not only costs to the economy as a whole but also personal costs.

- Loss of tax revenue – for every extra unemployed individual there will be a reduction in the amount of tax received by the revenue services in terms of both direct taxation – income tax and indirect taxes including VAT. This is because unemployed workers will reduce non-essential spending on non-essential products and services, concerned not only with their current status of unemployment but also with their future prospects and immediate security.
- An increase in government expenditure to support the unemployed – most unemployed individuals will become eligible for some form of unemployment or social security benefit, including job-seeker's allowance. This will be a drain on the economy, whereas previously the employee was funding the government in the form of both direct and indirect taxes, now it is the government funding the employee.
- Tax increases – if the level of unemployment remains high for a considerable period, the situation may become unsustainable and taxes may have to be increased. This will have a follow-on effect on the employed taxpayers, who will experience a reduction in their own disposable income and spend less on goods and services. This in turn will impact negatively on the sales of manufactured goods. Thus there may be a significant reduction in output.

- A reduction in demand in the housing market – unemployed workers may be unable to afford their mortgage repayments, leading to repossessions. Those planning to purchase new properties may be deterred from doing so which may result in less houses being built.
- Potential to send an economy into recession.
- The loss of output may lead to a reduction in GDP.
- There will be negative effects on wage inflation with the possibility of wage freezes or even cuts for those in work – also known as wage compression.
- A reduction in output of goods and services that could have been produced by those who have become unemployed. It follows that an economy is performing considerably below its potential if there is a high level of unemployment.

Test yourself 2.1

a) Define GDP.

b) Define GNP.

c) How do high levels of unemployment affect the economy?

d) What are the potential negative consequences of high unemployment?

3. Inflation, deflation and hyperinflation

Money is only worth what it can purchase. Thus money acts as a medium of exchange where individuals or entities are able to exchange their money for goods and services. If the price paid for a good or service remains constant in the short term, matters should be fine. However, there are factors that may force the price of these goods and services to rise over a particular period. If the price rise is small – perhaps 1% annually – then matters still may not be bad. This gives rise to the term inflation.

Inflation may be stated as the rate of increase in prices for goods and services. It is effectively a rise in prices with an associated fall in the purchasing power of money. More specifically, it is a sustained increase in the general price level of an economy. It leads to an increase in the cost of living as prices rise and the purchasing power of each unit of money falls.

If the currency in an individual's pocket will not buy as much today as it could have done yesterday, there has been a price rise with a certain amount of inflation.

For example, if a mobile phone costs £110 today whereas it cost only £100 exactly a year ago, we could state that the annual level of inflation for this particular product is 10%. Yet different products or services may have different price rises above or below 10%. A country's level of inflation would be based not merely on only one or two items, but rather on a large basket of items. The current level of inflation in the UK in 2018 is approximately 2%.

A certain level of inflation is acceptable in any economy, particularly if people's earnings keep up with inflation and if they receive pay rises at or above the inflation rate. However, where wages are frozen for many years, this can lead to a fall in the standard of living. The strategies used to control inflation are money supply and interest rates.

If money supply is increased, there will be more money in circulation within an economy chasing goods and services, this will force prices to increase and thus the inflation rate. Of course if money supply is reduced the reverse will be true.

The annual inflation rate is stated as the annual percentage change in price levels and is measured in the UK by using government statistics including the RPI (Retail Prices Index) and CPI (Consumer Price Index). In the UK, inflation rates have varied considerably. In April 2018, the rate was approximately 2%, whereas in 1974 it peaked at 25%.

Problems associated with inflation include:

- erosion of the real value (purchasing power of money) and the real value of financial assets denominated in money terms, particularly non-bearing or low-interest-earning bank deposits;
- the undermining of one of the key functions of money that is to be a store of value – thus its value falls; and
- the loss of another key function of money, that of being medium of exchange, in the event that people refuse to accept a particular currency money may fail in its function as a medium of exchange. This would be particularly the case if hyperinflation ensued.

Hyperinflation is a still inflation, but it is characterised by the prices of goods and services rising greatly and rapidly by in excess of 50% in any single month. It is this severity that separates it from ordinary inflation. The process may begin when a country's government prints money in order to pay for spending. As the money supply increases prices rise leading to inflation, however, rather than ceasing printing money in order to reduce the resultant inflation, the government continues printing.

A modern-day example of a country suffering hyperinflation is Venezuela, where the International Monetary Fund (IMF) predicts that prices will rise by 13,000% during 2018.

Deflation is essentially the reverse of inflation when prices for goods and services fall over time. It is a sustained fall in prices within a defined period. Consequently, money becomes a commodity with increased value as more can be purchased today than could be purchased yesterday. Initially, this may seem good for individuals particularly those who have a considerable amount of disposable income; however, it may ultimately lead to a fall in demand and it is probably an indicator of an imminent recession or in extreme circumstances a depression, which will result in falling wages and job losses.

Continued falling prices will act as a deterrent to people from spending on products and services in the hope that they will be able to purchase them more cheaply later. This will exert pressure on manufacturers to lower prices, resulting in lower wages for the workers and less investment.

3.1 Consumer Price Indices

CPIs are important indicators of how economies are performing and as such used by governments, businesses and society as a whole. They may influence interest rates, wages and state benefits demonstrating the effect of inflation on household budgets.

CPIs are monthly indicators showing the rate of either inflation or deflation. Following on from the discussion of inflation in the preceding section, consumer price inflation may be explained as the rate at which the prices of goods and services bought by households rises or falls.

The figure is produced monthly in the UK by the Office for National Statistics and estimated using the consumer price indices. The best way to understand these indices is to consider a large basket of goods and services purchased by households. Movements in these indices will indicate the changing cost of this basket whether resulting in inflation or deflation. It is important to remember that this is only an estimate of the changes of the total cost of the basket.

There is a wider figure, the Consumer Prices Index – Housing (CPIH), which is a more comprehensive measure of inflation. It includes those costs connected with owning and maintaining a home including council tax.

The Retail Price Index (RPI) is a general measure of inflation and is used, in the UK, as the basis of indexation of pensions, state benefits and index-linked bonds.

3.2 Retail Sales Index

The Retail Sales Index (RSI) measures the monthly movement in the average weekly turnover of retailers over a four- or five-week period (in the UK). This monthly measure is often taken as an indicator of consumer confidence, as it records purchasing trends. Currently, goods sold over the internet are not included in this index in the UK. At some point, this figure must be included so that the RSI reflects demand. Many goods ordered and supplied through the internet are sourced directly from overseas, which makes accurate recording difficult.

3.3 Public sector net cash requirement

The Public Sector Net Cash Requirement (PSNCR), formerly known as the Public Sector Borrowing Requirement (PSBR), represents the annual fiscal deficit. Notably it represents the shortfall between public sector revenues and expenditure. In the UK, it is a measure of the public sector's net financing requirement, quantifying the amount the government needs to borrow to cover all of its expenditure requirements – that is, the gap between tax receipts and government spending. PSNCR can be measured as an amount of money, or a percentage of GDP.

Governments have a number of methods to finance the PSNCR:

- increasing the narrow money supply (producing more notes and coins);
- issuing government securities (gilts); and
- overseas borrowing.

In the UK, the PSNCR for April 2018 was £7,840 million.

3.4 Money supply

Money supply may be defined as the total quantity of money in circulation within an economy. The measure of the money supply is important because of its influence on:

- price levels;
- inflation; and
- the business cycle.

There are a number of different measures which may be used in relation to the level of money supply. The specific measure used depends on the country in question and although M0 is now obsolete in the UK it does not prevent it being used in other jurisdictions or being re-introduced in the UK at a later date. The range is generally from M0 to M4 (five in all).

- M0, in the UK, ceased to be used when the Bank of England introduced its Money Market Reform in May 2006. M0 data are no longer produced. The last weekly observation for the M0 series was 17 May 2006, and the last monthly observation was April 2006. M0 is also referred to as the monetary base. This term refers to the fact that the money measured by M0 supplies was the base on which other forms of money, such as bank deposits, were based. It was the amount of money in circulation in notes and coin, plus the banks' till money and the banks' balances at the Bank of England.
- M1 includes all the components of M0 plus those assets which can be converted to cash at very short notice comprising those financial assets which can be used directly as a means of payment; however, they may additionally be used as a store of wealth.
- M2 is equal to M1 plus sterling time deposits with up to three months' notice, or up to two years' fixed maturity.
- M3 is a very broad measure of the domestic money supply that includes M2 items plus any large time deposits and money market fund balances held by institutions.
- M4 is the main broad measure of money supply in the United Kingdom. It includes everything in the M2 figure plus:
  - other deposits with an original maturity of up to five years;
  - other claims on financial institutions including bank acceptances;
  - debt instruments issued by financial institutions including commercial paper and bonds with a maturity of up to five years; and
  - 95% of the Major Financial Institution (MFI) difference.

Controlling the money supply is important in the control of an economy. This stems from the fact that money is used in nearly all economic transactions. An increase in the money supply leads to:

- a lowering of interest rates;
- an increase in economic activity;
- a rise in stock markets;
- an increase in consumer confidence;
- expansion of an economy;
- a rise in prices; and
- inflation

3.5 Interest rates

Interest is the charge made for a loan and is usually expressed in terms of percentage per year. The higher the interest charge, the more expensive it becomes to borrow money. Since commerce in a modern society depends on borrowed money to 'oil' the flow of transactions and goods, the level of interest can therefore be used indirectly to control an economy. If an economy enters an inflationary period due to increasing demand as a result of money becoming easy and cheap to borrow (see money supply, section 3.4), then the raising of interest rates eventually reduces the demand pressure through the cost of borrowing and making saving money on interest-bearing bank and building society accounts more attractive. Conversely, where an economy is likely to move into recession, a reduction of interest rates should stimulate demand in order to correct the movement. A change in interest rates is an indirect tool as it takes several months to have the desired impact on an economy. For this reason, many governments 'overreact' in the use of interest rates for control of an economy.

3.6 Quantitative easing (QE)

Quantitative easing is a form of monetary policy implemented if it is deemed necessary by a central bank such as the Bank of England in the United Kingdom to stimulate an economy when interest rates are already extremely low. The aim of quantitative easing (QE) is to kick-start an economy in order to reach a specific inflation target. Sometimes QE is referred to as 'asset purchasing'.

Quantitative easing (QE)
An instrument a central bank uses to bring down interest rates for companies and households by creating money electronically in the economy.

There is often a misconception that QE involves the printing of physical money in the form of notes. This is not the case; instead it is the purchasing of assets using money which has being created electronically. The QE process creates money electronically in order to make large purchases of assets from the private sector including pension funds, domestic banks and the assets will consist of government bonds (gilts) which have a high degree of liquidity.

As the asset purchases are in huge nominal volumes, this will push up the price of these assets – gilts and consequently reduce the yields – (returns). This is supposed to encourage those who sell the assets to use the money to buy other assets with higher yields, such as equities or corporate bonds. As more of these assets are bought, their prices will rise and their yields will fall, causing yields in general to fall. It is hoped that the companies issuing these securities benefit from cheaper borrowing, and consequently they will borrow, spend and invest more in the economy as a whole.

Those selling assets have more money in their bank accounts as a result. Commercial banks can use these new funds to finance new loans, encouraging more spending and investment.

If inflation appears to be too high, the assets purchased may then be sold through quantitative easing to reduce the amount of money and spending in the economy. The mechanics of quantitative easing are as follows:

- The central bank in the UK will purchase financial assets usually government bonds (gilts), with money it has created electronically.
- It then uses this electronic money to buy these financial assets from investors such as banks or pension funds.
- This increases the overall amount of useable funds in the financial system. Making more money available is supposed to encourage financial institutions to lend more to businesses and individuals.
- It can also push interest rates lower across the economy, even when the central bank's own rates are just about as low as they can go. This in turn should allow businesses to invest and consumers to spend more, kick-starting the economy.

Both the Bank of England and the US Federal Reserve embarked on a QE programme in the wake of the 2007/08 financial crisis in an attempt to stimulate economic growth.

- Between 2008 and 2015, the US Federal Reserve in total bought bonds worth more than $3.7 trillion.
- The UK created £375 billion ($550 billion) of new money in its QE programme between 2009 and 2012.
- In August 2016, the Bank of England announced that it would purchase £60 billion of gilts because of uncertainty over Brexit.

Disadvantages of quantitative easing include the following:

- It is difficult to manage and understand whether or not it has actually been effective.
- QE pushes up the market price of government bonds and reduces the yield, or interest rate, paid out to investors. In other words, investors have to pay more to get the same income.

- If market interest rates are lower, this will depress the value of a currency because it becomes less attractive to foreign investors.
- It has been suggested that the cash injected by the bank went to the more affluent.
- A key issue is that pumping more money into the economy could ultimately lead to an inflation or hyperinflation scenario.
- When inflation is close to zero, upward pressure on prices can be seen as beneficial; however, some politicians and economists have opposed the idea of QE in principle, as they consider that in the longer term, there is a risk that it could create too much inflation.
- The main risk is **hyperinflation**, which has been discussed earlier in this chapter.

hyperinflation
Very rapid inflation that leads to a complete loss of confidence in the sustainable purchasing power of a country's currency. It can lead to economic collapse.

Advantages of quantitative easing include the following:

- The extra money provided by the central bank should eventually boost spending.
- Unlike interest rates (which can only drop to zero), there is no limit to the amount that a central bank can provide, but the chance of inflation has to be monitored.
- With low interest rates, nothing else is likely to work.
- If it is effective, QE may shorten a recession and prevent deflation.

Test yourself 2.2

a) How can interest be used to control the economy?

b) What will cause the PSNCR to vary in normal times?

c) What are the definitions of money supply?

Stop and think 2.2

An increase in money supply can lead to positive and negative effects on an economy. What are these effects?

4. The business cycle

The business cycle is also known to as the trade cycle, economic cycle or even the boom bust cycle. It actually refers to fluctuations in GDP trade and economic activity, and may be considered as upwards and downward movements of GDP.

It is composed of four distinct stages:

1. growth (expansion);
2. peak;
3. contraction (recession); and
4. trough.

The growth/expansion phase is characterised by economic growth increased employment and an upward movement in prices. Ultimately, during expansion the business cycle must reach a peak where the economy is working close to capacity (maximum output). There may be full employment and inflation is evident. There will then be some form of correction where there is a slowing of growth, unemployment begins to increase and prices begin to fall. The slow-down then stops at the trough phase, where the economy reaches its bottom point. The business cycle then starts again, moving into expansion.

The following points should be noted.

- An expansion is the period from trough to peak.
- A recession is the period from peak to trough.

Business cycles are considered to be irregular and vary in:

- frequency;
- magnitude; and
- duration.

Test yourself 2.3

What are the stages of the business cycle?

5. Supply and demand

It is the inter-reaction of supply and demand that will affect the price of something, such as a share price. Demand means the quantity demanded at a particular price. As the demand for a particular share rises, then the price will rise due to the 'limit in supply' of shares available to trade. Supply affects prices as there is a limit to the total number of shares – for example, issued share capital available for trading at a specific time in a particular company on a stock market.

There are two laws of supply and demand and it is the interaction of these two laws which underpins virtually all economic events.

5.1 The laws of supply and demand

The law of supply states that the quantity of goods supplied rises as the market price of those goods rises and conversely the amount supplied will fall as the price of those goods and services falls. The typical supply curve will slope upwards from left to right. A company issues a set number of shares to be traded on a stock market as required by quotation rules. If, after a period of trading, demand for shares in the company is high, the company can issue more shares at a higher price, thereby raising capital for investment in production or acquisitions. Raising more capital for investment is one of the basic features of a stock market.

The law of demand states that the quantity of a good or service demanded falls as the price rises, while the quantity of a good or service demanded rises as the price falls. This can be observed from the typical demand curve, which slopes down from left to right. An exceptional demand curve is one that slopes upward from left to right. This reflects a situation where demand for a commodity (an item that can be bought or sold) is greater at a higher price. It often happens with shares. If a share price that has been low for a period starts to rise slightly, this may prompt a change in attitude to the company with the fear that the price may increase in the future, thus raising demand for the shares. If this continues, it may lead to speculative buying, with the price rising strongly until a level is reached where investors start to question future returns.

Equilibrium price

The equilibrium price occurs when supply and demand are equal. It is a function of markets to reach an equilibrium price that balances the demand with the supply of goods and services. An equilibrium price is that at which a seller can sell all that he/she wants to and a purchaser can buy all that he/she demands. Sellers would naturally like to charge higher prices for goods and services, however, even if there is no competition, consumers will demand less at higher prices. Consumers will want to pay less for goods and services, and if they do pay less, suppliers will produce less and some demand therefore may be unsatisfied. At the equilibrium price, the same will be supplied as demanded.

If the equilibrium price is correct in a market, there will be enough of the items available to satisfy demand at that price, as all buyers can be satisfied and all sellers will be able to dispose of their entire stocks of the items at the equilibrium price. At a price higher than the equilibrium price, sellers will be left with items unsold, and at a price lower than the equilibrium price, demand will exceed supply and a shortage of items will result.

The market price is where the equilibrium price equals the actual price due to temporary influences of the forces of supply and demand. However, when conditions of supply and demand have settled down so that the rate at which an item is consumed is equal to the rate at which it is produced, then a long-period equilibrium price will be established and this is known as the normal price.

Test yourself 2.4

a) **Outline the laws of supply and demand.**

b) **What is the difference between market price and normal price?**

5.2 Elasticity of demand

The elasticity of demand or supply means the degree of responsiveness of demand or supply relating to a change in price. Where a small change in price results in a large change in quantity demanded, then demand is said to be elastic. However, if a considerable change in price makes little difference to the quantity demanded, demand is considered to be inelastic. Demand is perfectly inelastic if the same quantity is demanded whatever the price.

Measurement of elasticity of demand

Where a change in the price of an item brings about a corresponding change in the quantity demanded, the elasticity of demand is equal to unity. Elasticity is greater than unity where the result in a change in price leads to a greater corresponding change in quantity bought. Elasticity is less than unity where the result in a change in price leads to a lower corresponding change in quantity bought. In addition, elasticity is less than unity when an increase in price results in a total outlay greater than before. Therefore, when elasticity is considered to be perfect, elasticity will be equal to infinity; conversely, when inelasticity is perfect, elasticity will be equal to zero.

5.3 Responsiveness of demand to price changes

Five factors influence the responsiveness of demand to changes in price.

1. **Possibility of substitution** – the most important influence on elasticity of demand is whether there are substitutes for a commodity. The substitute must be in the same price range.
2. **Degree of necessity** – whether an item is a necessary or a luxury is not an important determinant of elasticity of demand. An expensive item may be inelastic because there are no substitutes. Also, demand for items such as rice, bread and potatoes is inelastic because of a lack of substitutes rather than the fact they are considered necessities.
3. **Consumers' income** – a person with a high disposable income (plenty of money left over after paying the bills) is likely to be inelastic in their demand for most items. However, most people have to make a choice with items they purchase due to the limitations on their disposable income. For most people, items regarded as a necessary can be considered more inelastic compared to items that are more expensive and luxurious.
4. **Cheap items** – the smaller the proportion of a person's total income expended on an item, the more inelastic the demand for it.
5. **Habit** – a person's purchasing habit may be difficult to change immediately even if the price of the items they buy rises. A good example of this

characteristic is tobacco, as smoking is an inelastic demand for many people.

Test yourself 2.5

a) **What is meant by elasticity of demand and how is it measured?**

b) **Name the five factors that influence the responsiveness of demand to changes in price.**

6. The perfect market theory

A frequent assumption made in economics is the idea of a perfect market, also known as the efficient market theory. The following five conditions have to be fulfilled for a perfect market.

1. **Homogeneous commodity** – the commodity dealt in must be such that any one unit is exactly the same as any other. There is no opportunity for substitution. Although all ordinary quoted shares on a stock market are the same for a company under the quotation rules, stock markets are divided into sectors. The companies within a sector are not all the same, enabling shares in one company to be substituted for shares in another within the same sector.
2. **A large number of buyers and sellers** – for a sector that is in favour, there are normally a large number of buyers in the market. If a company is out of favour, there may be many sellers in the market. Most of the time, stock markets will satisfy this requirement.
3. **Buyers and sellers are in close contact with one another** – this requirement is satisfied within individual and global markets. The internet ensures that all buyers and sellers have ample opportunity to be aware of information likely to influence companies and markets on a worldwide basis. Some markets provide 24-hour dealing.
4. **No preferential treatment** – in a perfect market, there should be no preferential treatment of clients or discrimination by either buyers or sellers. There must be no opportunity for insider dealing, which is illegal in all markets. It is impossible to stop the use of insider information completely, as in practice, markets rely on information to function and there is always an opportunity for information not available in the public domain to filter into a market. Market participants must be on their guard to avoid using information that could be considered insider information, as abuse of this is heavily punishable in all countries. If this were not the situation, then confidence in markets would be lost.
5. **Transferability of a commodity** – entitlement or ownership of shares, bonds and other commodities are nowadays easily transferable not only within a market but also across the world. Costs may be involved, especially due to currency exchange rates. However, because markets

arbitrage
The simultaneous buying and selling of investments in different markets in order to take advantage of differing prices for the same asset.

are not perfect, there is an opportunity for **arbitrage** between markets worldwide to exist as a profitable business.

It is questionable whether the five conditions above are fulfilled. Also, in spite of information being available more or less equally to all market participants, it is questionable whether the perfect market does exist in reality. It does not seem to exist in markets for small company shares, such as the Alternative Investment Market (AIM).

The reason for this is simply that people are different and therefore they interpret the same piece of information in many ways. One has only to read research on a particular sector or company from different analysts to appreciate this fact. If markets were efficient, then 'stock market bubbles' would not occur. Efficient market theory, also known as efficient market hypothesis (EMH), is useful to understand as it gives a valuable description of how a perfect market would work and provides a basis for judging what happens in reality. Economist Paul De Grauwe suggests that individuals have severe cognitive limitations and do not understand much about the complexities of the world in which we live. The result is that in good times, individuals underestimate risk, and in bad times, they overestimate it. Markets, on this assumption, are far from rational.

Test yourself 2.6

a) **What five conditions are required for a perfect market to exist?**

b) **Why does a perfect market not exist in reality?**

Chapter summary

- Investment decisions need to take into account the likely performance of an economy and the companies operating within that economy.
- The measures of economic activity commonly used to inform investment decisions include: gross domestic product (GDP); gross national product (GNP) and balance of payments.
- Inflation can have a significant impact on economic performance. The main tools used to control inflation are money supply and interest rates.
- Quantitative easing arises when a central bank makes cash available to stimulate economic growth.
- The business (or economic or trade) cycle is made of four stages: growth, peak, recession and trough.
- Share prices are affected by supply and demand. There are three laws of supply and demand:

1. The lower the price, the greater the quantity that will be demanded.
2. The higher the price, the greater the quantity that will be supplied.
3. The equilibrium price occurs when supply and demand are equal.

- The perfect (or efficient) market theory requires five conditions to be fulfilled. It is questionable whether the perfect market can actually exist in reality.

Test yourself answers

Test yourself 2.1

a) GDP (gross domestic product) is the measure of the total value of goods and services produced in an economy. It is widely used by economists to measure the health of an economy.

b) High levels of unemployment have an effect on an economy through:

- loss of output;
- loss of tax revenue;
- increase in government expenditure to support the unemployed; and
- loss of profits to companies.

Test yourself 2.2

a) Interest is the charge made for a loan and is usually expressed in terms of percentage per year. The higher the interest charge, the more expensive it becomes to borrow money. Since commerce in a modern society depends on borrowed money to 'oil' the flow of transactions and goods, the level of interest can therefore be used indirectly to control an economy. In the UK economy, one of the key interest rates, the 'base rate', is set by the Monetary Policy Committee of the Bank of England. If an economy enters an inflationary period due to increasing demand as a result of money becoming easy and cheap to borrow, then the raising of interest rates eventually reduces the demand pressure through the cost of borrowing and making saving money on interest-bearing bank and building society accounts more attractive. Conversely, where an economy is likely to move into recession, a reduction of interest rates should stimulate demand in order to correct the movement. A change in interest rates is an indirect tool, as it takes several months to have the desired impact on an economy. For this reason, many governments 'overreact' in the use of interest rates for control of an economy.

b) The Public Sector Net Cash Requirement (PSNCR) in normal times will vary with the business cycle. For example, the banking crisis turned into a credit crisis, resulting in many world economies entering into recession. This has led to an increase in the PSNCR and, therefore, a higher level of national debt.

c) M0, in the UK, ceased to be used when the Bank of England introduced its Money Market Reform in May 2006. M0 data are no longer produced. The last weekly observation for the M0 series was 17 May 2006, and the last monthly observation was April 2006. M0 is also referred to as the monetary base. This term refers to the fact that the money measured by M0 supplies was the base on which other forms of money, such as bank deposits, were based. It was the amount of money in circulation in notes and coins, plus the banks' till money and the banks' balances at the Bank of England.

- M1 includes all the components of M0 plus those assets that can be converted to cash at very short notice, comprising those financial assets that can be used directly as a means of payment; however, they may additionally be used as a store of wealth.
- M2 is equal to M1 plus sterling time deposits with up to three months' notice, or up to two years' fixed maturity.
- M3 is a very broad measure of the domestic money supply that includes M2 items plus any large time deposits and money market fund balances held by institutions.
- M4 is the main broad measure of money supply in the UK. It includes everything in the M2 figure plus:
  - other deposits with an original maturity of up to five years;
  - other claims on financial institutions including bank acceptances;
  - debt instruments issued by financial institutions including commercial paper and bonds with a maturity of up to five years; and
  - 95% of the Major Financial Institution (MFI) difference.

Test yourself 2.3

The four stages of the business cycle are:

1. growth (expansion);
2. peak;
3. recession (contraction); and
4. trough.

Test yourself 2.4

a) There are three laws of supply and demand:

1. The lower the price, the greater the quantity that will be demanded.
2. The higher the price, the greater the quantity that will be supplied.
3. The equilibrium price occurs when supply and demand are equal.

b) The market price is where the equilibrium price equals the actual price due to temporary influences of the forces of supply and demand. However, when conditions of supply and demand have settled down so that the rate at which an item is consumed is equal to the rate at which it is produced, then a long-period equilibrium price will be established. This is known as the normal price.

Test yourself 2.5

a) The elasticity of demand or supply means the degree of responsiveness of demand or supply relating to a change in price. Where a small change in price results in a large change in quantity demanded, demand is said to be elastic. However, if a considerable change in price makes little difference to the quantity demanded, demand is considered to be inelastic. Demand is perfectly inelastic if the same quantity is demanded whatever the price.

Where a change in the price of an item brings about a corresponding change in the quantity demanded, the elasticity of demand is equal to unity. Elasticity is greater than unity where the result in a change in price leads to a greater corresponding change in quantity bought. Elasticity is less than unity where the result in a change in price leads to a lower corresponding change in quantity bought. In addition, elasticity is less than unity when an increase in price results in a total outlay greater than before. Therefore, when elasticity is considered to be perfect, elasticity will be equal to infinity and conversely, when inelasticity is perfect, elasticity will be equal to zero.

b) Five factors influence the responsiveness of demand to changes in price:

1. possibility of substitution;
2. degree of necessity;
3. consumers' income;
4. cheap items; and
5. habit.

Test yourself 2.6

a) The five conditions that have to be fulfilled for a perfect market are:

1. homogenous commodity;
2. a large number of buyers and sellers;
3. buyers and sellers in close contact with one another;
4. no preferential treatment; and
5. transferability of a commodity.

b) It is questionable whether the five conditions are fulfilled. In addition, in spite of information being available more or less equally to all market participants, it is questionable whether the perfect market does exist in reality. It does not seem to exist in markets for small company shares, such as the Alternative Investment Market (AIM).

The reason for this is simply that people are different and therefore they interpret the same piece of information in many ways. One has only to read research on a particular sector or company from different analysts to appreciate this fact. If markets were efficient, then 'stock market bubbles' would not occur. Efficient market theory, also known as efficient market hypothesis (EMH), is useful to understand as it gives a valuable description of how a perfect market would work and provides a basis for judging what happens in reality. Economist Paul De Grauwe suggests that individuals have severe cognitive limitations and do not understand much about the complexities of the world in which we live. The result is that in good times, individuals underestimate risk, and in bad times, they overestimate it. Markets, on this assumption, are far from rational.

Part two

Chapter 3
Company finances and new issues

Chapter 4
Assessing returns on shares

Company formation and value

Overview

This Part covers the different company types and how companies finance their overall operations and growth by using different sources of funds and different strategies, such as mergers and acquisitions.

This is followed by a look at the wider picture that investors need to consider when making investment decisions and the valuable sources of information available to help them make those decisions.

Learning outcomes

At the end of this Part, you will:

- know about different company structures in the UK;
- understand how companies finance their overall operations and growth;
- know about the securities markets; and
- understand sources of information available to assess the value of share prices.

Chapter three
Company finances and new issues

List of topics

1. Company structures
2. Capital structure: debt capital and share capital
3. Ordinary shares
4. Preference shares
5. The primary market and new issues
6. Admission to the London Stock Exchange
7. Rights issues
8. Capital and income distributions
9. The secondary market
10. Mergers and acquisitions

Introduction

In order to achieve its overall corporate objectives, a company may employ a variety of capital structures by using a range of different strategies. The choice may involve the use of guarantees, shares or debt. There are a number of different share types, including ordinary, preference, and deferred shares.

The advantages and disadvantages of each of these are discussed within this chapter. When new ordinary shares are issued by a company, this will necessarily reduce the existing shareholders' overall control. Ordinary shareholders have certain rights under the Companies Act 2006. The options and process for bringing new shares to the market are also described, and the operation and importance of the secondary market is introduced. The chapter concludes with an overview of mergers and acquisitions (M&A).

1. Company structures

1.1 Types of UK company structures

Before discussing the various capital structures employed by companies, it is perhaps pertinent to outline the various types of company structures that exist. In the UK, a company cannot operate in any form unless it has been incorporated and registered as a company at **Companies House** (the registrar of companies in the UK, and the regulator of company registration). Similar registrars exist in other jurisdictions and will operate in a similar manner. When companies have been registered at Companies House, a certificate of incorporation will then be issued.

Companies House
The UK registrar of those companies incorporated in the United Kingdom. It is an executive agency of the Department for Business, Innovation and Skills.

In the UK, there are four basic types of company structure. Where it has been decided to form any one of these which is limited by shares, the founders/owners must then agree to take some or all of these shares. Outside the UK other corporate structures exist, such as **hybrid companies**, found mostly in offshore centres (see section 1.2).

hybrid company
A cross between a company with a share capital and a company limited by guarantee.

The four main types of UK company structures are as follows.

1. *Private unlimited companies*

A private unlimited company is one that may or may not have share capital. There is no limit as to its members' liability. In this instance, the disclosure requirements will be less rigid than for other types of company. Private unlimited companies can neither offer their share capital to the general public nor be quoted on recognised stock exchanges.

2. *Private companies limited by guarantee*

A private company limited by guarantee is a company that does not have any share capital. As such, its members are guarantors rather than shareholders.

A company is limited by guarantee when its members agree to guarantee a specific amount of their own assets to the company in the event of the company being wound up. As there is no share capital, these companies cannot be quoted on recognised stock exchanges. They do not have to have 'limited' or '(Ltd)' after their name, provided they have been granted an exemption.

3. *Private companies limited by shares*

Private companies limited by shares clearly do have share capital, however, the shareholders' liability is limited to the amount of the fully paid share. In other words, the shareholders do not have to contribute any additional capital should that company go into **liquidation**. There may be instances in which the share capital is only partly paid, and in such circumstances, the shareholders would have to contribute any shortfall as though the shares were fully paid.

liquidation
The process whereby a company is 'liquidated' and its assets turned into cash. Liquidation may be voluntary or involuntary (as in the case of bankruptcy). Assets will be sold, liabilities paid and any balance returned to the equity holders. There is a statutory order of payout.

Private companies limited by shares can neither offer their shares to the general public nor be quoted on recognised stock exchanges. Their shares may be transferred with the permission of the company directors, however, these are not freely transferable like shares in quoted public limited companies (plcs).

Their shares may be obtained from both the company and existing shareholders subject to the conditions above. In order to transfer shares in a private limited company, it is necessary to complete a stock transfer form, coupled with the share certificate with stamp duty having to be paid. The name of a private company limited by shares must end its name with 'limited' or '(Ltd)'. Other jurisdictions will have their own conventions.

4. Public limited companies

Public limited companies are those that do have share capital and again the shareholders' liability is limited to any amount outstanding for their shares. The shareholders do not have to pay any outstanding debts of the company. Public limited companies can offer their shares to the general public and can be quoted on recognised stock exchanges. However, there is absolutely no obligation for the plc to take either of these courses of action, and they can remain unquoted plcs.

In the event that a company decides to become a plc, it must fulfil stringent requirements. The company must have at least two directors who can also be members of the company. One director must be a person rather than another company and there must be at least one company secretary who is suitably qualified.

Before conducting any business or exercising any borrowing powers, the plc must obtain a trading certificate confirming that it has satisfied the minimum allotted share capital requirement, which is currently £50,000. Public limited companies must have the suffix 'plc' or 'public limited company'. It is also a requirement that 25% (£12,500) must be fully paid before the Registrar of Companies will issue a certificate.

recognised investment exchange
An investment exchange that has been approved by the UK's FCA.

It is not a requirement that a company should first become a private limited company and subsequently re-register as a plc. It may be set up as a plc straight away, provided it conforms to the legal requirements pertaining to its capital. However, it cannot obtain a listing on a **recognised investment exchange** until it has also fulfilled the relevant listing requirements (see section 5.2). A great number of plc are effectively privately owned until they obtain a listing on either the LSE or AIM, because they are unable to sell their shares until either of these events have occurred.

At the outset, the owners of the company must decide what the most appropriate corporate structure will be in order for the company to fulfil its overall corporate objectives.

Stop and think 3.1

Understanding the legal status of different types of UK companies limited by shares, and the terminology used to describe them, is important.

- **A private company cannot offer shares to the public.**
- **A public limited company can offer its shares to the public.**

- **A quoted company has its shares traded on a recognised investment exchange (for example, the London Stock Exchange (LSE), but also AIM, Nasdaq, etc.).**
- **A listed company has its shares traded on the UK Official List (for example, the LSE Main Market).**

Because a private limited company cannot offer its shares to the public, it can be neither quoted nor listed. A public limited company can offer its shares to the public, but does not necessarily have to do so through a recognised investment exchange; it may, therefore, choose to be neither quoted nor listed.

1.2 Hybrid companies

Hybrid companies have evolved from UK company law and are to be found mainly in offshore jurisdictions, including the Isle of Man, Gibraltar and the British Virgin Islands.

They are financial structures created by the fusion of two distinct types of corporate entity: a company limited by shares and a company limited by guarantee. There are three parties to a hybrid company.

1. Shareholders

The shareholders own the legal title to the shares and so control a company, as they possess all of the voting rights. However, they will not receive any **dividend payments** or return of capital when the company is wound up. In essence, the shareholders will perform duties similar to those of the trustees of a **trust** and they will control the company without actually owning the equitable rights to the shares, although the shares will be registered in their names.

2. Guarantors

Guarantors (also referred to as members or guarantee members) will receive all the benefits relating to capital and income distributions. In return for these privileges, the guarantors will agree to contribute a fixed nominal amount towards the company's debts (if any), in the event that the company is wound up. The guarantors acquire a contingent (potential) liability.

The guarantors are invited and elected by the directors, and it is their membership fees that inject money into the hybrid company. The membership fees will be calculated so that they are equal to the amount of the investment required. Distribution and rights upon liquidation belong to the guarantors.

The guarantee members will receive the benefits in a similar manner to the beneficiaries of a trust and they are able to transfer their rights to third parties.

3. Directors

The rights and responsibilities of each class of member will be stated in carefully drafted **articles of association** which will cover the scope of the directors' powers. The directors make income distributions, however, it is not

dividend payments
These are usually made in twice-yearly instalments (the interim dividend and the final dividend) to the ordinary shareholders of a company and are usually made out of profits.

trust
A structure whereby the legal title of assets is transferred by an individual (settlor) to trustees for the benefit of third-party beneficiaries. The trustees will look after the assets for the benefit of the third-party beneficiaries with the settlor sacrificing all control of the assets. Trusts are mainly used as tax-planning tools and for succession planning.

articles of association
The internal rules of a company covering what has to be done, the roles and responsibilities of the company directors, and the positions required to perform their relevant duties.

the shareholders who will benefit, but the guarantors. In common with all companies, income payments will be made at the discretion of the directors.

Uses of hybrid companies

Hybrid companies are used:

- as an alternative to trusts – they may be used by residents of civil law jurisdictions where trusts may not be recognised;
- in a similar manner to trusts and are located mainly in offshore jurisdictions;
- as tax-planning vehicles because they do not have to be included as part of an estate's declaration to Her Majesty's Revenue & Customs (HMRC), as there are no assets;
- for the deferral of capital gains tax;
- to lessen personal or company taxation; and
- to guarantee members' interests after their death using various provisions.

If one guarantee member dies, the benefits can be transferred to another member, thus avoiding the payment of inheritance tax. Legally there are no succession issues. Each hybrid company, however, will be tailored to the requirements of the investor, subject to the restrictions of the jurisdiction. Hybrid companies will guarantee to meet company liabilities up to a specific fixed amount with rights and obligations of each class of member structured to cater for their individual requirements.

1.3 Alteration of company status and re-registration

As a company evolves, its directors may decide that it is appropriate to change their company's status from a private limited company to a public limited company. However, a company can change its status from:

- a private limited company to a private unlimited company;
- a private limited company to a public limited company;
- a public limited company to a private limited company limited by shares;
- a public limited company to a private unlimited company; or
- a private unlimited company to a private limited company.

Where a private limited company is re-registering as a plc, it must conform to the authorised share capital requirement for a plc, which is currently £50,000. The law relating to re-registration is contained in Part 7 of the Companies Act 2006.

Test yourself 3.1

a) **Name the four main types of company structures that exist in the UK.**

b) **What are hybrid companies?**

2. Capital structure: debt capital and share capital

The term 'capital structure' may sound rather daunting; however, it is a very straightforward concept and companies' capital structures are in constant states of flux.

Capital structure is the manner by which a company is financed. It is the combination of cash, **debt capital** and **equity capital**, and is the method by which a company obtains various forms of finance in order to allow it to function and to attain its corporate aims and objectives.

debt capital
The percentage of debt contained within a company's capital structure. This may include debentures and long-term bank borrowings.

equity capital
The percentage of a company's capital structure that is financed by share capital. This would include both ordinary and preference shares.

There is no single capital structure that will suit every company, and the structure may not always be what the directors of the company want. For instance, not all companies will be able to issue corporate bonds, debentures or **commercial paper,** as they might be small companies, and lenders may be unwilling to provide finance by any of these methods.

commercial paper (CP)
Often referred to as 'corporate IOUs' and used by large companies as a cheaper alternative method to bank borrowing. It is issued as a method of raising short-term unsecured finance. CP has fixed maturities between one and 270 days.

The capital structure for a large quoted plc will be very different to that of a small private limited company. A company's capital structure will be a constant balancing act for its directors. For example, in a company where the directors do not wish to give away any equity or control of the company, they may decide that bank borrowing or the issuance of bonds (types of debt capital) is preferable to a further share issue. Another consideration may be the cost of organising share issues, especially for new public issues, known as **flotations**.

flotation
The selling of some or all of the shares in a company which is being brought to market for the first time on a recognised investment exchange.

However, a company may have a need to expand or to finance major capital projects, and thus may be forced into issuing shares if its directors are unable to obtain bank finance or issue bonds.

2.1 The main types of capital finance

The two main types of capital finance are debt capital and share, or equity, capital.

Gearing

Debt capital and preference shares represent prior claims on a company. Debt interest repayments and preference share dividends must be paid before any payment can be made to the ordinary shareholders. These prior claims will weaken the balance sheet because they represent increased liabilities. If the level of debt capital is too high, it may destabilise the company and even force it into involuntary liquidation.

The relationship of debt capital to equity capital is referred to as gearing. It is quite normal for companies to have some element of **gearing**, but the level should be closely monitored not only by its directors, but also by corporate analysts. Gearing may be expressed as a ratio:

gearing or leverage
The use of a resource, often borrowed funds or debt, in a way that the potential positive or negative outcome is enhanced. The objective is to increase a return substantially.

$$\frac{\text{Total long-term borrowings}}{\text{Ordinary shareholders' funds}}$$

The components of the long-term borrowing figure would include long-term loans and preference shares. By contrast, the ordinary shareholders' funds would additionally include ordinary shares and reserves. The resulting figure is then shown as a percentage.

The aim of the gearing ratio is to show to investors and analysts alike the relationship of total net borrowings against ordinary shareholders' funds. There are a number of variants of the formula, however, the underlying factor is to indicate the level of debt to equity – that is, how much the company is relying on borrowed funds to support its operations.

When a company has a high level of debt to equity, it is said to have a level of gearing (be highly geared) by contrast if the level of debt to equity is low, the company is said to have a low level of gearing (be low-geared).

2.2 Debt capital

Debt capital is the extent to which a company depends upon various forms of debt in order to finance its assets. In essence, it is a reliance or part-reliance on borrowed money. The greater the proportion of debt capital to overall capital, the more leveraged the company is and the more highly geared it is said to be. The most important features of debt capital are that it must be paid back at predetermined dates, and regular payments of interest must be serviced. If interest rates are high, this may have a catastrophic effect on the company's cash flow and ability to pay. Conversely, if interest rates are low, this may represent a relatively cheap form of external finance; it is cheaper than dividend payments.

Debt capital may include any or all of:

- bank borrowing in the form of fixed term loans, revolving credit lines or overdrafts;
- corporate bonds (discussed in Chapter 8) and commercial paper (discussed in Chapter 7); and
- debentures.

2.3 Share capital

Share capital includes ordinary shares and preference shares. Private companies limited by guarantee will not have shares in their capital structures.

Test yourself 3.2

a) What are the two main types of capital finance?

b) Explain 'gearing' in relation to the capital structure of a company.

c) What is debt capital?

3. Ordinary shares

Ordinary shares are the most common form of stock in the UK. They are fixed units of the share capital of a company and are the most important component of a company's capital structure. They are used not only to finance expansion but also to reduce reliance on debt. If a company does not have any debt it is not concerned with interest payments.

Ordinary shares, or equities, are so-called because the ordinary shareholders own the equity of the company. They are thus entitled, after prior charges such as preference share dividends and bank interest, to all distributed profit. If, at some point in the future, liquidation should occur, the ordinary shareholders will be entitled to any residual assets, but only after all other creditors have been satisfied.

Ordinary shares may also referred to as voting shares, although there may be some classes of ordinary share that have no voting rights, each ordinary share represents an equal share in the company. These may be designated A or B shares. Each ordinary share of the company will have the same nominal value; consequently all shareholders have parity which is directly proportional to their total holding.

Ordinary shares, having been issued initially in the **primary market,** by one of the five authorised methods, may subsequently be traded freely in the **secondary market** (the market for second-hand securities), enabling investors to make a profit, break even or limit their loss.

primary market
Where shares or bonds are issued for the first time. In the gilts market this would be the issuance by the DMO through its auctions.

secondary market
The market for second-hand securities. Securities are bought and sold between investors rather than the original issuer. The securities must have been issued in the primary market first.

The ordinary shareholders will provide capital in exchange for their shares. From the company's perspective, this will be its issued share capital, and forms the equity capital of the company.

Each individual share will possess an equal right to share in the distributed profits of the company. If, for example, a company has issued 1,000 ordinary shares, each share will be entitled to receive 1/1000 of the distributed profits – this is different from 1/1000 of the overall profits. Preference shareholders must receive their fixed dividends before ordinary shareholders receive their dividends, and some of the profits will normally be retained for future growth.

3.1 Advantages and disadvantages of ordinary share ownership

For shareholders, the risks of share ownership include the following.

Company default

The company may become insolvent and be unable to pay its debts; consequently its shares may become worthless, eliminating all shareholder investment. In the shorter term, there may be no dividend payments resulting in no receipt of income, which might have been expected. British Petroleum (BP) had to suspend its dividend after the Deepwater Horizon oil rig disaster (see Making it work 3.1), and Lloyds Bank plc had to suspend payment of its dividend when it was taken into part-government ownership during the credit crisis of 2007/08.

Corporate takeovers

Companies may be taken over or become the target of a takeover, causing a rise in share price for the target company. However, the share price of the acquiring company will tend to fall.

Nationalisation

Railtrack was nationalised by the UK government (it was put into administration on 7 October 2001) and shareholders received only a fraction of their investment. In 2008, Northern Rock and Bradford & Bingley Building Society were both taken into state ownership, and the shareholders did not receive any compensation whatsoever, losing all of their investment.

Bad publicity

Share prices may be adversely affected by bad publicity. For example, the share price of Signet (formerly Ratners) famously plunged in 1991 its chief executive officer (CEO) made a speech in which he addressed a conference of the Institute of Directors. In this speech he commented that their products were sub-standard.

Market forces

Sector shares (banking shares) have been particularly susceptible to increased share price volatility following the 2007/08 credit crisis. These include:

- shares across national markets particularly in unstable countries or those with a weak balance of payments; and
- shares across international markets.

Other disadvantages of owning ordinary shares

- The opportunity cost of unearned bank interest on the capital used to purchase the equities.
- The company's failure to pay dividends as expected.
- A fall in a company's share price resulting in a reduction in the value of a shareholder's portfolio, which may not be able to recover for many years.
- All risks will increase the longer the stock is held, even in well-established companies where there have been no previous indicators of any failure.
- There is no obligation for the company to pay dividends or even to return the shareholders' capital.
- Ordinary shareholders rank below preference shareholders in both the payment of dividends and the order of pay out upon liquidation; in the event of liquidation, they may receive nothing at all.

Making it work 3.1: The effect of an environmental disaster on share price

On 20 April 2010, there was a major accident on the BP Deepwater Horizon oil rig near the coast of Louisiana, USA.

This resulted in tens of thousands of barrels of oil pouring into the Gulf of Mexico, which caused a devastating environmental incident.

The President of the United States, Barack Obama, intervened with the result that BP had to set aside US$13.5 billion for compensation claims. This resulted in BP cancelling the payment of its ordinary share dividends. This in turn has had a considerable downward pressure on the price of BP shares, which almost halved in value between April and July 2010, although the price later recovered somewhat.

Because UK pension funds invest heavily in BP (almost 1/7 of all dividend income derived from the FTSE 100 companies is received from BP), this, in turn, threatened both current and future pensions, as the pension funds rely on the receipt of these dividend payments to make their own payments to pension holders.

Ultimately, BP incurred a $32.2 billion liability in July 2010 and in order to cover this, the company has had to sell some of its assets in Vietnam (a pipeline project) and Venezuela to TNK-BP, its Russian joint venture. It also aimed to sell $30 billion in non-core businesses by the end of 2011 to cover its compensation claims.

Consider:

- the short-term and long-term effects on BP's share price; and
- how the BP directors might manage their public relations issues.

As of May 2018, the price of BP shares has rallied to 558 pence per share.

However, there are significant advantages of ordinary share ownership:

- The ordinary shareholders do not have any duties to perform.
- Ordinary shares carry a higher potential return, based on risk.
- The liability of ordinary shareholders is limited to the amount they have contributed for their shares. If the company becomes bankrupt, the shareholders will not have to provide any additional finance (provided that the shares are fully paid).
- There is the prospect of the payment of interim and final dividends.
- There is also the prospect of capital growth.

Advantages to the company of issuing ordinary shares

There is no fixed dividend to pay as is the case with preference shares, and all payments are made at the discretion of the directors. If profits are small or losses have been incurred, the directors may decide not to make the payments, thus preventing any further cash drain.

Disadvantages to the company of issuing ordinary shares

Disadvantages include a potential high administration cost of issuing, particularly with large flotations, and a reduction of control of the company.

3.2 The rights of ordinary shareholders

Ordinary shareholders benefit from a number of rights that attach to ownership of their shares. They have the right:

- to share in the profits of the company, although such profits may be either retained or distributed at the discretion of the directors;
- to transfer their ordinary shares freely in the secondary markets in the case of plcs;
- to receive notice of annual general meetings (AGMs) and any other shareholders' meetings, including extraordinary meetings;
- to attend and vote at these meetings;
- to appoint a proxy on their behalf to attend meetings;
- to receive annual reports and accounts;
- of pre-emption, which entitles the ordinary shareholders to subscribe for new ordinary share capital and convertible loan stock, in direct proportion to their existing holdings (convertible loan stock can be converted in ordinary shares, thus diluting a holding); and
- to share equally in the assets of the company after all liabilities have been paid if the company is liquidated.

Test yourself 3.3

a) **What are ordinary shares?**

b) **Identify three shareholder rights under UK law.**

c) **From the perspective of an investor, give three advantages and three disadvantages of owning ordinary shares.**

4. Preference shares

4.1 Definition of preference shares

Preference shares, which are sometimes referred to as preferred stock, are often likened to debt. However, they are legally classed as share capital and as such are treated for tax purposes in the same manner as ordinary shares. The terms of issue for, and characteristics of, preference shares are usually explained in detail within a company's articles of association.

Preference shares can be issued by both private and public companies limited by shares. Preference shares derive the name because they are 'preferred' over ordinary shares in a number of significant ways, including the following:

- Preference shareholders have an entitlement to an annual fixed dividend (a percentage of the nominal amount), whereas ordinary shareholders do not.

- In the event of liquidation, preference shareholders have prior claims in respect of both repayments of capital and outstanding dividend payments, although this right must be included in the company's articles of association.

Preference shares comprise less than 1% of the overall share market, and are issued and used by companies, usually financial institutions, as a means to obtain external finance without having to relinquish any control of the company, as is the case with ordinary shares. They are another method of obtaining capital without having to borrow from a bank or issue bonds. Both of these methods would require absolute contractual obligations to make regular interest payments. However, companies do have to make the preference share dividend payment.

Preference shares have a nominal or face value for instance, £1 with fixed dividends, perhaps 5%. The fixed dividend is set at the time of issue and is a fixed percentage of the nominal amount.

4.2 Designation and types of preference shares

Cumulative and non-cumulative preference shares

Preference shares may be designated as either cumulative or non-cumulative in relation to the payment of their fixed dividends. Cumulative means that if dividends are not paid in any one year, then the current year's dividends, together with any previous non-payments, must be accumulated and paid before any future ordinary share dividend payments are made. By contrast, there is no legal obligation to pay the non-cumulative preference share dividend. However, they do have preference over ordinary shareholders in relation to the current year's dividend. In each year, if a business makes sufficient realised profits to permit the dividend to be lawfully paid, the company is obliged to pay the preference share dividend for that year.

Whether preference shares are designated as cumulative or non-cumulative will be stated in the company's articles of association and on the preference share certificate itself at the time of issue.

Redeemable and irredeemable preference shares

Under usual circumstances, irredeemable preference shares will not have a **redemption date**. This is because, having been issued, the only liability of the company is to service the fixed dividend payments. There is no obligation to return the capital, unless of course the company goes into liquidation; in this case, there would be an obligation to return the principal should sufficient funds be available. However, this will only ever be the nominal amount.

redemption date
The same as the maturity date, the date when the bond is redeemed.

In contrast, for redeemable preference shares, the company will have to return the capital on a predetermined date. This redemption date will be specified on the share certificate.

All designations of preference share of quoted companies can be bought or sold through stockbrokers.

4.3 Categories of preference share

Convertible preference shares

Convertible preference shares can be converted into ordinary shares at a predetermined future date under specific terms and conditions. This right will be stated from the outset. Sometimes the conversion can be called at the directors' discretion. The effect on ordinary share dilution must be considered.

Participating preference shares

Participating preference shares are those where the holders have the right to participate in or receive further dividends over and above the stated fixed dividend. These dividends will usually be linked to the level of profits of the company.

Investment suitability

Preference shares were traditionally purchased by institutional investors. However, they may also be used by private investors focused on income rather than capital gains, although capital gains are still very much possible. They are particularly appropriate for higher rate taxpayers.

If default ensues in relation to the dividend payment, the preference shareholders cannot force the company into liquidation.

4.4 Advantages and disadvantages of preference shares

Investor advantages

- Preference shares usually provide higher returns than bonds issued by the same company and there is generally less risk than with ordinary shares in the company.
- Preference shareholders receive a fixed percentage of the nominal amount annually. This dividend must be paid, as previously noted, before the ordinary share dividend. There is no need for the investors to wait for the directors' announcement to ascertain the amount of the dividend, because it is known from the outset.
- Even if no ordinary share dividend is declared, the preference share dividend should be paid, because non-payment will be viewed very unfavourably in the markets.
- Upon liquidation, preference shareholders rank above the ordinary shareholders for return of capital and current and accrued dividend payments.
- Upon liquidation, investors will receive only the nominal amount rather than a market price, because that is the liability of the company. If the preference shares were purchased below par, the investor will make a capital gain (assuming that the company, on being wound up, is in a position to pay out the full face value of the preference shares).
- The preference share dividend is paid out of post-tax company profits and is thus franked investment income.

Investor disadvantages

- Preference shareholders are members of the company, but they generally have no right to vote or attend AGMs unless dividends of cumulative preference shares are in arrears.
- Unless the preference shares are participating preference shares, the preference shareholder will only ever receive a fixed percentage of the nominal value, even if a company performs extremely well.
- Upon liquidation, investors will receive only the nominal amount. If shares were purchased above par, the investor will make a capital loss.

Issuer advantages

- The company does not relinquish any control as is the case with ordinary shares.
- Preference shares are not secured against any of the company's assets.
- Dividend payment may be suspended if the company has not earned sufficient profits to finance the dividend. This may be detrimental rather than fatal. If bank loan or bond interest payments are missed, the company may be forced into administration by its creditors.
- Known fixed commitments – the amount of preference share dividend.
- Allow the issuer to bolster the balance sheet when interest rates are low.
- If the preference shares are non-cumulative, arrears of dividends do not have to be paid to the preference shareholders.
- Preference shares do not ordinarily carry rights to profits beyond the fixed entitlement or to receive any capital surpluses beyond the nominal amount of the share.

Issuer disadvantages

- The company may offer higher rates of return in order to attract investors.
- If profits are reduced, the issuer may still be obliged to make the fixed dividend payment.
- The payment of preference shares dividend is not tax deductible, as is the case with debt interest payments.

Test yourself 3.4

a) Why are preference shares so called?

b) What are the main disadvantages to the investor of holding preference shares?

5. The primary market and new issues

5.1 Primary and secondary markets

new issues
The issuing of new securities, either for a company coming to the market for the first time or as a rights issue for an already-listed company in order to raise additional capital.

The securities markets are categorised as either primary or secondary. The primary market is the market for **new issues,** whereas the secondary market (as its name suggests) is concerned with buying and selling second-hand securities (in this respect it may be thought of as being the second-hand market for securities).The secondary market is introduced within this chapter, but will also be covered in more detail in Chapter 5.

Within the primary market (the new issues market), there are two main scenarios:

1. new corporate applicants (existing plcs that have never previously had a stock market listing or quotation of any type) who wish to obtain a listing for the first time, which may be achieved by one of five permitted methods (see section 6 of this chapter); and
2. companies that already have a stock exchange listing and wish to bring new securities to the market – for instance, in a **rights issue** (see section 7 of this chapter).

rights issue
A method by which a company can obtain additional capital (cash) by selling new shares. Rights issues give the right to existing shareholders to subscribe for new shares in a company in direct proportion to their existing holding. Allocations are made in the form of a rights letter.

5.2 New issues

The term 'new issues' refers to the bringing of new securities to the market for the first time. This includes rights issues, which are described in section 7.

Reference has already been made in the chapter to the fact that there are various types of corporate structure. Unquoted public limited companies may decide that it is appropriate to become a quoted company, thus making their shares available to the public through a recognised investment exchange.

If the directors of a company do decide that it is time to obtain a stock exchange quotation, they must undergo a thorough vetting process for the company. The requirements are far more stringent than those for remaining an unquoted plc.

Floating a company (i.e. obtaining a listing for the first time) can be a very expensive process; there is usually a minimum cost of £500,000, but this could run into many millions of pounds.

Although it is feasible to become a plc from the inception or start-up of a company, it is not possible to become a quoted plc, given that there are a number of regulatory and market requirements that must be fulfilled. For example, in order to obtain a listing on the main market (or Official List) of the London Stock Exchange, a company must satisfy specific criteria. There will be the listing requirements of the United Kingdom Listing Authority (UKLA), which is a division of the Financial Conduct Authority (FCA). These requirements will be set out in their rules and will necessarily include the following.

- Incorporation: The company must be incorporated under relevant laws, which in the UK means already being a plc.

- Accounts: The company seeking a listing must have published or filed audited accounts covering a three-year period. This period must end no more than six months before a planned floatation.
- Track record: The company must have an independent trading and revenue earning record covering a three-year period.
- The directors: The company must show that the directors possess the appropriate collective experience to run all areas of the business.
- Working capital requirement: The company must demonstrate that it has enough working capital not only for its immediate needs but also for the next 12 months, and must also have a market capitalisation of not less than £700,000.

5.3 The reasons for bringing new securities to the market

Some companies may wish to become quoted without the need to raise additional finance, as they may require some other non-financial benefit, as discussed below.

A new issue involves the sale of new securities specifically in order to raise additional capital. This could be the issue of new securities from a company already quoted on a recognised investment exchange, or alternatively by way of a rights issue.

It can also be in the form of a flotation, bringing a company to market for the first time – perhaps a previously unquoted plc that meets the requirement of a recognised investment exchange and now wishes to come to the market. Thus, the company will obtain a listing on its chosen exchange. The shares will be offered to the general public for the first time, although obviously shares already exist and are held by the current private shareholders.

As companies expand, they will start to experience a number of constraints. The key issues that companies may have to deal with include:

- the need to raise additional finance for major capital projects;
- replacement of debt capital with share capital; and
- lack of marketable shares.

If any of these issues arise, at this stage the company's directors may decide that the time is right to offer the company's shares to a wider public with these being listed on a recognised stock exchange. A private limited company is not compelled to become a plc, but it would have to re-register as a plc if it subsequently wished to offer its shares to the public, whether through a recognised investment exchange or not.

If the directors of a company do opt for a flotation, they must carefully consider and appraise the numerous advantages and disadvantages that could arise. This can be an expensive and time-consuming process.

The directors' decision as to whether the company's shares should be listed on a recognised stock exchange is very significant and must be based on the stage of the company's life cycle.

Directors may decide to opt for a flotation of their company for the following reasons:

- The original founders of the company may wish to release some or all of their original capital, which may be difficult while their shares are held within a private limited company structure.
- The company may need to raise additional capital in order to finance expansion, which may not be possible through bank finance.
- Existing venture capitalists and private equity firms may want their stake returning and be looking for an exit strategy, as their focus is always short term.
- The previous sources of capital may no longer be available (for instance, bank borrowing) and perhaps the existing shareholders are unable or unwilling to commit any additional capital.
- The company many not want any element of gearing.
- The directors may wish to retain key staff through share ownership schemes. Consequently, the company shares must be marketable.
- There is a need to be competitive with other companies that already have a stock exchange listing.
- The company's profile can be raised in the press.
- There is greater access to the capital markets.
- Marketability of shares is improved.
- There is a perception of financial stability.

New issues are the sale of new securities. The purpose of new issues due to raise capital through the issue of new shares from an existing company or an unlisted plc joining the market for the first time. A rights issue is a new issue, not an IPO (Initial Public Offering).

A flotation refers only to the bringing of the securities of a previously unlisted company to the market for the first time. This is also referred to as an IPO.

In 2017, there were 106 successful IPOs in London, raising $15 billion. Successful IPOs that year included:

- Allied Irish Bank, which raised euro 3 billion;
- Pirelli (an Italian motoring company), which raised euro 2.4 billion; and
- Eddie Stobart (a logistics company), which raised £393 million.

Potential IPOs in 2018 included:

- Aston Martin – a UK privately owned luxury car manufacturer is potentially seeking a flotation of £4–5 billion in order to facilitate expansion and also enter the lucrative SUV market. This flotation may take place in London or New York;

- AJ Bell – a UK investment platform provider; and
- Softbank Corp – will float its mobile telephone business in Tokyo and potentially London.

Making it work 3.2: Betfair plc

Betfair plc is an online betting exchange formed in 2000. It was previously an example of an unlisted plc with its shares held by a small group of shareholders. In late 2010, Betfair decided to obtain a stock exchange listing by offering 15.2% of its shares to the general public.

- Total number of shares in issue: 106.58 million.
- Number of shares offered to new investors initially: 16.20 million.
- Number of shares retained by existing shareholders: 83.80 million.

It is important to be aware of the following points:

- Betfair was an unlisted plc that had been trading for more than ten years and satisfied the listing requirements of the UKLA.
- The rationale for the listing was to obtain additional finance.
- Betfair did not offer all of its shares to investors – in this case only 15.2%. It was stated at the time that a further 10.8% might be offered at a later date, bringing the total to 26%.
- As Betfair's shares were being brought to market for the first time this is referred to as a flotation or an IPO.

Test yourself 3.5

a) **What is the difference between a primary and secondary securities market?**

b) **Outline three reasons why directors might decide to float their company.**

6. Admission to the London Stock Exchange

Admission to the Main Market of the London Stock Exchange for those companies wishing to have their securities listed is a two-stage process.

1. Their securities need to be admitted to the Stock Exchange Official List by the UKLA, a division of the FCA.
2. They need to be admitted to trading by the stock exchange.

Both stages have to be completed before shares can be listed on the stock exchange.

There are five permitted issue methods for an unlisted company bringing its securities to the market for the first time. These are:

1. an introduction;
2. a placing;
3. an intermediaries offer;
4. an offer for sale (a public offer); and
5. an offer for subscription (a public offer).

introduction
A method whereby an unlisted company can obtain a stock exchange listing without raising any capital or issuing shares. It would be used where the shares of a company are already widely held in the public domain. It is a marketing operation and would be used where there will be a guaranteed secondary market.

market makers
Organisations, usually investment banks or stockbrokers, that stand ready to make markets in particular securities. They buy and sell the securities on their own behalf and will always have a bid and offer price available.

offer for sale
A method by which a company can raise capital via a new issue. This method usually involves an issuing house who will buy the securities and then sell them at a slightly higher price to the general public.

offer for subscription
An offer of shares to the general public and institutional investors alike. Shares are offered directly to the public without using an issuing house. The public may apply for shares, offered by the company, at a fixed price or alternatively will be invited to tender.

Some of these methods may also be used for issuing new securities of already listed companies.

1. An introduction

An **introduction** is the cheapest and easiest of the five permitted issue methods. It is not a new issue at all, but is used as a method for a company to obtain a stock exchange listing. The company joins the stock market but without raising any new capital; consequently, it is not seen to be a marketing operation. It is, however, a method by which already-established overseas companies and listed on their own national exchanges can gain access to the London Stock Exchange Official List. The stock exchange will only permit a listing where there is a wide spread of shares available and where more than 25% of its shares are in public hands.

There are no underwriters' fees (see section 6.1) and minimal requirements for advertising the issue, which may be in the form of a box advertisement. On the negative side, because the advertising requirements are not as stringent as for the other methods, the opportunities to raise the company's profile are diminished considerably.

A usual condition for an introduction is that some of the larger current shareholders ensure that sufficient of their own shares are available to **market makers** in order that a market can be made when dealing commences. An introduction may also be used where two previously listed companies have merged to form a new company. In this instance, the newly formed company's shares will be brought to market by means of an introduction.

2. A placing

The company, through a sponsor or broker, will offer its shares to a small number of institutional investors only (pension funds, insurance companies and financial institutions including banks), in order to raise capital. This will obviously be a lot cheaper than either an **offer for sale** or an **offer for subscription**, as will be explained later.

A placing may well result in the company's shares being held by a narrower shareholder base than either an offer for sale or an offer for subscription, and this in turn may result in considerably less liquidity.

The only advertising requirement is that a box advertisement is placed in a newspaper advising that the shares have been sold.

The majority of companies now tend to favour placings, as these can be for any amount and do not have to be underwritten. Placings are often used together with a rights issue by the same company.

Making it work 3.3: Bank of Ireland

The Bank of Ireland, which was supported by taxpayers during the financial crisis of 2008, announced that it was to raise €3.9 million in order to expedite its recovery. This is an example of a company that is already listed 'placing' its new securities.

It achieved this as follows.

- A rights issue (to existing shareholders): €1.9 billion.
- New shares were placed with institutional investors: €0.5 billion (326.8 million shares).
- Conversion of the Irish Government's preference shares to ordinary shares: €1.5 billion.

3. *An intermediaries offer*

An intermediaries offer is very similar to a placing, the difference being that the sponsor or broker will offer the shares to other stockbrokers in addition to institutional investors. These stockbrokers will then offer the shares to their own clients, thus increasing the shareholder base and in turn marketability.

4. *An offer for sale*

Public offers may be sub-categorised into offers for sale and offers for subscription.

A public offer is when a company's shares are offered to both private and institutional investors alike. The offer will be underwritten so that any shares not taken up by the public will be purchased by the institutions. Underwriters will charge a fee for this service.

Of the various methods of making new issues, public offers are the most expensive, given that the aim is to raise as much capital for the company as possible. The main feature of a public offer is that it brings in private investors, which will greatly increase the liquidity of a company's shares, and should raise significant amounts of capital.

An offer for sale involves the appointment of an intermediary, where a company appoints a sponsor issuing house to manage the issue. The issuing house will normally buy the new securities and then offer them to the public and institutional investors at a slightly higher price than it paid. Most offers for sale will be new securities being brought to the market, but can occur where existing shareholders wish to dispose of their current holdings. All of the administrative issues will be overseen by the issuing house.

Offers for sale may involve subscription by either a fixed price or an offer for sale by tender.

Offers for sale using a fixed price means that investors will be invited to subscribe for shares at a fixed price determined by the company's financial advisors and sponsor. The price will be calculated using perhaps sector comparisons and market conditions.

When the price has been determined, the new securities will be offered to the public. Subscribers must state the number of shares they wish to purchase at or above this fixed price. If the issue is oversubscribed, allocations will be scaled down as specified in the issue **prospectus**. If the issue is undersubscribed, all of the investors will receive the amount applied for, and the remainder will be taken up by the underwriters.

prospectus
A document that sets out in accordance with legislation the terms and constitution of a company which is applying for its shares to be issued on a recognised stock exchange.

An offer for sale by tender will also involve the use of an intermediary issuing house. However, in this instance, the issuing house or sponsor will establish a minimum tender price. Potential investors will be invited to subscribe at or above the minimum tender (offer) price. The subscribers will state the number of shares they wish to purchase at this minimum selling price. Allocation will then be made to those subscribers who have tendered at or above the minimum tender price.

Worked example 3.1

An issuing house offers for sale by tender on behalf of its corporate client, ABC plc. The tender issue is for 1,000,000 ordinary shares at a minimum tender price of £3.60 per share.

Applications are received from subscribers as follows.

- 250,000 shares @ £3.60 (the minimum tender price)
- 350,000 shares @ £3.70
- 400,000 shares @ £3.80 (this will be the actual tender price)
- 450,000 shares @ £3.90
- 150,000 shares @ £4.00

When all the applications have been received by the issuing house, the tenders will be ranked.

All of those who bid at £4.00, £3.90 and £3.80 will be successful, and the entire issue will be taken up.

The subscribers at £3.70 and £3.60 will be unsuccessful, and will receive none of the ordinary shares. If the unsuccessful applicants are still determined to purchase the shares, they may do so in the secondary market through a stockbroker.

The successful subscribers do not pay the price they actually offered. Rather, they pay the lowest price that disposes of the entirety of the offer. In this example, all successful subscribers will pay £3.80. This is sometimes referred to as the 'actual tender price' or 'strike price'.

If there had been more subscriptions at £3.80, then there would have to have been an element of scaling down the allocations.

5. ***An offer for subscription***

The requirements for an offer for subscription are the same as an offer for sale. These are issues of new securities offered directly to the public by the company itself. They may include issues by the Bank of England and loan stock issues, whereas issues of ordinary shares made in this manner would have included those made by investment trust companies.

Although similar to an offer for sale, an offer for subscription is where a company directly invites investors to subscribe for its shares. This method is generally used by new companies and, if a minimum amount of capital is not raised, the offer will be withdrawn. There are no sponsors or issuing houses involved and the offer is only partially underwritten. Most companies are not able to run such offers themselves, as they lack the necessary expertise.

6.1 Underwriting

Although some new issues can fail, it is of paramount importance that they succeed and that they are fully subscribed. Ideally, dealings will commence at a premium with investors realising a profit immediately. However, as there is a chance (although small) that matters can go wrong at the last minute, offers for sale of equities have to be underwritten.

There are instances of new issues not being fully subscribed, shares trading at a substantial discount and offerings being withdrawn very close to the anticipated flotation date. This could be for any number of reasons, including:

- insufficient investor interest in the offering;
- perceived over-pricing of the issue price;
- lack of confidence in the general sector or market; or
- better offers from other parties.

Underwriting is a form of insurance policy to ensure that the new issues succeed. It involves institutional investors (investment banks, pension funds and insurance companies) agreeing to take up any shares for which the public does not subscribe. The take-up proportion of each underwriter will be agreed from the outset.

Usually the issuing house (sponsor) itself will be the principal underwriter, followed by a series of sub-underwriters. Underwriting commission is the greatest expense of any new issue and is usually in the region of 2% of the new issue proceeds. The issuing house will generally retain 0.5% of the proceeds and pass the remaining 1.5% to the sub-underwriters. Although the percentage taken appears to be small, it is a very lucrative business in the case of a multi-billion pound rights issue (see section 7). This commission is payable whether or not the underwriters are called upon to take up any unsubscribed shares.

Another way in which a rights issue can be made to succeed and thus reduce the need for underwriters is to issue the securities at a deep discount. This, however, will not be too popular with the existing shareholders.

Test yourself 3.6

a) **In the UK, what are the five permitted issue methods for bringing new securities to the market?**

b) **Explain an offer for sale by tender.**

c) **Explain underwriting relevant to new issues.**

7. Rights issues

A rights issue is a way in which a company can raise additional capital by selling new shares. This is usually for a specific purpose, such as business expansion, but may also be used as a means to reduce reliance on existing debt capital, particularly if interest rates are high.

Rights issues derive their name because the existing ordinary shareholders have an absolute statutory right contained within the Companies Act 2006 to subscribe for the new shares in the company prior to those shares being offered to external investors. This is in order that they can prevent their existing percentage shareholding from being diluted, while at the same time maintaining their existing level of control. This right is referred to as the **right of pre-emption**.

right of pre-emption
The legal right of existing shareholders to subscribe, prior to general release, for new equity capital of the same class or any class of security (warrants and convertible loan stock), which may potentially have a diluting effect on their percentage shareholding. This would include rights issues.

These rights will not only have the effect of increasing the assets of the company, as they must be paid for in cash, but they will also reduce the value of each existing ordinary share and the percentage control of existing shareholdings. If an investor does not take up the rights, the size of the share portfolio will remain the same and the overall cash value of the portfolio should remain constant. If the value of the rights is included should remain constant as it will be comprised of the existing shares and the rights which will have a value.

A rights issue is an alternative to bank borrowing or increasing debt capital by other means and is relatively inexpensive from the company's perspective, as new capital is raised in the form of cash. A rights issue is a category of new issue, discussed earlier in this chapter (section 5.2).

The rationale underpinning a rights issue is that the current shareholders must be allowed to maintain their existing percentage control of the company, should they so wish.

However, the existing ordinary shareholders are only allowed to subscribe for the new shares in direct proportion to their holding; this is a right and not an obligation, and existing ordinary shareholders are not compelled to contribute any additional capital. However, should they not subscribe for the new shares, their overall control of the company will diminish.

Each of the new shares will possess the same rights as the old shares – for example, in relation to voting rights and receipt of dividend payments. The shares are **fungible** in that each share will be identical and indistinguishable from another.

fungible
Interchangeable and not able to be told apart (for example, £10 notes). Fungible securities of the same class are therefore interchangeable and indistinguishable.

7.1 Method of issue

The new shares will be offered to the existing shareholders in direct proportion to their existing holding. For instance, they may be offered one new share for every four 'old' shares currently held.

In order to encourage the existing shareholders to subscribe for the new shares, they will be given the right to subscribe for them at an often substantial discount to the prevailing market price. This is generally in the region of a 15–20% discount on the closing market price on the day before the announcement of the rights issue.

The rights to the new shares now become fully tradable securities in their own right, as they give the holder or the potential holder the right to purchase new shares at a discount to the prevailing market price.

Worked example 3.2

If the market price of a certain share prior to the announcement of the rights issue were £10.00 and the rights issue allowed existing shareholders to subscribe for new shares at £8.00 (representing a discount of 20% on the closing price of the previous day), this will necessarily result in the 25% more shares being issued.

If an investor has a portfolio containing 10,000 ordinary shares of a particular company and each of these shares has a market price of £10.00, the investor will now be entitled (although not obliged) to subscribe for 2,500 new shares (one for every four currently held).

The rights will be allocated to the existing shareholders in the form of a 'rights letter'.

Obviously, the market price of the 'old' shares cannot remain the same because 2,500 new shares will be issued which will dilute the 'old' share price. Consequently, the price of these shares will fall (assuming that there are no other factors which will affect the share price). A new theoretical share price may now be calculated thus:

Existing portfolio holding	10,000 shares at market price of £10.00	= £100,000
New shares	2,500 shares at £8.00	= £20,000

The combined holding of 12,500 shares will now have an aggregate price of £120,000.

There are many external factors that might exert influence on the share price, but the theoretical price of all of the shares (old and new combined) should now be £9.60 per share.

$$\frac{£120,000}{12,500} = £9.60$$

The shareholders will now have the right to subscribe for the new shares at £8.00 when the market price is £10.00. The theoretical market price, as we have calculated above, is £9.60.

The current shareholders with a holding of £100,000 will have to pay £20,000 if they are to maintain their current percentage holding, and the company will receive £20,000 in the form of cash, which will be reflected by an increase in issued share capital (this will be included in the balance sheet).

This will result in the share price of the existing holding (10,000 shares) falling to £9.60, representing an apparent loss per share of 40p or a total loss of £4,000.

This will be offset by the gain on the rights issue: £9.60 – £8.00 = £1.60 per share (£1.60 × 2,500 = £4,000). However, the current shareholder is only entitled to subscribe for one new share for every four currently held. This £1.60 gain will be spread over four shares, and the gain per share is £1.60 / 4 = £0.40. These figures (in theory) should always balance. Each right is clearly worth 40p and is a fully tradable security in its own right.

Buying and selling prices for the rights will be provided by the majority of stockbrokers. If the new price of the share is £9.60 and the current market price is £10.00, then the most that an investor should ever pay in the secondary market for a single right should be 40p.

Worked example 3.3

In March 2017, Tullow Oil announced a 25 for 49 issue. The purpose of this rights issue was to raise £600 million to reduce debt and fund exploration.

The terms of the rights issue were 25 'new' ordinary shares for every 49 currently held. The price of each new share was set at £1.30 and the closing price of the existing shares was £2.37 on the day prior to the company's announcement. This represented a 45.2% discount which is considerably outside market practice.

For an investor with a holding of 245,000 the implications could be as follows:

Existing shareholding value is 245,000 x £2.37= £580,650.

Under the terms of the rights issue this investor is entitled to apply for

$$\frac{£245,000}{49} \times 25 = 125,000 \text{ new shares}$$

The maximum entitlement to 125,000 new shares would cost £125,000 × £1.30 costing = £162,500.

Thus if the investor took up his full entitlement of 125,000 the total portfolio value would be.

Total number of shares (existing and new) 245,000 + 125,000 = 370,000.

Total cost = 245,000 @ £2.37 = £580,650 plus

125,000 @ £1.30 = £162,890

Total portfolio value 370,000 costing £743,540 = £2.01 – Theoretical ex-rights price.

However, the price actually fell from £2.37 to £2.03.

7.2 Nil-paid value (nil-paid form)

In the first instance, the existing shareholders are given rights to subscribe for new shares at a stated price. As the shareholders have paid nothing for these rights, they are referred to as **nil paid**.

nil paid
Under a rights issue, existing shareholders are given rights to subscribe for new shares at a specific price. The rights themselves become fully tradable securities. As the existing shareholders have paid nothing for these rights, they are referred to as nil paid.

If an existing shareholder receives a notification of a rights issue from a company in which he has a shareholding there will be five possible courses of action:

1. To take up all of the rights, as allocated in the rights' letter. This course of action would maintain the shareholder's percentage holding and thus will also maintain their same degree of control, although this is via an increased number of shares. This will necessarily mean that additional capital will have to be contributed. Although the value of each individual share will in theory fall, the size of the shareholding will increase, as will the value of the portfolio in cash terms. The investor's bank balance will fall by the amount paid for the rights.
2. To take up a proportion of the rights while selling the remainder. An investor's percentage control of the company will diminish. Additional cash will still have to be contributed. In this instance, the total number of shares held will increase and the cash value of the shareholding will increase, however, the percentage control of the company still decreases. Although the investor's bank balance will reduce, cash will also be received by selling some of the rights.
3. To sell all of the rights. This will dilute the shareholder's percentage holding but they will not have to contribute any additional capital and will receive

money for the sale of these rights. This will increase their bank balance, although the value of the share portfolio will decrease.

4. To do nothing. The company will sell the rights on the shareholder's behalf and send the proceeds to them. The value of the shareholder's portfolio will fall, as will their percentage holding, but their bank balance will increase.
5. To sell sufficient rights and use the resulting capital received to exercise some rights to purchase a percentage of the shares. In this case, there is no capital contribution. The cash value of the shareholder's portfolio will remain unchanged, although there will be an increase in the number of shares held, but with reduced control, as no additional capital was provided. There may be some impact on bank balance. This is often referred to as 'tail swallowing'.

The existing shareholders may purchase additional rights in the secondary market over and above their allocation in order to increase their percentage holding even further; this will reduce their bank balance.

7.3 Cum rights and ex rights

Ordinary shares may be designated and traded either cum rights or ex rights.

Cum rights

Securities are traded on the stock exchange before the ex-rights cut-off day. This means that, if an investor purchases shares cum rights, they will receive shares together with the rights to buy new shares. The price that the investor will pay will be the market price, which factors in the value of those rights.

Ex rights

An investor purchasing shares will buy without receiving the right to participate in the rights issue. This price will obviously be lower and will be the price less the value of the rights. This price is referred to as the ex-rights price of a share. It is similar to the theoretical market price subsequent to a rights issue.

7.4 The implications of rights issues

A rights issue in order to finance expansion will generally be viewed favourably by both shareholders and the markets.

Rights issues are undertaken by issuing houses, which will arrange to have them underwritten, usually by City institutions. These will in turn guarantee to take up any shares for which the existing shareholders have not subscribed. This will be on a pro-rata basis and will be agreed by the various underwriters and sub-underwriters at the outset.

If shareholders do not exercise any of their rights or, alternatively, sell some or all of their rights, their percentage holding in the company will have reduced because, although they have the same number of shares or less as before, there are now more shares in circulation. These shares have a reduced value. Shareholders ought not to lose out as they will receive the proceeds of their rights, thus increasing their bank balance, although control of the company will decrease.

Making it work 3.4: Prudential plc

On 17 May 2010, Prudential plc announced proposals to merge with AIA Group. This was effectively a reverse takeover.

This merger was to have been part-financed by the largest rights issue in UK corporate history and was intended to raise £13.8 billion (net of costs; £14.5 billion including costs).

The rights issue was fully underwritten by Credit Suisse, HSBC and J.P. Morgan Cazenove (the three lead underwriters) together with a syndicate of sub-underwriters.

Specific details of the issue

Prudential plc was to have issued 13,964,557,750 shares.

The terms were to have been 11 rights shares for every two existing shares already held. The issue price for the new shares was to have been 104p per share.

This represented a significant discount of 80% to the closing price of 542.5 pence on 14 May 2010. This discount of 80% was considerably out of line with market practice, where a discount is usually in the region of 15% to 20% to the current share price.

The subscription price of the new shares also represented a significant discount of 39.3% to the theoretical ex-rights price.

Proposed timetable

17 May: Announcement of rights issue and publication of rights issue prospectus.
4 June: Record date for entitlement under the rights issue.
7 June: Expected date of despatch of provisional allotment letters.
8 June: Dealing in rights issues shares, nil paid commenced on LSE.
8 June: Existing shares marked 'ex rights' by LSE.
23 June: Last date in UK for acceptance, payment in full and registration or renunciation of provisional allotment letters.
24 June: Announcement of the result of the rights issue.
24 June: Dealings in rights issue shares, fully paid, commence on the LSE – rights issue shares credited to **CREST** stock accounts.

CREST
The electronic settlement system for gilts, equities and other corporate securities in the United Kingdom.

However, on 2 June 2010, the Prudential announced the cancellation of its proposed rights issue. This raised a number of important considerations.

- Although the proposed rights issue was cancelled, the Prudential still incurred significant costs, in the region of £450 million. This will have included a break-fee of £153 million.
- Investors who bought the shares on a cum-rights basis before the markets closed on 1 June might not have bought the shares had there

been no rights entitlements attached. However, the proposed rights issue was conditional on the passing of the rights issue resolution at the general meeting, which was to have been held on 7 June. This is a clear case where investors should have studied the fine detail of the issue conditions. The failure of the deal also had a considerable negative effect on the reputation of the Prudential.

8. Capital and income distributions

8.1 Capitalisation issues

scrip issues
These increase the number of shares in circulation by reducing the price of the shares in direct proportion. There is no dilution of a shareholder's current percentage holding. This is a process to make shares which appear expensive more marketable.

Capitalisation issues are similar to **scrip issues** (also known as bonus issues) and are essentially only bookkeeping exercises.

In this situation a company will issue new shares to its existing shareholders in direct proportion to their current holding, perhaps a one-for-one or one-for-two. Consequently, there will be an increase in the issued share capital. The cash value of the total shareholding will not fall, but the value of each individual share will.

For clarity, existing shareholders will not provide any additional capital and there is no extra funding received by the company, consequently there is no matching increase in the value of the company.

reserve account
An account or accounts comprising funds set aside for specific purposes such as the purchase of capital equipment.

The rationale underpinning of this corporate action is that reserves such as revenue reserves or share premium accounts are converted into share capital – that is, they are capitalised. Any increase in share capital will be matched by a reduction in a **reserve account**.

Under usual circumstances, a shareholder with a holding of, for example, 10,000 shares of £2.00 under a one-for-one capitalisation issue would subsequently have 20,000 ordinary shares of £1.00.

The purpose of a capitalisation issue is to make a company's shares more attractive to investors, who may be more inclined to purchase 100 shares at £2.00 rather than 10 shares at £20.00. The improved marketability may also have a positive effect on a share price given that new investors may be attracted to the 'lower' price. For example, where they could not afford one share at £20.00 because they only had £19.00, they could at now least afford nine shares at £2.00.

stock split (or share split)
A corporate action where a company issues additional shares to existing shareholders. There is a reduction in the nominal value of each share in direct proportion to the increase in number of additional shares issued.

In the event a company states that it will maintain its future dividend payments, this means that the shareholder will receive the same percentage dividend, but on an increased number of shares.

8.2 Stock split

A **stock split** involves the company issuing additional shares to existing shareholders in direct proportion to their holding. This corporate action requires approval by the board of directors.

A stock split or subdivision involves reducing the nominal value of shares and at the same time increasing the number of shares. There is no new capital raised, and there is no capitalisation element with reserves remaining unaltered. If a shareholder had 100,000 shares with a nominal value of £2.00, this would be changed to 200,000 shares with a nominal value of £1.00, assuming a two-for-one split.

There will be no effect on a company's overall market value or shareholders' percentage ownership, although there would be a reduction in the market price, which would be in direct proportion to the new shares issued.

The reason for a stock split is to make a company's shares more marketable while retaining reserves, resulting in the company's shares being more accessible to a broader spectrum of investors.

8.3 Stock consolidation

Essentially this is the reverse of a stock split. This corporate action involves increasing the nominal amount of the shares. Again, there is no effect on a company's market value or shareholders' percentage holding. However, there should be an increase in the market price of the share relating to the share reduction.

This course of action would be taken when a company's share price has fallen to an unacceptable level and needs to be brought back to an appropriate level. The overall result is a reduction in the number of shares in issue, with a matching increase in the share price.

8.4 Dividends

Dividends are the amounts of money distributed by companies to shareholders based on an amount per share. A dividend is not the profit earned by a company; instead it is the amount that the directors decide to allocate to each share. The amount of money paid to the shareholders is referred to as a dividend payment and is subject to income tax. During the year, the company may pay one or more dividends. Generally, in the UK at least, there are two dividend payments paid six months apart: the interim and final dividend.

While shareholder approval is not required for the interim dividend, it most certainly is for the payment of the final dividend, which is usually agreed at the AGM. Shareholders have no power to increase a final dividend that has been recommended by the directors, but they do have the ability to reduce or cancel it.

Special dividends

Special dividends are paid on a one-off basis and are usually much larger than the usual dividend. They are used as a means of returning surplus capital to the shareholders and must be given to all shareholders in direct proportion to their holding.

8.5 Deferred shares

Deferred shares (also referred to as founders' shares) are part of the ordinary share capital. They are 'deferred' in relation to the payment of the dividend, which may be suspended for up to ten years. During this period, even though the holder may receive no income, there may still be considerable capital growth. After the deferred period, both ordinary and deferred shares will become fungible.

Although the holders of deferred shares do not receive dividends for a number of years, it is customary for these shares to have considerably increased voting rights. It is also notable that the deferred payments take priority over lower-ranked ordinary shares.

Test yourself 3.7

a) **What is a rights issue?**

b) **What is the purpose of a capitalisation issue?**

c) **How does a dividend differ from a company's profits?**

d) **Explain the term nil-paid value.**

9. The secondary market

Historically, the UK secondary market, like the US market, was a physical market, but now it is conducted via screens, telephones and computers terminals. It is the market in second-hand securities and is used for those securities that have already been issued and bought at least once. By definition, it would not be used for 'new issues'.

It is vital that there is an efficient and well-regulated secondary market because, without it, there would be no means of disposal for those securities already purchased by investors in the primary market. Thus, without the secondary market, potential investors are less likely to buy shares in the first instance.

In the UK, the LSE provides an active and efficient secondary market for trading in a vast range of securities.

The main participants in the secondary markets are:

- investors (individual or institutional), who buy and sell securities for their own purposes, perhaps for long-term investment, speculative purposes or some other reason;
- brokers, who act on behalf of investors and their own account, and may hold shares on behalf of their clients in nominee accounts; and
- market makers, who by their very nature create markets in securities in which they trade, on their own behalf, with investors.

If investors know that there is an efficient secondary market, they will be more inclined to buy in the primary market.

This secondary market is generally exceptionally liquid, with both buying and selling prices made available throughout the trading day. It must not only be a level playing field for investors, it must also be seen to be so.

A distinction may be made between the primary and the secondary markets. In the primary market, companies issue their securities for the first time by one of the permitted methods referred to in section 6 of this chapter. In the secondary markets, investors may trade among themselves through an intermediary.

10. Mergers and acquisitions

Mergers and acquisitions alone make up an entire field of study, and many books and papers have been written on this topic. It is, however, a corporate strategy used for business expansion.

This area is often referred to as 'M&A', or 'Mergers and Takeovers', and is essentially split into three distinct categories:

1. acquisitions (also referred to as takeovers);
2. mergers and de-mergers; and
3. consolidations.

10.1 Acquisitions (takeovers)

In this instance, one business buys another business, known as the target company, and then the purchasing company will control that acquired company. The acquiring company will wholly absorb that target company, and generally the target company will lose its name. The assets, liabilities, rights and responsibilities of the target company will then become the responsibility of the acquiring company.

A company will become a target when its share price is less than the total value of assets. The acquiring company believes it is getting a bargain, and that perhaps it can make better use of these assets.

10.2 Mergers and de-mergers

In a merger, two businesses join together. The control of the enlarged company is shared between the owners of the original two companies.

A de-merger is where one large company is split into a number of smaller companies. This is often a tactic employed to prevent hostile takeovers.

10.3 Consolidations

Two or more companies join together to become a new entity with a new name. Each of the original companies will sacrifice their previous company names. The business reasons for mergers and acquisitions are:

- expansion which will ultimately benefit the company;
- business rationalisation and improved growth;
- cost reductions; and
- business diversification.

10.4 Financing acquisitions

underlying (asset)
Assets upon which derivative instruments are based.

Shares in a target company may be paid for either in cash or alternatively with shares in the acquiring company or some other security. If the shares are paid for in cash, the shareholders of the target company must consider whether the offer is adequate in relation to the value of the **underlying** assets. A takeover paid for in cash might give rise to a capital gains tax liability, whereas for a takeover paid for with other securities, this will not be the case.

Test yourself 3.8

a) Who are the main players in a secondary market?

b) Identify the three main areas of M&A activity.

Chapter summary

- There are four main types of companies registered in the UK.
- Hybrid companies bring together two different types of entity: a company limited by shares and a company limited by guarantee.
- Companies employ various types of capital structure in order to achieve their overall corporate objectives. This is a matter for the company directors to decide upon and will be a combination of share capital and debt capital.
- Gearing (or leverage) is the relationship of debt capital to the total shareholders' funds. An element of gearing is usual in most companies, but this should be monitored closely. A company with a high proportion of debt capital is said to be highly geared.
- Companies use a number of methods to raise share capital, perhaps by the issuing of ordinary and preference shares.
- There are a number of advantages and disadvantages attached to each of these share types, from the perspective of both the issuer and the investor.
- In the UK, there are five permitted methods for bring new securities to the market: an introduction, a placing, an intermediaries' offer, an offer for subscription and an offer for sale. Rights issues are a class of new issue.
- It is vital that there is an efficient and well-regulated secondary market for securities because, without it, there would be no means of disposal for those securities purchased by investors in the primary market.

Test yourself answers

Test yourself 3.1

a) The four main types of company structures that exist in the UK are:

1. private unlimited companies;

2. private companies limited by guarantee;

3. private companies limited by shares; and

4. public limited companies.

b) Hybrid companies are financial structures created by the fusion of two distinct types of corporate entity: a company limited by shares and a company limited by guarantee.

Test yourself 3.2

a) The two main types of capital finance are debt capital and share (or equity) capital.

b) The relationship of debt capital to equity capital is referred to as gearing. It is quite usual for companies to have an element of gearing, but the level should be closely monitored not only by its directors, but also by corporate analysts. Gearing may be expressed as a ratio:

$$\frac{\text{Total long-term borrowings}}{\text{Ordinary shareholders' funds}}$$

c) Debt capital is the extent to which a company depends upon various forms of debt in order to finance its assets. In essence, it is a reliance or part-reliance on borrowed money.

Test yourself 3.3

a) Ordinary shares are the most common form of stock in the UK. They are fixed units of the share capital of a company and are the most important component of a company's capital structure. They are used not only to finance expansion but also to reduce debt.

b) Ordinary shareholders benefit from a number of rights. They have the right:

- to share in the profits of the company, although such profits may be either retained or distributed at the discretion of the directors;
- to transfer their ordinary shares freely in the secondary markets in the case of plcs;
- to receive notice of annual general meetings (AGMs) and any other shareholders' meetings including extraordinary meetings;
- to attend and vote at these meetings;
- to appoint a proxy on their behalf to attend meetings;
- to receive annual reports and accounts;
- of pre-emption, which entitles the ordinary shareholders to subscribe

for new ordinary share capital and convertible loan stock, in direct proportion to their existing holdings (convertible loan stock can be converted in ordinary shares, thus diluting a holding); and
- to share equally in the assets of the company after liabilities have been paid if the company is liquidated.

c) Advantages of owning ordinary shares include:
- ordinary shareholders do not have any duties to perform;
- ordinary shares carry a higher potential return;
- the liability of ordinary shareholders is limited to the amount they have contributed for their shares. If the company becomes bankrupt the shareholders will not have to provide any additional finance (provided that the shares are fully paid);
- the prospect of the payment of interim and final dividends; and
- the prospect of capital growth.

Disadvantages of owning ordinary shares include:

- ordinary shareholders rank below preference shareholders in both the payment of dividends and the order of payout upon liquidation.
- in the event of liquidation, they may receive nothing at all;
- the company may become insolvent and be unable to pay its debts; consequently its shares may become worthless, wiping out all shareholder investment;
- the opportunity cost of unearned bank interest on the capital used to purchase the equities;
- the company may fail to pay dividends as expected;
- a company's share price may fall, resulting in a reduction in the value of a shareholder's portfolio, which may not be recovered for many years;
- all risks will increase the longer the stock is held, even in well-established companies where there have been no previous indicators of any failure; and
- there is no obligation for the company to pay dividends or even to return the shareholders' capital.

Test yourself 3.4

a) Preference shares are so-called because they are 'preferred' over ordinary shares in a number of significant ways. For example:
- Preference shareholders have an entitlement to an annual fixed dividend (a percentage of the nominal amount), whereas ordinary shareholders do not.
- In the event of liquidation, preference shareholders have prior claims in respect of both repayments of capital and outstanding dividend payments, although this right must be included in the company's articles of association.

b) The main disadvantages to the investor of holding preference shares include the following.

- Although preference shareholders are members of the company, they generally have no right to vote or attend AGMs unless dividends of cumulative preference shares are in arrears.
- Unless the preference shares are participating preference shares, even if a company performs extremely well, the preference shareholder will only ever receive a fixed percentage of the nominal value.
- Upon liquidation, investors will receive only the nominal amount. If shares were purchased above par, the investor will make a capital loss.

Test yourself 3.5

a) The primary securities market is the market for new issues whereas the secondary market, as its name suggests, is concerned with buying and selling second-hand securities (in this respect it may be thought of as being the second-hand market for securities).

b) Reasons why directors might decide to float their company include the following.

- The original founders of the company may wish to release some or all of their original capital, which may be difficult while their shares are held within a private limited company structure.
- The company may need to raise additional capital in order to finance expansion, which may not be possible through bank finance.
- Existing venture capitalists and private equity firms may want their stake returning and be looking for an exit strategy, as their focus is always short term.
- The previous sources of capital may no longer be available (for instance, bank borrowing) and perhaps the existing shareholders are unable or unwilling to commit any additional capital.
- The directors may wish to retain key staff through share ownership schemes. Consequently, the company shares must be marketable.
- There is a need to be competitive with other companies that already have a stock exchange listing.
- The company's profile can be raised in the press.
- There is greater access to the capital markets.
- Marketability of shares is improved.
- There is a perception of financial stability.

Test yourself 3.6

a) In the UK, there are five permitted issue methods for an unlisted company bringing its securities to the market for the first time, which are:

1. an introduction;
2. a placing;

3. an intermediaries offer;
4. an offer for sale (a public offer); and
5. an offer for subscription (a public offer).

b) An offer for sale by tender will involve the use of an intermediary issuing house. The issuing house offers shares to the public by inviting subscriptions from investors. Investors state the price they are willing to pay. After all bids are received, the issuing house establishes the price. All investors pay this price.

c) Underwriting is a form of insurance policy to ensure that the new issues succeed. It involves institutional investors (investment banks, pension funds and insurance companies) agreeing to take up any shares for which the public does not subscribe. The take-up proportion of each underwriter will be agreed from the outset. Usually the issuing house (sponsor) itself will be the principal underwriter, followed by a series of sub-underwriters.

Test yourself 3.7

a) A rights issue is a way in which a company can raise additional capital by selling new shares. The existing ordinary shareholders have an absolute statutory right contained within the Companies Act 2006 to subscribe for the new shares in the company prior to those shares being offered to external investors.

b) The purpose of a capitalisation issue is for a company to increase the number of its shares in circulation without raising more capital from existing shareholders.

c) Dividends are the amounts of money distributed by companies to shareholders based on an amount per share. A dividend is not the profit earned by a company; instead it is the amount that the directors decide to allocate to each share. The amount of money paid to the shareholders is referred to as a dividend payment and is subject to income tax. During the year, the company may pay one or more dividends. Generally, in the UK at least, there are two dividend payments paid six months apart: the interim and final dividend.

d) The term nil-paid value is used in relation to rights issues. In the first instance, the existing shareholders are given rights to subscribe for new shares at a stated price. As the shareholders have paid nothing for these rights, they are referred to as nil paid.

Test yourself 3.8

a) The main participants in the secondary markets are:

- investors (individual or institutional), who buy and sell securities for their own purposes, perhaps for long-term investment, speculative purposes or some other reason;
- brokers, who act on behalf of investors and their own account, and may hold shares on behalf of their clients in nominee accounts; and
- market makers, who by their very nature create markets in securities in which they trade, on their own behalf, with investors.

b) The three main areas for mergers and acquisitions activity are:

1. acquisitions (also referred to as takeovers);
2. mergers and de-mergers; and
3. consolidations.

Chapter four
Assessing returns on shares

List of topics

1. Price and value
2. Sources of information
3. Annual reports and accounts
4. Stock market announcements
5. Principal shareholder ratios

Introduction

This chapter explains the difference between price and value, and the importance of this distinction is described. Investors and investment advisers are exposed to vast quantities of information, and so they need to be able to understand and make sense of the information available. The main sources of investor information are outlined in this chapter. The publication of company accounts is vital in allowing investors to relate share prices to profits and dividend payments. Most stock exchanges will also require listed companies to declare certain information to the market. Such announcements can have an effect on share prices that ranges from negligible to dramatic. This chapter then concludes with a discussion of four key shareholder ratios. The significance, applications and limitations of each of these is thoroughly explained. The crucial message of this chapter is that investors should not consider any one piece of information in isolation before making any investment decision.

1. Price and value

The terms 'price' and 'value' are often confused.

1.1 Price

Price is relatively straightforward to explain. It is generally a monetary amount set by and required by a seller or influenced by the forces of supply and demand (in the case of shares). Price is not necessarily the amount that the seller will actually receive, but rather the amount they would like to receive or believe they could receive in payment for a good or service. It is the seller that sets a price, not the buyer. However, a buyer does have a number of options, including to pay the asking price, decline the offer or negotiate with the seller to reduce an asking price. This will be applicable to relatively straightforward transactions – for example, the purchase of a second-hand car.

However, on 1 May 2018 an investor who considered Marks and Spencer's ordinary shares to be undervalued purchased 50,000 at a price of 284.90 (pence) costing £ 142,450. If, the same investor subsequently sold the 50,000 ordinary shares on 25 May 2018 when the price had reached 310.70 (pence) he would have made a profit of £12,900 (£155,350 – £142,450). This would represent a return in excess of 9% in less than a month. In this instance the investor's belief that the ordinary shares were undervalued was true.

1.2 Value

Value is less straightforward to define because it is subjective and rather conceptual. It is possible that price can be equal to value but it very rarely is, and value does not necessarily have to be quantified (measured) in monetary terms – although it should be in the case of ordinary shares. Many sources refer to investments as either being undervalued or overvalued when they actually mean under-priced or overpriced.

Perhaps the only true way of expressing value is, rather crudely: 'What can I actually get for this if I resell it?' 'What is its worth?'

Making it work 4.1: Price and value for concert tickets

The cheapest ticket price for Michael Jackson's series of concerts at London's O2 Arena in 2009 was £32. In this instance the price was fixed. When in the possession of various buyers, the price paid was still £32, but values ascribed to these tickets by different parties would be entirely different. A genuine fan might have regarded it as 'priceless', whereas a ticket tout may have given it a value of £500 because that is what they believed they could get for it. This perceived value may then become a tout's asking price, but in reality the tout may only get £200, so this is the true value to the seller. Then, after Michael Jackson's death, there was a period when the price was equal to value because the price of the ticket was equal to the amount that would be returned to the fans by the promoter. Note, however, that the interaction of the forces of supply and demand are always present.

We now need to apply this rationale when considering how to assess returns on shares.

Share undervaluation will generally only be from the buyer's or practitioner's perspective, given that such buyers may anticipate huge growth potential. Although the price may be high, the shares may still represent good value. It would be correct to say from the share buyer's perspective: 'Ultimately, what am I going to get out of this: good income returns [dividends] or perhaps good capital growth?'

In a similar vein, an investor may buy shares in a company at a very low price, believing that they represent very good value. If, however, the company has huge debts and cannot repay its liabilities, that company may be forced into administration. The investor may receive little or none of their investment back. Even though the price of the shares was low, so also was their true value.

2. Sources of information

In today's volatile financial markets, a huge number of sources of investor information are available. This means it will be necessary to be able to distinguish between relevant and irrelevant information, and it is important that buyers and sellers alike consider and appraise such information objectively, and try to be vigilant for:

- any indication that a share is under-priced;
- warning signals that a share is over-priced; and
- reasons why they should buy, hold or sell their equities.

Different classes of stakeholder will require different types of information, which they will use for their own specific purposes. Investors need information to assist them with their investment decisions, whereas financial advisers and stockbrokers require up-to-date information in order to provide accurate advice to their clients. It is necessary to be able to separate the wheat from the chaff.

Irrespective of the quality of information available, it should be remembered that there is no guarantee as to the future performance of any share. Prices can fall as well as rise. Terrorist activity such as 9/11 can cause international equity markets to endure a downwards spiral and financial markets may go into 'meltdown'.

It is imperative for investors to know how and where to look for current and relevant information, in order to reach their own conclusions and so make informed decisions. The ratios provided later in this chapter will assist with such decisions.

2.1 Stock exchanges

In addition to providing a market for the buying and selling of shares both in the primary and secondary markets, stock exchanges also provide a great deal of information including up-to-date share prices, reports and regulatory information.

The main UK stock exchange is the London Stock Exchange (LSE). Other stock exchanges include:

- Germany – Gruppe Deutsche Börse AG;
- France – Euronext Paris;

- USA – New York Stock Exchange (NYSE); and
- Japan – Tokyo Stock Exchange (TSE).

2.2 Financial information subscription service providers

Bloomberg and Reuters provide share prices covering many international markets and sectors, and in the UK, share prices are updated every 15 seconds. Information provided by Bloomberg includes:

- current mid-market prices (the average of the buying and selling prices);
- the day's high and low;
- 52-week high and low;
- number of shares issued;
- market capitalisation;
- price/earnings (P/E) ratio;
- dividend yield; and
- company profiles.

2.3 Independent financial advisers

Independent financial advisers (IFAs) are always good sources of information. They can provide recommendations that may turn out to be good or bad but, either way, IFAs ought to be able to provide you with the current prices and informed information not only for ordinary shares but also for a wide range of other financial products including pensions and tax advice. They should have access to company reports and accounts.

2.4 Newspapers and other useful publications

In the UK, a considerable amount of information may be elicited from the quality press whether through hard copies or online editions. They include recommendations, share tips, buy, sell and hold advice, warnings and other well-written journalistic articles.

As the hard copies may already be out of date at the time of reading, they should not be used as indicators of the current market price, given that a lot can happen in 24 hours, although information may include the previous day's closing price, **earnings per share** (EPS – see section 5.1) and the price/earnings (P/E) ratio (see section 5.2). There may still be quality information that may encourage investors to buy or avoid shares.

earnings per share (EPS)
The amount of net profit attributable to each single issued ordinary share after deductions including interest, tax, preference share dividends and any minority interests.

Some useful websites are:

- the Bank of England *www.bankofengland.co.uk*;
- the Financial Conduct Authority *www.fca.org.uk*;
- the Debt Management Office *www.dmo.gov.uk*; and
- the British Bankers Association *www.bba.org.uk*.

Useful publications include:

- *Governance + Compliance* – the ICSA magazine (www.icsa.org.uk/products-and-services/governance-and-compliance);
- *Investors Chronicle* – providing share tips, information relating to market sectors, trends' data and many research tools (www.investorschronicle.co.uk);
- *The Economist* – (www.economist.com); and
- *Citywire* – provides news and information about investing for personal investors, financial advisers, wealth managers and fund selectors. It is also available as an app for use on an iPhone, iPad or other similar device (www.citywire.co.uk).

Other information sources include:

- television and radio – look out for specialist business or investor programmes;
- the internet and company web pages;
- stockbrokers – those providing advisory services;
- seminars and courses and lectures;
- specialist investment blogs; and
- webinars.

Test yourself 4.1

a) What is the difference between price and value?

b) Identify three key sources of information relating to share value.

3. Annual reports and accounts

Annual reports and accounts are invaluable sources of information relating to a company's current and future business strategies. In the UK, the Companies Act 2006 section 447 dictates the filing obligations of quoted companies. The directors must deliver annually to the registrar a copy of:

- the company accounts;
- the **directors' report**, which must be prepared as required under section 415 (duty to prepare directors' reports); and
- the directors' remuneration (payment) report.

directors' report
A report provided by the directors of a company which is intended to provide all stakeholders with explanations and interpretations of the figures contained within the statement of comprehensive income and other matters of significance.

The submission must also include a copy of the auditors' report relating to each of these points. The audited accounts must provide a 'true and fair view'. If auditors have any difficulties compiling their reports, they may qualify them, which companies do not want. This may alert stakeholders to potentially difficult situations.

3.1 The directors' report

The directors' report may provide far more information than the Companies Act 2006 requires. It is intended to provide all stakeholders with explanations and interpretations of the figures contained within the **statement of comprehensive income** (formally known as the profit-and-loss or P&L account). The report also highlights other matters of significance, including a review of the year's activities, and the company's likely future strategic direction.

statement of comprehensive income
An account that indicates whether a business made a profit or loss in a given period.

3.2 The directors' remuneration report

This is self-explanatory, providing details of the directors' pay and other benefits. The publication of company accounts is vital, allowing investors and analysts to relate share prices to dividends and profits, thus allowing them to decide whether shares are overpriced or under-priced. The price/earnings ratio (P/E ratio or PER) is calculated using figures contained within the statement of comprehensive income. If a company is highly geared, it must be able to service its debt repayments, and must possess the relevant liquid assets to allow this. The company's borrowing figures may be ascertained from the **statement of financial position** (formally known as the balance sheet).

statement of financial position
A snapshot of a company's account balances – both assets and liabilities – shown at a given date.

The company accounts must include the statement of financial position, the statement of comprehensive income, a cash-flow statement and a statement of changes in equity (SOCIE). It is an additional requirement of the Companies Act 2006 that accounts must be made available on the company's website.

3.3 Statement of financial position

The statement of financial position is a snapshot of a company's financial state of affairs at a given date. It is a summary sheet of all of the individual account balances, and its components are capital, assets and liabilities taken from these individual accounts.

In its simplest form, a business may be valued according to the total of its assets minus its total liabilities. The statement of financial position may be used to ascertain inventory (stock) totals, work in progress, levels of receivables (debtors) and payables (creditors). The statement is used to show whether a company is highly geared, perhaps with too much reliance on debt.

A simple view may be that equity equals assets. However, this will change if outsiders have contributed finance. Equity would then be equal to assets minus liabilities. Assets are described as either current or fixed, whereas liabilities are referred to as current or long term.

A key issue here is that the amounts shown in the statement of financial position may already be out of date because they have not been valued for some time. If assets are later found to have been undervalued, this would affect the share price positively. If they had been overvalued, there would be a negative effect on the share price.

Similarly, liabilities such as loans may be understated. The value of intangibles (things that are not physical and able to be touched), such as patents, copyrights and licences, must also be considered. The importance of marketing strategies and business acumen may be included under intangible assets.

Additionally, investors should look at the consolidated statement of financial position, which includes the account balances of all of subsidiary companies.

For the purpose of the ICSA investment examination, the methodology for valuing and revaluing various assets and the accounting adjustments that may need to be made under relevant accounting regulations will not be considered. It is only necessary to be aware that a business is made up of capital and a collection of assets and liabilities, the value of which may already be out of date when published, but it is at least useful as a snapshot.

This statement of financial position is also an indicator of what a business may be worth if forced into liquidation. If the liquidation happens quickly, investors may receive considerably less than the stated book values for its assets.

One positive feature of the balance sheet is that it does at least allow investors and analysts to calculate various ratios, which will be indicators of how a business is performing.

current ratio
The ratio of current assets (including inventory/stock) to current liabilities.

acid-test ratio
The ratio of current assets (minus inventory/stock) to current liabilities.

Two straightforward, but very important, ratios are the **current ratio** and the **acid-test ratio**, both of which are calculated using figures from the statement of financial position and are liquidity rather than shareholders' ratios.

The current ratio

$$\text{Current ratio} = \frac{\text{Current assets}}{\text{Current liabilities}}$$

The purpose of the current ratio is to show how easy it is for a company to be able to service its current liabilities with its current assets. It is calculated dividing current assets – those that will become available within 12 months – by current liabilities, those that are due and payable within 12 months.

The acid-test ratio

The acid-test ratio is calculated using the same figures as used in the current ratio. However, the difference is that the numerator is adjusted by the balance of stock, as follows:

$$\text{Acid-test ratio} = \frac{\text{Current assets} - \text{inventory}}{\text{Current liabilities}}$$

The purpose of this ratio is to show how liquid a business is using cash-only balances and receivables (debtors). After all, it may be very difficult trying to realise inventory, and conversely it may not be easy for a company to settle its current liabilities when inventory is excluded. There is a very high chance that a business may fail if it cannot service its current liabilities.

3.4 Statement of comprehensive income

The statement of comprehensive income is used to calculate the gross and net profits of a company, and is therefore the basis of many of the calculations used in the ratios outlined later. It is a financial statement rather than an actual account and is used to compare actual with expected results.

The items included in the statement of comprehensive income include gross profit (which is the excess revenue received over the cost of goods sold) and net profit, which is the gross profit plus any non-sales revenue less total expenses.

In addition, the statement of comprehensive income may be used:

- to help a business to plan ahead and make adjustments to its existing strategies;
- as a measure of a business' relative success or failure; and
- to calculate any taxes due on profits which must be paid to the revenue authorities.

Test yourself 4.2

a) What is the purpose of a company's statement of financial position?

b) How would you calculate an acid-test ratio?

4. Stock market announcements

A company may be valued by reference not only to its share price but also to its market capitalisation, which is the total amount of outstanding shares multiplied by the market price per share.

Basic supply and demand factors affect share prices, and stock market announcements can have a significant positive or negative effect on share prices. The main sources of information are naturally stock markets (for example, the LSE in the UK). In addition to this, there are numerous organisations that make these announcements.

In the UK, FE investigate (www.investegate.co.uk) is a company press-release announcement service providing up-to-the-minute information relating not only to the FTSE 100 but also to the FTSE 250 and techMARK. There are some useful search options and its archive service is particularly helpful. Searches may be activated by company, category and sector. The Financial Times website also provides similar information.

Announcements may have a significant effect on share prices ranging from slight to dramatic. However, many announcements will already have been discounted by equity traders who have correctly anticipated the information.

Stop and think 4.1

Look out for stock market announcements and assess what effect these have on a company's share price after the announcement.

4.1 Classes of stock market announcement: the London Stock Exchange

Numerous types of stock market announcement will be made via the company, and approved for release by an exchange like the LSE. These announcements will then be made available not only on the LSE website, but also on the company's own website and those of other specialist web providers. The requirements below apply to the LSE, but are typical of the kinds of information other exchanges might expect to make available.

The classes of announcement would include:

- issue of new ordinary shares;
- short-selling disclosures;
- results of extraordinary general meetings (EGMs);
- rights issue price announcements;
- board changes;
- interim results; and
- share buy-back schemes.

The results will be listed for each company by date and time of announcement, and also the source of announcement. Announcements may not have the expected outcome that a particular company was anticipating.

Profit announcements

An announcement that a company's annual profits have doubled may send share prices soaring, whereas an announcement that profits have halved may cause share prices to crash. There is a need to be conscious of a sector as a whole.

In May 2018, Marks and Spencer announced a sharp fall in annual profits, revealing a significant fall in clothing sales and extensive store closure costs. Pre-tax profits at the retail giant fell significantly by 62% to £66.8 million after a £514.1 million bill for restructuring, including £321 million to pay for the first phase of its restructuring plan. A third of its core clothing and home stores is scheduled to close by 2022 and M&S advised that a further £150 million of closure costs would follow. Following this announcement, it might have been expected that the share price would have fallen. In fact, the price rose by over 2% because the market perceived the action taken by the management as positive.

General announcements

Positive news about a company generally causes share prices to rise because it increases interest, whereas negative press releases can cause share prices to fall to zero.

Restructuring announcement

Restructuring announcements may include large-scale redundancies. This can impact on share prices depending on why such a decision is made. If the decision is as the result of falling markets, reduced demand and falling profits, share prices may fall. Alternatively, if as the result of this restructuring there is a considerable improvement in efficiency and hence profitability, share prices may rise. Restructuring decisions are often viewed by investors as buy signals for shares, because the management is seen as having taken tough decisions.

Share buy-back announcements

Share buy-back schemes can have varying effects depending on their rationale. It will be necessary to assess the reason for a buy-back and to try to interpret the message that is being sent to the market. It would be necessary to ascertain whether or not the buy-back is being financed out of surplus capital or by increased debt. A buy-back financed by debt will signal a change in a company's capital structure reducing reliance on equity. Some companies may buy back shares because they consider the value of their shares is too low, but this cannot be looked at in isolation. Share buy-backs may cause investors to sell their shares, thus reducing the price.

Test yourself 4.3

Identify three types of announcements required by the LSE.

5. Principal shareholder ratios

A ratio may be defined as the quantitative relationship between two numbers that shows how many times one number either contains or is contained by the other number. The ratios that are now discussed are of relevance to shareholders, and in each case the price used will be the mid-market price of the share quoted on a recognised investment exchange.

5.1 Earnings per share (EPS) ratio

It is compulsory for all UK public limited companies to publish quarterly reports stating their earnings per share (EPS) figures.

EPS, as its name suggests, is the amount of net profit attributable to each single issued ordinary share. More specifically, it is the total amount of income earned by each share of the company, after specific deductions. It follows that the greater the number of issued shares the less can be allocated to each individual share. It is also the case that the higher the EPS figure the greater the profitability of the company.

Thus, rather than being expressed as a number or percentage, the result is always expressed as a monetary amount (for example, £ or $), and it is based on net profit after deduction of interest, tax, the preference share dividend and any minority interests.

$$\text{EPS} = \frac{\text{Net profit after interest, tax and preference share dividend and minority interests}}{\text{Number of issued ordinary shares}}$$

It is possible to use a weighted average for the number of issued shares over the reporting period, but it is also possible to use the number of shares outstanding at the end of the reporting period.

Worked example 4.1

If a company has net profit of £25 million in any given year and has issued 10 million ordinary shares in the same year, its EPS will be:

$$\text{EPS} = \frac{\text{£25 million}}{\text{10 million}} = \text{£2.50 earned per share}$$

Assumptions

- EPS may or may not be calculated before any adjustment for exceptional items.
- It may be calculated using a variety of accounting techniques.

It should be stressed that the earnings used in the EPS ratio are the net profits that have the potential to be paid to the ordinary shareholders. This does not necessarily mean that this amount will actually be distributed to them. More often than not, a large percentage of the earnings will be retained for future investment. Dividend payments are determined at the discretion of the directors and have to be approved by the shareholders. However, if the directors decide that no dividend payments will be made, this decision cannot be overturned by the shareholders. But the directors have to stand for re-election by the shareholders annually, and the latter can therefore vote the directors out if they are disgruntled at having received no dividend or an insufficient dividend.

Applications of EPS

EPS is most useful as a means of comparing and contrasting shares in public limited companies. It is an indicator of the health of a company, and is perhaps the most widely used of all of the shareholder ratios, being considered by many investors as the most significant ratio.

It also allows analysts and current and potential shareholders to compare and contrast earnings in a company year by year. It may be used as:

- an indicator of a company's profitability;
- a comparison tool between companies in the same industry/sector;
- an indicator of a company's ability to sustain the payment of its ordinary share dividend;

- a precursor to calculating the P/E ratio (discussed in section 5.2); and
- a way to compare and contrast different companies' ability to make profits.

EPS indicators

Assuming all other factors are equal between two companies, the company with the higher EPS figure will be preferred, and in theory the market price of that share ought to be higher. Shareholders will be looking for a positive trend over time. A negative trend may indicate little or no growth in the shares of a company.

5.2 Price/earnings ratio

The price/earnings ratio (also referred to as P/E ratio or PER) is a key tool for investors and analysts alike. It is an indicator of how many years' earnings could be purchased with one ordinary share at the prevailing market price of that same share. It also indicates how many years it will take to recoup the current market price of a share from the current earnings attributable to the shareholders. This would assume static earnings per share over the period. The result is expressed as a number rather than a percentage.

It is perhaps better to think of this ratio as the price/earnings per share ratio, as in order to calculate the P/E ratio, we must first calculate the EPS ratio (see section 5.1).

$$\text{P/E ratio} = \frac{\text{Current market price of one ordinary share}}{\text{Annual earnings per share}}$$

Worked example 4.2

If the market price of one ordinary share of Company A were £3, and the annual EPS were £0.45, then it follows that:

$$\text{P/E} = \frac{300}{45} = 6.66$$

Therefore, the market price of the share covers its earnings by a multiple of 6.66 times. This indicates that it will take 6.66 years to buy the share at the current market price with the current year's earnings. For companies with no earnings, the P/E ratio is not relevant.

This P/E ratio may be either historical (based on known figures) or forward, based upon prospective earnings. It is historical when earnings are used from a company's most recent 12-month period, whereas a forward P/E ratio may be calculated using analysts' projected earnings for the next 12 months.

Assumptions

- The market price used is the mid-market price quoted at the close of business on the previous business day and is quoted ex-dividend.

- The ratio will change on a daily basis, given that market prices may fluctuate significantly.
- Figures can be compared year on year within the same company, with other companies or within the same sector, or indeed the market as a whole. The ratio allows companies to be compared and contrasted regardless of their size.

Applications of P/E ratio

- To elicit what the price of a share ought to be in relation to EPS.
- To show a share's relative cheapness or expensiveness.
- To establish what the average (the mean) is for the industry, and then question why it is higher or lower for a particular company.

P/E ratio outcomes

A low P/E figure indicates that a stock may be undervalued. It suggests that investors do not expect any earnings growth in the near future and they perhaps believe a fall in earnings is likely or the market price has already fallen, and therefore the P/E ratio has fallen.

A high P/E figure:

- tends to be associated with growth stocks;
- indicates that the market price of a share is high relative to its earnings per share, and possibly the market price has risen because there is an expectation or anticipation of improved earnings;
- indicates that a stock may be overvalued;
- suggests that the same proportion of a company profits will cost more, as the earnings do not change although the market price does and indicates how much an investor is prepared to pay for a company's earnings. A figure of ten means that, in paying the current market price for each share, the investor is paying ten times the amount of the current earnings. So, in essence, the investor will recoup the share price in ten years' time (assuming earnings are static, which in practice is unlikely to be the case).

Suppose two companies in the same sector are being compared and contrasted. Company A has a P/E ratio of ten, whereas Company B has a P/E ratio of five (all other factors being equal).

This suggests that, for the same amount of investment, you will receive from Company B twice the earnings as you would receive from Company A. However, there may be many reasons for this, which should be analysed.

Limitations of P/E ratio

Some companies using debt may have lower P/E ratios and may appear cheaper even though they have similar prices, but this may mask large debts. In such circumstances, caution should be exercised by looking at the wider picture in order to calculate to what extent a company is financed by external capital.

5.3 Dividend yield

Dividend yield (DY) is sometimes just referred to as the yield. It indicates the percentage of its earnings a company's directors are prepared to distribute to shareholders from excess revenue (income). DY is used to measure the annual gross rate of return (per ordinary share) paid to ordinary shareholders. Most significantly, DY represents the current year's return on the shareholders' investment.

$$\text{Dividend yield} = \frac{\text{Actual gross annual dividend paid per share – including interim and final instalments}}{\text{Current market share price as at time of dividend payment}} \times 100$$

In the UK, the numerator and denominator of the ratio are both expressed in pence.

Worked example 4.3

If the market price of one ordinary share of Company A were £3.00, and the total amount of dividends paid per share were £0.22, then:

$$\text{Dividend yield} = \frac{22}{300} \times 100 = 7.33\%$$

It is the measuring of the real rate of return calculated by dividing the dividend actually paid to the shareholders by the market price of the share and then multiplying by 100.

Assumptions

- DY may be calculated using either historic or projected figures.
- DY is shown as gross but paid as net.
- DY is expressed as a percentage rather than a number.
- The current market share price used is ex-dividend.
- Dividends are paid out of current earnings.

Applications of dividend yield

- DY is used by shareholders to measure the real rate of return received on their investment.
- DY allows investors to compare and contrast the dividend received against the current market price of the share.
- DY is used to compare and contrast the level of attractiveness of those ordinary shares that actually pay dividends.
- DY can be used to compare not only the attractiveness of ordinary shares between similar companies, but also the attractiveness of different classes of investment such as corporate bonds and bank deposits.

Considerations

- DY should be used in conjunction with the other shareholder ratios.
- Well-established companies tend to have higher DYs whereas younger start-ups tend to have lower yields.
- There cannot be a dividend yield if a company does not pay a dividend.
- A company that does not make a dividend payment in a particular year is not necessarily in financial difficulty, as it may be reinvesting its profits.
- There is a need to exercise caution with companies paying dividends above the market norm, as they may have failed to meet earnings forecasts.
- A high yield does not necessarily mean that the shares are cheap. It can mean or imply that a dividend will be reduced or even missed in the near future. Alternatively, companies are perhaps trying to attract investors.
- High yield is associated with high risk and for those shares where there is a high yield, there may also be a reduced dividend or even no dividend payment at all in the near future. There may also be a chance of reduced profits or even the possibility of an imminent loss.

5.4 Dividend cover

Dividend cover is used to assess the financial health of a company, and indicate the stability of the current dividend payment and indeed the likelihood of an increase in future payments. It is the measure of the ability of a company to pay its ordinary shareholders a dividend, and show how many times the ordinary share dividend is covered by the net profits after tax (or, alternatively, the number of times the net profits can pay the current ordinary share dividend).

If, for example, dividend cover is four times, it follows that one-quarter of net profits is available for distribution as ordinary dividends, whereas three-quarters are retained by the company for future investment.

There are essentially two ways of expressing the formula, and both will have the same result.

$$1.\ \text{Dividend cover} = \frac{\text{Net profit after payment of tax and preference share dividends}}{\text{Total value (currency) of ordinary dividends paid and proposed (gross)}}$$

$$2.\ \text{Dividend cover} = \frac{\text{Earnings per share (pence)}}{\text{Dividends per share (pence)}}$$

The result is shown as a number (though as a multiple rather than as a percentage or an amount). The net profit (the numerator) is shown as a monetary amount (for example, £6 million). The ordinary dividend (the denominator) is also a monetary amount rather than the number of shares in issue.

Worked example 4.4

If a company were to earn £6 million (after tax, and preference share dividends) and if the total amount of the ordinary share dividends proposed and paid were £1.5 million, then:

$$\text{Dividend cover} = \frac{\text{£6 million}}{\text{£1.5 million}} = 4$$

Therefore in this example, the ordinary share dividend is covered four times, with £1.5 million being paid out in dividends (whereas £4.5 million is retained).

This means that 25% of net profits are paid out as dividends (pay-out = 25%) and 75% of net profits are retained (retention = 75%).

Assumptions

- If a loss is made, no calculation of dividend cover can be made (although some analysts provide negative figures).
- If no dividend payment is proposed or made, dividend cover cannot be calculated.
- If the earnings are greater than the dividend, dividend cover will be greater than one.
- If the earnings are less than the dividend, dividend cover will be less than one.
- Dividend cover of less than one means that a company cannot cover its dividend from the earnings of the year in question. Investors would then need to ascertain how the dividend is actually being covered; typically, this will be from previous years' retained earnings.
- A high ratio implies that a company is retaining a considerable proportion of its earnings.

Applications of dividend cover

- To relate the total dividend payments to total earnings.
- To show how easy it is for the company to be able to afford its dividend. The greater the amount paid out means the less available for retention.
- As an indicator of continued profitability.

A dividend is usually paid out of the current year's earnings. However, it is possible that a company can declare a dividend that exceeds its net profit after taxation and preference share dividend (indeed, the company could have made a loss). In this case, payment would typically be made from previous years' retained earnings.

Indicators

Dividend cover should not be viewed in isolation and investors should consider the norm for the industry sector.

Low dividend cover implies that a company is not retaining sufficient funds within the company – perhaps investment is too low. If the company's fortunes were to take a sudden downturn, it might not be able to maintain its current dividend payments, or might even have to reduce future payments.

High dividend cover implies that a company is retaining a considerable proportion of its earnings, and may indicate that a company could have paid out more in dividends. However, the directors have decided to retain more for future investment.

Where a company pays out a dividend greater than its earnings, the dividend is said to be either uncovered or not fully covered, which in certain circumstances will be acceptable to investors. Generally, ratios tend to be at least 2:1, but there is considerable variation and indeed a cover of at least two implies that a company has sufficient funds to maintain its dividend. Income investors (as opposed to growth investors) will want a low level of cover, as they will want larger dividend payments, whereas investors seeking capital growth will want a higher cover because of retained earnings.

Test yourself 4.4

a) **How is EPS calculated?**

b) **What are the main applications of P/E ratios?**

c) **Explain both dividend cover and dividend yield.**

Chapter summary

- Understanding the difference between price and value is essential to an understanding of how investment decisions are reached.
- In today's dynamic and volatile financial markets, a great many sources of share information are available which may assist in making various investment decisions or the provision of advice to clients. It is important to distinguish between relevant and irrelevant information, and to remember that buyers and sellers alike should consider all such information objectively.
- Sources of information include stock exchanges, subscription services and newspapers. Companies' annual reports and accounts are invaluable sources of information relating to both current and future business strategies. The Companies Act 2006 section 447 dictates the filing obligations of quoted companies. However, it is important to understand the limitations of the statement of financial position, which is only a snapshot of a company's financial position at a particular point in time.

- Basic supply and demand factors affect share prices, and stock market announcements can have a significant positive or negative effect on share prices.
- Shareholder ratios offer another method of assessing share value and four key ratios are particularly important: price/earnings, earnings per share, dividend yield and dividend cover. None of these should be used in isolation, and the applications and limitations of each of these should be considered.

Test yourself answers

Test yourself 4.1

a) Price is a monetary amount set by and required by the seller or influenced by the forces of supply and demand (in the case of shares). Price is not necessarily the amount that the seller will actually receive, but rather the amount they would like to receive or believe they could receive.

Value, unfortunately, is less straightforward to define because it is subjective and rather conceptual. It is possible that price can be equal to value but it very rarely is, and value does not necessarily have to be quantified (measured) in monetary terms – although it should be in the case of ordinary shares. Many sources refer to investments as either being under-valued or over-valued when they actually mean under-priced or over-priced.

b) Sources of information about share value can include:

- stock exchanges;
- financial information subscription service providers;
- independent financial advisers;
- newspapers and other useful publications;
- television and radio – look out for specialist business or investor programmes;
- the internet and company web pages;
- stockbrokers – those providing advisory services;
- seminars and courses and lectures;
- specialist investment blogs; and
- webinars.

Test yourself 4.2

a) The statement of financial position is a snapshot of a company's financial state of affairs at a given date.

b)

$$\text{Acid-test ratio} = \frac{\text{Current assets} - \text{inventory}}{\text{Current liabilities}}$$

Test yourself 4.3

Types of announcements required by the LSE include:

- issue of new ordinary shares;
- short-selling disclosures;
- results of extraordinary general meetings (EGMs);
- rights issue price announcements;
- board changes;
- interim results; and
- share buy-back schemes.

Test yourself 4.4

a)

$$\text{EPS} = \frac{\text{Net profit after interest, tax and preference share dividend and minority interests}}{\text{Number of issued ordinary shares}}$$

b) The main applications of price/earnings ratios are to:

- elicit what the price of a share ought to be in relation to EPS;
- show a share's relative cheapness or expensiveness; and
- establish what the average (the mean) is for the industry and then question why it is higher or lower for a particular company.

c) Dividend cover is used to assess the financial health of a company, and indicate the stability of the current dividend payment and indeed the likelihood of an increase in future payments. It is the measure of the ability of a company to pay its ordinary shareholders a dividend, and show how many times the ordinary share dividend is covered by the net profits after tax (or, alternatively, the number of times the net profits can pay the current ordinary share dividend).

Dividend yield (DY) is sometimes just referred to as the yield. It indicates the percentage of its earnings a company's directors are prepared to distribute to shareholders from excess revenue (income). DY is used to measure the annual gross rate of return (per ordinary share) paid to ordinary shareholders. Most significantly, DY represents the current year's return on the shareholders' investment.

Part three

Markets, foreign exchange and derivative products

Overview

Part 3 begins by looking at the role, operation and regulation of stock markets and trading platforms, the procedures around dealing and settlement requirements, and the importance of counterparties.

Aspects of the derivatives market – futures, options, warrants and interest-rate swaps, contracts for difference and turbos – are then examined, as well as pricing, rights and contractual obligations of relevant parties involved, and the reasons why derivatives instruments are so attractive to investors.

Part 3 will then explore the money market and its inherent instruments and participants, followed by the foreign exchange markets, products and strategies.

Learning outcomes

At the end of this Part, you will:

- understand the role, operation and regulation of stock markets and trading platforms;
- understand the derivatives market and derivative instruments;
- know about money markets and money market instruments; and
- understand principles of foreign exchange.

Chapter five
Markets, dealing and settlement

List of topics

1. Quote or order-driven dealing on a regulated market
2. Recognised investment exchanges (RIEs)
3. London Stock Exchange (LSE) trading systems
4. Dealing platforms and the effect of MiFID II
5. Large international exchanges and multilateral trading facilities (MTFs)
6. Settlement
7. Counterparties and clearing houses
8. Data vendors

Introduction

This chapter looks at the role and operation of stock markets and trading platforms, the procedures around dealing, settlement requirements and the importance of counterparties. The largest markets in the world are in the USA, Europe and Japan, but China is not far behind. Details of some of the more important stock exchanges are outlined in this chapter. The vast changes in market communication and the adoption of computerised dealing on a worldwide basis, with new laws and regulations, mean that change will continue for several years. In Europe, the introduction of MiFID II, the European Union (EU) directive designed to increase competition and enable passporting to exist in Europe, is continuing to have a major impact. MiFID II was introduced in January 2018, and will continue to have a major impact on markets, settlement and use of counterparties. This section of the syllabus is changing rapidly, as markets recover from the financial crisis; the impact of Brexit will need to be considered. It is also necessary to be aware of all changes and keep up to date using the resources listed in the directory of web resources.

1. Quote or order-driven dealing on a regulated market

When new shares are quoted on a stock market (exchange) and governments or corporations issue bonds (or debentures), a secondary market develops, allowing trades in these new shares and bonds to take place. Shares in the major companies quoted on a stock market are highly liquid – that is, they are available to buy and sell in large and small quantities. Trades are undertaken on either a quote-driven basis or an order-driven(price-driven) basis.

A quote driven market is one where registered market makers are required to display both bid and offer prices on the shares they trade in together with the maximum bargain size to which the displayed prices relate. The main advantage of quote driven markets is they provide liquidity, in that there is an absolute guarantee that a trade will be executed, unlike a price driven market. Disadvantages include the lack of transparency and the fact that deals have to be routed through brokers, as there is no electronic execution. SEAQ is an example of a UK quote-driven market.

All companies quoted on this type of dealing system have a normal market dealing size, which is determined by the stock exchange. The screen quote will be at this size, or larger, depending on the market maker's position – that is, how many shares the market maker owns or needs to buy to keep their position in balance.

The screen page for the particular company will normally have a yellow band showing the highest bid price and the lowest offer price, and which market maker(s) is/are making these prices and at what size. The highest bid and lowest offer are known as the touch price. The broker then contacts the market maker showing the best screen price, depending on whether their client is a seller or buyer of the shares in the quoted company at that price and size, and a deal is done.

Order-driven markets are essentially the opposite of quote-driven markets; stockbrokers place orders to buy or sell a certain number of shares at a particular price on a matching-order system, again computer-based, like SETS (described in section 3.3). Many stock markets around the world operate an order-driven system. Unlike quote-driven markets, where only the prices of registered market makers are displayed, all buyers and sellers display the prices at which they will trade a particular security, together with the quantity of that security. It must be stressed that one of the key drawbacks of an order driven system is that there is no guarantee an order will actually be executed.

Test yourself 5.1

a) What are the differences between quote and order-driven markets?

b) Explain how you would trade, both in a quote-driven and an order-driven market.

2. Recognised investment exchanges (RIEs)

In the United Kingdom a recognised investment exchange (RIE) is a recognised body under part XViii of the Financial Services and Markets Act (2000), which has been granted a recognition order by the FCA. An RIE is an exempt person for the purposes of the general prohibition in FSMA section 19. This means it does not require permission from the FCA or PRA to carry on regulated activities as part of its business as an investment exchange, or for the purposes of, or in connection with, providing clearing services in the United Kingdom. Examples of RIEs may be found in the Financial Services Register, and include:

- the London Stock Exchange;
- the London Metal Exchange;
- LIFFE Administration and Management;
- the London Metal Exchange;
- ICE futures;
- BATS Trading Ltd;
- CME Europe Ltd;
- Euronext UK markets Ltd; and
- ICAP Securities and Derivatives Exchanges Ltd.

Businesses require capital to commence operations and, if successful, more capital to expand. At first they are able to raise capital from wealthy friends and family, banks and even venture capitalists. However, if they are successful and continue to expand, they have to look for other sources of capital. This can be achieved by obtaining a listing on a recognised investment exchange, as outlined in Chapter 3. Not only can companies raise more capital by doing this, but their existing shareholders are also able to sell their shares (or some of them) if they wish.

Recognised investment exchanges are organised institutions for the trading (buying and selling) of shares (stocks) and bonds. Although such stock markets have existed for centuries for the funding of trading ventures, the Industrial Revolution brought about expansion that required the raising of capital beyond the means immediately available to family-run private companies. These companies obtained the funding for their proposed expansion by selling shares to interested investors via a stock exchange. This is still the case today, although the procedure of 'listing' on an exchange is more complicated, as a company has to comply with many regulations. Most companies that seek to raise money through the issue of shares will have a track record of several years of successful trading. However, new smaller companies are able to raise funds for investment on what is known as a 'junior' market like the Alternative Investment Market (AIM) in London. A successful company is able to raise additional capital for investment through a secondary issue on a stock market. The major investors on stock markets are funds, and other institutions (banks, insurance companies, pension funds) which require a return on their investment at an acceptable level of risk.

Stock and share certificates were evidence, in the last century, of a stake in a company or, in the case of bonds, that the investor had lent money to a government by buying government stock. UK government stock certificates in the early days had a gold edge to them, which gave rise to the name they are known by today: gilts. Certificates have now been replaced in most markets by an electronic record of holdings on behalf of investors.

To obtain a listing in any world market, companies have to fulfil a number of stated requirements (see Chapter 3). In addition to raising capital, liquidity in a particular market sector is often the prime reason a company may list in New York, London, Frankfurt, or the Far East (for example, Shanghai or Singapore).

3. London Stock Exchange (LSE) trading systems

Merchants began dealing in stocks and shares in the seventeenth century. Other forms of trading existed before the seventeenth century, as noted in section 5.11 on Deutsche Börse. An informal market developed in the City of London over the years, resulting in 'New Jonathan's' coffee house, which developed into a stock exchange in 1773. The London Stock Exchange was formally constituted in 1802, with 550 subscribers and 100 clerks. London was the largest stock exchange in the world until the First World War. It is still the most important exchange in Europe, and benefits from its time zone in relation to other world markets: it closes as New York opens and opens as the Far East markets close, which puts the LSE at the centre of the global financial market, catering for some of the largest and most successful companies in the world.

The LSE is one of the world's most dynamic regulated stock exchanges. London caters not only for new companies raising capital on the stock market, through an Initial Public Offering (IPO), but also for further capital raising, known as secondary issues. Companies can join the main market, or the AIM, which is designed to cater for smaller companies.

Full details about how companies join the LSE (a process known as obtaining a listing) and an overview of the secondary market are given in Chapter 3.

3.1 The changing role of traditional stock markets

Historically, stock markets, such as London, were owned and operated by their members. Over the years, the profile of shareholders of companies changed from individuals to institutions, and companies that raised money on the exchanges moved from being mostly 'local' to 'international'. This change required greater capital for stock markets to operate effectively and in London the stock exchange underwent a major change in 1986. More capital was injected through outside investors and changes in ownership of stockbroking firms. Also, fixed commissions were replaced with negotiated commissions (at lower rates) and the 'two tier' system of jobbers and brokers was replaced with a single 'tier' of brokers. These changes reflected the requirements of the government of the day and of the institutions. These institutions often traded in large volumes of shares and required a market of sufficiently large liquidity, with the capability of carrying out dealing instructions efficiently. The changes also helped to prevent trade moving from London to other exchanges around the world.

3.2 The Alternative Investment Market (AIM)

AIM is the LSE's international market for smaller growing companies, and is the most successful global growth market. Since its launch in 1995, in excess of 3,600 companies from around the world have joined AIM. These companies have raised in excess of £98 billion of development funds since the inception of AIM. The focus of the AIM is to assist smaller and growing companies to expand. A wide spectrum of businesses including early stage venture capital backed companies and more established companies join AIM in order to seek access to this growth capital.

AIM is designed mainly for the equities of small and medium sized growth companies with potentially less-diversified business models or those that may not possess a proven track record which would enable them to qualify for the main market. Mindful of this AIM companies may be considered higher risk compared to more established companies traded on the main market. However, they may provide excellent investment opportunities for those wishing to purchase these equities.

AIM is far more than an IPO market; rather, it provides companies with high quality, long-term international liquidity, combined with the ability to fund future growth. In the region of 60% of the money raised on AIM has been through further issues, which demonstrates not only companies' confidence in the markets, but also that of investors. In addition to offering growing companies the advantages of a world-class public market, it provides a regulatory environment which is designed specifically to match their needs. It has a balanced approach to regulation, which is specifically suited for smaller companies. The rules are concise and principles-based, with a 'Nomad' – a nominated adviser – responsible for advising the company on the interpretation and compliance with rules.

The admission process

When a company has decided to seek a quotation on AIM, the first requirement is to identify and appoint a Nomad, who will assist the company in its endeavours to come to the AIM. A Nomad would have a thorough understanding of the needs, aims, objectives and aspirations of the company seeking admission to AIM. Additional advisers, brokers and law firms, accountants PR and Marketing will also be required to support the process. The company must provide admission documentation, which includes information pertaining to its directors, financial position, business activities and strategy, which will be prepared in consultation with the Nomad.

Some of the reasons why AIM has been successful for small companies are as follows:

- It allows access to capital at flotation, and for raising capital through further share issues.
- It creates a market for companies' shares.
- It broadens the shareholder base.
- It allows existing shareholders to sell or reduce their holding – this is important for family business and individual taxation purposes.
- It offers a market valuation of a business.
- Share incentive schemes can be introduced for employees.
- Shares can be used for acquisition purposes.
- It provides access to institutional and private investors.
- International companies trading for at least 18 months on an AIM Designated Market, in another country, may use their existing annual report and accounts for a complementary listing.
- It raises the profile and increases the credibility of a company.

There are no minimum requirements as to the size of a company, its track record or the number of shares required to be issued. However, in return, a company must accept that with a quotation:

- market conditions can change and this can affect share prices;
- directors are accountable to shareholders and should be prepared for more openness, especially regarding financial position;
- the company will be subject to closer scrutiny;
- the company's performance will be monitored more closely;
- the company will need to keep all investors aware of future plans and developments (without giving details to competitors); and
- the company may become the subject of a hostile takeover.

Similar developments have taken place in other stock markets, such as Neuer Börse in Frankfurt and Le Nouveau Marché in Paris.

Test yourself 5.2

a) What is a recognised investment exchange?

b) Identify five potential benefits for companies trading on AIM.

Stop and think 5.1

Which stock exchanges are likely to grow most in the coming years and why?

3.3 LSE trading systems

The LSE operates three trading services for Main market and AIM securities. All three operate within the rules of the LSE.

SETS

The Stock Exchange Electronic Trading System (SETS) is the LSE's flagship, and fully electronic, order book. SETS has integrated market executable quotes, with both buying and selling prices, and central counterparty clearing, which permits anonymous pre and post-trading. It trades FTSE100, FTSE 250, FTSE Small Capital index constituents, exchange-traded funds, and liquid AIM. It also executes the trades.

Those investors trading a particular security (for example, shares) enter the price at which they are willing to buy or sell the security and the quantity they wish to buy or sell. If a buyer enters details that can be matched by a seller, then a deal is executed. If the price entered by the buyer is too low, then the order will be shown on the screen. It will remain there until either a seller changes their price in order to complete the bargain, or a new seller places an order that meets the price entered by the buyer.

A buyer may not be able to complete their purchase if the seller was only offering a smaller quantity of shares at the buyer's price. In such a situation, the buyer would purchase the quantity on offer, and the balance would remain on the system until another seller or sellers enable the deal to be completed. The SETS system is mainly used for shares that are traded frequently, but some business has moved to other trading systems discussed below.

Advantages of SETS:

- It is highly accessible to trading participants.
- Order book users are able to place various order types such as limit, quote, and deal, directly onto the order book, allowing the users to participate directly in the price formation process. This is in contrast to SEAQ, where it is the market makers only who participate in the price formation process.

SETSqx

SETSqx (Stock Exchange Electronic Trading Service, quotes and crosses) is a trading service which has been designed specifically for those securities that have less liquidity than those traded on SETS. It combines a periodic electronic auction book with stand-alone non-electronic, quote-driven, market making, providing guaranteed liquidity in at least one Exchange Market Size throughout the trading day.

It is appropriate for those instruments that have less liquidity and are more dependent on market maker quotes providing investors with the ability to access prices in less liquid securities. Additionally, it provides investors with a choice of trading in either quote-driven, or order book, service. Orders are scheduled at five times throughout the trading day. Electronic orders can be named or anonymous on submission, and for most securities, order book executions will be cleared centrally.

SEAQ

SEAQ (Stock Exchange Automated Quotations) is a quote(price)-driven dealing system. Although SEAQ is one of the LSE's systems, it is focused on pricing information.

Before explaining what SEAQ is, it is important to state what it is not. It is not a system that allows electronic execution, rather it is a merely a quotation or pricing information service, enabling two or more competing and registered market makers the opportunity to provide firm quotes (those prices at which they are obliged to deal), combined with an EMS in a particular share. Only registered market makers display firm prices, both bid and offer, at which they are prepared to deal and indeed must deal. The firm quotes are in relation to AIM securities; notably not securities traded on either SETs or SETqx. SEAQ may additionally be used for some fixed income securities, where at least two competing registered market makers provide their firm quotes.

Market makers may provide from their own stock or match with another order. Although market makers provide spreads, they change throughout the trading day.

SEAQ is appropriate for less liquid instruments, relying solely on market maker quotes, notably AIM securities, which are traded neither on SETS or SETSqx.

SEAQ *screen*

There is a yellow strip on the display screen, showing the best bid and offer prices, together with the corresponding volume and number of orders at that price. Where there are two identical prices, the best price shown might actually be a combination of best price combined with the lowest EMS. The SEAQ screen also displays which section of the LSE trading system the stock is traded in, e.g. AIM.

The prices shown on the screen are only those of the bid and offer prices provided by the market makers, rather than those of the entire market.

Advantages of SEAQ:

- Only the registered market makers can participate directly on screen in the price formation process.
- There is guaranteed liquidity provided throughout the trading day by those registered market makers in the shares for which they provide firm quotes.
- Market makers ensure the provision of two-way prices in at least one EMS (Exchange Market Size). *EMS (exchange market size) which is set by the LSE for each security traded on SEAQ is the minimum size at which market makers are obliged to trade.*
- Registered market makers are obliged to deal at their quoted prices.
- A unique selling point, in contrast to SETS, is that SEAQ provides guaranteed liquidity by those market makers who will provide two-way prices throughout a trading day. There is a requirement to have at least two competing market makers.
- Guarantees that an order will be executed, even in a relatively illiquid market.

- Stocks have to have at least two recognised market makers in order to be eligible for trading on SEAQ.
- Investors will have to deal with brokers, who will select the market maker offering the best price. If there is only one market maker offering a price, this will not be displayed on SEAQ, and the broker would deal with this single recognised market maker.
- This system provides liquidity to otherwise illiquid shares.

Disadvantages of SEAQ:

- Although it is a price posting system, it does not allow electronic execution.
- One of the main drawbacks is the lack of overall market transparency.
- It is only available for second-hand securities, therefore would not be used for new issues, including IPOs and rights issues. There would not be any IPO prices, and is only really appropriate for more illiquid shares.

Test yourself 5.3

Explain the difference between SETS and SEAQ.

4. Dealing platforms and the effect of MiFID

Dealing in shares used to be undertaken on a person-to-person basis, either face-to-face or by telephone. However, as markets became fully computerised, dealing has transferred from stock market floors to offices. Stock markets used to be 'a closed shop' to outsiders, even after the introduction of computers. Large buying or selling orders (trades), undertaken by institutions like pension funds in the UK, were difficult to complete, partly due to the rules regarding transparency. There was a time delay in reporting trades, but market professionals could often work out what was happening and potentially make unscrupulous profits by moving prices against the institution trying to complete a large trade. Various methods were tried to overcome problems associated with buying or selling large quantities of shares without affecting the market and the share price. None was completely successful. However, the introduction of the **Markets in Financial Instruments Directive (MiFID)** allowed European markets to introduce new dealing platforms, which made large deals possible.

Markets in Financial Instruments Directive (MiFID)
A European Union law that provides harmonised regulation for investment services across the 30 member states of the European Economic Area.

4.1 What is Mifid II?

Mifid II, which succeeds Mifid I, is a European Union (EU) directive. Introduction having been delayed by a year, it came into force on 3 January 2018. Mifid I itself replaced the Investment Services Directive for all members of the European Economic Area (EEA) (i.e. EU member states plus Iceland, Norway and Liechtenstein). Mifid II is, essentially, EU legislation that regulates firms that provide services linked to financial instruments, including shares, units in collective schemes and derivatives, and the venues where those instruments are traded. It is designed to afford greater protection for investors, and enhance transparency into all asset classes, including equities, fixed income, including bonds, exchange traded funds and foreign exchange products, and derivatives, including contracts for difference.

The rules contained within Mifid II cover nearly all areas of financial trading within the EU. Specifically, they will apply to all EU member states.

The main aims of Mifid II are to:

- make European financial markets safer with enhanced transparency;
- restore investor confidence following the 2007/2008 credit crisis;
- transfer a significant part of the OTC market to regulated trading venues, moving away from telephones to regulated exchanges – this would provide enhanced audit trails; and
- confront head-on unregulated and opaque areas of the financial markets, including bonds, foreign exchange and derivatives.

The extent of coverage includes:

- banks;
- fund managers;
- exchanges;
- trading venues;
- pension funds;
- high-frequency traders;
- brokers;
- hedge funds;
- retail investors.

Markets covered include:

- equities;
- foreign exchange;
- fixed income; and
- contracts for difference.

Powers include:

- enhanced pricing transparency for off-exchange markets;
- splitting of payments for analyst research and trading commission;
- more rigid standards for investment products;
- upper limits for dark pools; and

- to ensure more institutional reporting in real time – notably volumes and pricing.

Additionally:

- trading information must be stored for a minimum of five years;
- banks and financial institutions will have to show customers that they were offered the best prices available for their trade; and
- fund managers will have to pay separately for research and trading costs – this is referred to as unbundling.

MiFID II aims to build on MiFID I by introducing a sounder, more transparent and responsible financial system. MiFID II covers the following.

Authorisation, regulation and passporting
Firms authorised and regulated in their home state will be able to use the MiFID **passporting** system to provide financial services in other EU states.

passporting
The practice where collective investment funds may be marketed by their management house across European Economic Area (EEA) states, without having to separately 'set up' the fund in each state. It also allows investment firms to set up offices in other EEA member states and conduct cross-border business without the need for separate licensing in each jurisdiction.

Client categorisation
Clients are categorised into 'eligible counterparties': professional clients and retail clients.

Client order handling
Firms have to ensure they are acting in a client's best interest, especially when they gather together orders from different clients.

Pre-trade transparency
Companies have to comply with transparency for (a) order-matching systems by providing information on best price levels and (b) market makers, the best bids and offers.

Post-trade transparency
The price, volume and time of all trades in listed shares must be published, unless they qualify for delayed publication.

Best execution
Firms should be able to prove that they have taken reasonable steps to deal in the best interest for their client. The requirements for **best execution** include:

best execution
Occurs when a trade of a particular size is transacted at the best available price and cost in the market at the time of the trade.

- cost;
- speed;
- size;
- likelihood of execution and settlement; and
- any other consideration relevant to the execution of an order to achieve the best overall result for the client.

Multilateral trading facility (MTF)
An alternative trading venue to existing exchanges which does not have a listing process. MTFs require a rule book, trade transparency and an accessible notice of prices and charges. The legal status of MTFs was defined by MiFID.

systematic internalisers
These are investment firms which 'match', 'buy' and 'sell' orders they receive from clients in house, rather than placing orders with a central exchange.

transferable securities
Classes of investments which are negotiable on share exchanges or other dealing platforms. Shares and bonds fall into this category.

money-market instruments
Short-term low-risk financial instruments such as commercial paper, Treasury Bills and certificates of deposit (CDs).

UCITS
A set of European Union directives for collective investment funds available throughout the European Economic Area on the basis of a single authorisation in the fund manager's state.

options
Standardised derivative contracts purchased by a holder (the purchaser) from a writer (the seller) or third parties which give the holder the right (without any obligation) either to buy or to sell standard quantities of an underlying asset on or before a specified fixed future date.

Multilateral trading facilities

Before the implementation of MiFID, trading in shares and other financial instruments could only be undertaken on RIEs. The new rules recognised other organised trading facilities known as **multilateral trading facilities (MTFs)**. MTFs allow trades to be undertaken on a similar basis to RIEs but they do not act as counterparties to the transaction. MTFs are outlined in more detail in section 5.

Systematic internalisers

The new rules also allowed the introduction of **systematic internalisers** (SIs). These allow investment firms to deal on their own account, without using RIEs or MTFs, carrying out client orders in an organised, frequent and systematic way.

Financial instruments governed by MiFID II include:

- **transferable securities**;
- **money-market instruments**;
- Undertakings for Collective Investment in Transferable Securities (**UCITS**) schemes (see Chapter 9);
- financial contracts for differences; and
- **options, futures**, swaps, forward rate agreements and any other derivative contracts relating to currencies, interest rates or yields, commodities or other derivative instruments.

Market structure framework

A new framework to ensure that trading, where possible, takes place on a regulated platform.

Market transparency

Equity trading transparency is expected to increase, and transparency for non-equity instruments such as bonds and derivatives will be introduced.

Strengthened supervisory powers

To meet G20 commitments, new rules for commodity derivatives were introduced, to prevent market abuse and assist regulators and participants to obtain more comprehensive information on these markets.

Trading and clearing of financial instruments

A new framework for non-discriminatory access to trading and **central counterparties (CCPs)**.

Controls for algorithmic trading activities

Introduction of controls to safeguard against systemic risk through properly regulated market-making strategy.

Stronger investor protection
Strengthening of conduct rules and introduction of better organisational requirements for the benefit of clients. Also to enhance the distinction between independent and non-independent advice.

Effective and harmonised administrative sanctions
The use of strengthened cooperation to improve the effective detection of breaches of MiFID.

Third country firms
Access to EU markets, depending on assessment, may be granted to third-country jurisdictions by the European Commission.

4.2 Automated exchanges – algorithmic and high frequency trading.

In order for companies involved in financial services to comply with the MiFID directive, automated trading systems have been introduced. These systems use **algorithmic trading**, which takes price, venue, cost and speed of execution into account, as well as providing audit trails to allow firms to comply with MiFID.

In the USA, fully automated markets include the ICE (Intercontinental Exchange), NASDAQ OMX Group, Direct Edge, and BATS. These initially gained market share from the NYSE, until NYSE Euronext, an MTF platform, was introduced. ICE acquired NYSE Euronext in 2013. Deals once undertaken by human traders have been switched to computers using algorithmic or automatic trading. The use of computers has meant that the speed of trading, from the placing of an order to final confirmation (also known as the 'round trip'), has fallen to around three milliseconds in the USA. This change has resulted in a number of 'high-frequency' traders dealing in markets and completing trades in milliseconds. Some of these deals are known as 'flash' trading, and are likely to be controlled through limiting the size and number of trades undertaken in many trading centres. The speed or time required to undertake an automatic trade is known as 'latency'. A low-latency platform will undertake trades in three to five milliseconds or less. High-frequency traders use strategies that enable them to spot short trading patterns, as well as read supply and demand signals. As these strategies command a large percentage of the market share, not only in the USA but also in Europe, they are very profitable, through making the most of easily determined market trends, based on their innovative computer modelling.

Algorithmic trading (or automatic computer-based trading), also known as 'algo trading', can be used for trading, market making, arbitrage, and inter-market spreading. The computer algorithm automatically decides, when placing an order, on timing, price and quantity, with little or no human intervention. This form of trading is used by hedge funds, pension funds and collective funds. Institutional traders use algorithmic trading to divide large trades into smaller amounts in order to manage risk, market impact and opportunity cost. Algorithmic trading is normally associated with high-frequency trading. More trading is expected to be undertaken using the high-frequency trading

futures
Legally binding, standardised forward contracts between two parties (a buyer and a seller) to either buy or sell a predetermined quantity of a specified asset (commodity or financial asset) of a specific quality requiring the delivery of that specified asset on a fixed future date, the price of which will be agreed today by both the buyer and seller.

central counterparty (CCP)
A dealing system used in stock markets where deals are settled with a single party rather than between investors, thereby reducing settlement risk.

algorithmic trading
A type of trading based on the use of mathematical formulae which are designed to replicate and speed up the human decision processes that would normally be used to decide trading strategies.

method. As the amount of fully automated trading increases, brokers have indicated that it has become more difficult to monitor the risk of their clients' positions. The FCA has noted the benefits, including liquidity resulting from the efficiency of new technology, but warned of the increased risk in business interruption resulting from system failure. In the USA, in order for automated markets to operate efficiently (especially when institutions, brokers and banks are using their independently developed algorithms for trading), there needs to be a common base for communication. In 1992, a bilateral communications framework for equity trading between Fidelity Investments and Salomon Brothers was started. Having been developed over the years since then, it is now known as the Financial Information eXchange (FIX) protocol. FIX is a series of messaging specifications for the electronic communication of trade-related messages. Banks, broker-dealers, exchanges, institutional investors, investment industry utilities and information technology providers from around the world, with an interest in automated trading of financial instruments, continue to collaborate on the development of the FIX protocol. Without FIX, many of the automated dealing systems would not be able to communicate with one another, and the development of algorithmic trading would have been considerably slower.

4.3 Dark pools

dark pool
A type of electronic trading venue that allows big institutions to execute large trades away from an exchange's normal public, or 'displayed', order book.

The name **dark pools** may seem somewhat furtive, but in reality they are electronic networks allowing traders to execute large orders of shares anonymously. They allow non-displayed trading, where deals are executed away from the public order book (or 'displayed'), with prices posted post-execution, without the risk of other traders being able to work out the trader's, or their clients', strategies. If the other traders were able to do this, they may then try to force the price up or down, to profit from the order themselves. The main aim of dark pools is thus to minimise the impact on markets – critically, quotes are not revealed. It must be noted that not all of the operators of dark pools are traditional financial institutions.

Advantages are that:

- they should reduce overall trading costs, charging lower fees than traditional exchanges, as they are within a single firm;
- trading information is retained within a small group;
- they are useful for the exchange of large block trades; and
- they enable institutional investors to minimise their information leakage and realise more efficient executions.

Disadvantages are that:

- there is a lack of transparency – pre-trade prices are not displayed, the prices at which shares are offered for sale is not displayed;
- they have been described as being akin to private stock markets, where large institutions investors trade blocks of shares secretly;
- some dark pools may have been structured in such as a way as to let frequent traders know how the price of a particular security will move;

- they may result in the fragmentation of markets comprised of public exchanges; and
- brokers may place their own interests ahead of their clients, or favour one client over another.

Dark pools fall into three categories:

1. Independent
   They provide facilities catering for specific requirements such as reduced impact and exchange liquidity pools for block trades.
2. Exchange sponsored
   Offer dark pools which are aimed at high-frequency traders. They offer equal access.
3. Broker / dealer sponsored
   These dark pools offer increased versatility and are not bound by equal access rules. They match orders internally by using the mid point of bid-offer spreads.

Test yourself 5.4

a) Name the financial markets areas to be covered by MiFID II.

b) What are the requirements for best execution?

Stop and think 5.2

How successful do you think the introduction of MiFID II has been in Europe?

5. Large international exchanges and multilateral trading facilities (MTFs)

5.1 Intercontinental Exchange (ICE) and New York Stock Exchange (NYSE)

ICE acquired NYSE Euronext, in November 2013, to become the largest operator of global exchanges, dealing in asset classes including interest rates, equities and equity derivatives, credit derivatives, bonds, foreign exchange, energy, metals, and agricultural products. ICE was founded in 2002 to trade OTC in the energy markets. LIFFE (London International Financial Futures and Options Exchange) was founded in 1982, and acquired by Euronext (founded in 2000 by the merger of the Amsterdam, Brussels, Paris and Lisbon stock exchanges). Euronext merged with the NYSE Group in 2007.

The NYSE is currently the largest equity stock exchange in the world (in dollar terms), and the impact of movement in share prices in New York will be reflected on all other world markets. The NYSE can trace its roots back to Wall Street, where it was founded at the end of the eighteenth century. It is still known as 'Wall Street', although it is now located in Broad Street.

The Dow Jones Industrial Average (DJIA), or the 'Dow', is one of the two market indices that reflect the movement in NYSE shares. On 17 October 1987, the Dow dropped 508 points, a 22.6% loss in one day. Part of the loss was triggered by 'programmed trades' (the forerunner of algorithmic trading): when a share falls to a certain level, it activates a sell order in that share, to protect the investor against further falls. This process turned out to be 'self-feeding', because as the market fell, more shares were sold, which in turn triggered further selling orders. As a result of this, trading now stops for a specified time if the market falls 10 to 20%, and for the rest of the day if the fall is as much as 30%, in order for the market to evaluate the position. A 'flash crash' occurred on 6 May 2010, which led to the introduction of new rules from the US Securities and Exchange Commission (SEC), in an attempt to curb volatile trading. It will affect all stocks traded in Standard & Poor's Index and is known as a circuit breaker. The new circuit breakers are intended to prevent wild price swings and are based on rolling reference price movements over a five-minute time period.

The other main index is the NYSE Composite, which covers all common stocks listed, including American Depository Receipts (ADR), Real Estate Investment Trusts (REITs), Exchange Traded Funds (ETF), and foreign listings. The index is also the basis for the iShares NYSE Composite Index Fund (NYC), an ETF. Recently, ICE has acquired the Singapore Mercantile Exchange. In June 2014, Euronext was floated as a separate independent company, but LIFFE remains part of ICE.

5.2 NASDAQ OMX

The National Association of Securities Dealers Automated Quotation (NASDAQ) started life as the National Association of Securities Dealers (NASD). Electronic trading was introduced in 1971, and the words 'Automated Quotation' was added to the name. In 2006, NASDAQ separated from NASD and, the following year, combined with the Swedish-Finnish financial services company OMX-AB.

NASDAQ OMX is a leading participant in the exchange and technology sector, delivering trading, listing, financial market technology and public company services across six continents. It controls and operates the NASDAQ stock exchange in New York. It also operates eight stock exchanges in Europe (Copenhagen, Stockholm, Helsinki, Tallinn, Riga, Vilnius, Iceland, and Armenia), and has a 10% stake in the Oslo exchange. As well as OMX technology, which develops systems for financial transactions and is one of the world leaders in this field, its trading volume per hour is reported to be the highest of all exchanges in the world, making use of computerised trading. Many technology companies are quoted on NASDAQ, especially those situated on the west coast of the USA. NASDAQ is introducing the NASDAQ Volatility Guard to complement the introduction of S&P stock circuit breakers, resulting from market volatility, as explained above.

5.3 BATS Europe

BATS Global Markets Inc. is one of the leading equity market operators in the USA, operating four equities exchanges. It is an electronic-based, ultra-fast trade matching system, backed by investors including Citigroup, J.P. Morgan Chase and Morgan Stanley. It started trading in US equities in January 2006. BATS has full regulatory approval and competes directly with the NYSE and NASDAQ in the USA.

BATS launched a European service in London at the end of 2008 and, at first, was in competition with LSE Turquoise, NASDAQ OMX, and Chi-X. In 2011, BATS Europe and Chi-X Europe combined to form the largest MTF in Europe. In 2013 it became a recognised investment exchange (RIE) and is one of Europe's largest equity exchanges by market share. BATS Global Markets merged with Direct Edge (which was founded in 1998 and obtained full exchange status from the SEC in 2010) in 2014.

5.4 London Stock Exchange

The history of the London Stock Exchange (LSE) was outlined in section 3 of this chapter.

The London Stock Exchange Group operates a broad range of international equity, bond and derivatives markets, including the LSE, Borsa Italiana, MTS (Europe's leading fixed income market), and the pan-European equities platform Turquoise. Turquoise has been majority-owned by the LSE Group since February 2010. It is an equities MTF, which started trading on 15 August 2008. It is backed by nine major investment banks: BNP Paribas, Citibank, Credit Suisse, Deutsche Bank, Goldman Sachs, Merrill Lynch (now part of Bank of America), Morgan Stanley, Société Générale and UBS. The platform operates in 15 European countries and is based in London.

Turquoise offers:

- a displayed platform which is similar to existing exchanges;
- a public order book; and
- a 'dark pool' facility for its participants.

Turquoise provides a fully risk-managed clearing solution using EuroCCP, which is owned by the Depository Trust and Clearing Corporation of the USA and LCH. Clearnet.

LCH.Clearnet, a leading global CCP, is majority-owned by the LSE and clears a diverse range of OTC and exchange traded asset classes worldwide.

5.5 Chicago Board Options Exchange (CBOE)

CBOE Holdings is the world's largest option exchange, with an annual trading volume of over one billion contracts each year. The CBOE offers options in over 2,000 companies as well as stock indices and ETFs. Ninety-five per cent of orders by volume are traded electronically, with the balance through open outcry (the method of shouting and using hand signals).

5.6 Chicago Mercantile Exchange (CME)

The CME Group, formed from the CME, Chicago Board of Trade (CBOT) and New York Mercantile Exchange (NYMEX), is the world's largest futures and options exchange, with trades based on interest rates, equity indices, foreign exchange, energy, agricultural commodities, metals and alternative investment products such as weather. Most trades are executed on the CME Globex electronic trading platform. CME Clearing matches and settles its trades and acts as counterparty to every trade, thereby almost eliminating credit risk. The CME was founded in 1898 as the Chicago Butter and Egg Board. It merged with CBOT in 2007 and NYMEX in 2008.

5.7 Tokyo Stock Exchange (TSE)

The Tokyo Stock Exchange was founded in 1878, and has combined over the years with ten other stock exchanges in Japan. The exchange reopened in 1949, having closed after the Second World War, and the market expanded dramatically from 1983 onwards, to become the largest market in the world in 1990. The main index used on the exchange is the TOPIX Index, with a base level of 100 at 4 January 1968. A new series of TOPIX indices based on various sectors of the market with a base date of 1 April 1998 and level of 1,000 has been introduced. The TOPIX New Index Series comprises of seven sub-indices: TOPIX Core 30, TOPIX Large 70, TOPIX 100, TOPIX Mid400, TOPIX 500, TOPIX 1000 and TOPIX Small.

The TSE Group merged with the Osaka Securities Exchange in January 2013 to form the Japan Exchange Group JPX.

5.8 Singapore Exchange (SGX)

The Singapore Stock Exchange was established in December 1999, by the merger of the Stock Exchange of Singapore and the Singapore Monetary Exchange. The indices used are the MSCI Singapore Free Index and the Strait Times Index. The Strait Times is the main index. The SGX has many alliances with other exchanges around the world including, in the USA, one with the American Stock Exchange (AMEX) for ETFs, and one with the CME for round-the-clock trading of Eurodollars and Euroyen futures and options. It also has an alliance with the Baltic Exchange in London for freight settlement.

5.9 Hong Kong Stock Exchange (HKEx)

The Hong Kong Stock Exchange and Clearing Limited (HKEx) was founded in 1891, and has had various arrangements with other local exchanges over the years. In 2000, the holding company of the HKEx became Hong Kong Exchanges and Clearing. It is reported to be the third largest exchange in Asia. Companies that are incorporated in the People's Republic of China and approved by the China Securities Regulatory Commission for a listing in Hong Kong are referred to as 'H share' companies (the 'H' stands for Hong Kong). A company that has 30% of its shares held in aggregate, either directly or indirectly, by mainland Chinese entities is referred to as a 'red chip' company. In certain circumstances, the percentage can be as low as 20%. A 'red chip' company is not mainland registered, but an 'H share' company is a mainland China registered company. The main index of the HKEx is the Hang Seng Index.

5.10 Australian Securities Exchange (ASX)

The first stock exchange in Australia was founded in Melbourne in 1861. The Sydney Stock Market was founded ten years later in 1871. Various local exchanges were set up and operated around the continent on the back of mining booms over the years, before the final six important exchanges joined to form the Australian Stock Exchange in 1987. The S&P/ASX indices are calculated in real time by Standard & Poor's.

5.11 Deutsche Börse

A börse was founded in Frankfurt for currency trading in 1585, although the exchange can trace its trading origins back to the ninth century. Over the years the Frankfurt Stock Exchange (Frankfurter Wertpapierbörse – FWB) developed into one of the world's main exchanges, like those of London and Paris. In recent years, the exchange benefited from, firstly, the proximity of the Bundesbank, which decided on financial policy in Germany, and secondly, the establishment of the European Central Bank (ECB) in Frankfurt, following the introduction of the Euro in 2002. The Frankfurt Exchange became part of Deutsche Börse in 1993. Deutsche Börse also owns Eurex, the European futures and options exchange, and Clearstream, which provides integrated banking, custody and settlement services for fixed interest securities and equities. The Deutsche Börse therefore covers the entire security exchange process, from trading and clearing to settlement and securities, custody for equities, bonds and derivatives.

The Frankfurt Stock Exchange (FSE) introduced an electronic trading system, Xetra, and benefited from its development through expansion with partner exchanges: the Vienna Stock Exchange, Irish Stock Exchange and Budapest Stock Exchange. About 45% of the FSE's market participants come from abroad. Deutsche Börse has recently opened a representative office in Beijing. The main trading index is the DAX 30 (Deutsche Aktien IndeX 30).

5.12 Euronext

Early in the nineteenth century, the Paris Bourse was located at the Palais de la Bourse. Later in the same century the Paris stock markets were operated by the Compagnie des Agents de Change. In the late 1990s the Bourse launched Euronext, an alliance of several European stock exchanges. The first European integrated stock exchange was formed by the merger of Paris, Brussels and Amsterdam in September 2000. Euronext merged with the NYSE in April 2007 to form NYSE Euronext. NYSE Euronext was acquired by ICE in November 2013. In June 2014, Euronext became an independent European Stock Exchange. The main index of the Paris SE is the CAC 40 (Cotation Assistée en Continu).

5.13 Chinese Stock Exchanges

The China Securities Regulatory Commission confirmed that the combined total market value of the Shanghai and Shenzhen exchanges amounted to over $3 trillion at the end of May 2010, making China the third largest stock market in the world, after the USA and Japan. The Shanghai Stock Exchange (SSE) was founded in 1990. The SSE has now listed many companies referred to as 'red chips' . These are Chinese companies incorporated and listed outside the People's Republic of China.

The Shenzhen Stock Exchange was also founded in 1990 and is the second largest stock exchange in China. It is owned by the China Securities Depository and Clearing Co.

Test yourself 5.5

a) What are the main European stock exchanges?

b) What does LSE Turquoise offer?

6. Settlement

6.1 The need for settlement

Once a purchase or sale has been made, then the deal has to be settled – that is, the purchaser has to pay for the equity (or other instrument bought) and the seller has to provide good delivery. The seller must be able to deliver their stock within the required time limits in order to receive cash in settlement from the buyer, otherwise the seller will be liable to charges for late delivery. Settlement can, therefore, be defined as the delivery of securities against payment in order to complete a trade between two parties.

A central counterparty (CCP) covers the risk of delivery and payment for the deal. Clearing and settlement require good administration by the exchange or, if applicable, its approved service providers.

6.2 Stock exchange settlement

In the early years of exchanges, settlement was a paper process, and trading volumes were usually small; there were a few exceptions for 'bubbles', and higher-value dealing was centred on government bonds in the nineteenth and twentieth centuries, during the period of Industrial Revolution and wars. Changes to these patterns occurred after the two world wars. Major changes to the volume of equity traded in Europe started in the 1980s, with the opening up of the LSE to outsiders in 1986. Before this change, the stock exchange year was split into account periods. The normal account period ran for two weeks, with settlement of bargains about a week later. However, after the change in 1986, the LSE followed many other world markets by moving to, first a five-day, then a three-day, rolling settlement process (T+3). In this way, share transactions made on a Friday, for example, are settled three working days later, on the following Wednesday.

Settlement is vital to the functioning of a market, as it is the final stage in a transaction, with transfer of ownership of the security to the purchaser followed by registration in the shareholders' book of members (or equivalent).

6.3 Clearing of trades

Before the changes to the LSE in 1986, clearing of trades, and acting as counterparties to dealing, was undertaken by the markets themselves. This is still the case for regulated markets such as the LSE, Deutsche Börse and NYSE, but independent clearing houses for multilateral platforms have become a necessity, in order to handle the volume of business created by computerised trading. The 2007 banking crisis emphasised the need for transparency, effective clearing and settlement of trades, with counterparties able to assess risk and to have sufficient assets to cover their trading positions. The EU has also introduced a choice of companies for settlement and counterparties, giving users greater choice. A code of conduct was introduced by the EU in November 2007, to which all European exchanges, clearing and settlement houses have to keep. This is based on:

- price transparency;
- access and **interoperability**;
- unbundling; and
- accounting separation.

interoperability
The ability of different (trading) systems to work together.

There is a European Code of Conduct on Clearing and Settlement, which is a voluntary arrangement of the European stock exchanges, settlement agencies and central securities depositories (CSDs). Post-MiFID moves have demanded that clearing be competitive, transparent and cross-border (outside the EU country of origin). Interoperability and cross-border clearing are proving to be difficult to achieve, but there are positive developments, with competitive clearing imminent. The sub-prime crisis, and resulting bank crisis, has led CCPs to wider risk management roles by clearing standardised derivatives centrally, in order to reduce counterparty risk. LCH.Clearnet has already launched clearing for OTC interest rates swaps through SwapClear. Also, Intercontinental Exchange (ICE), the US-based international clearing house, has a strong presence in derivative clearing.

6.4 TARGET2

The Trans-European Automated Real-time Gross Settlement Express Transfer System – TARGET2 – is a European cross-border settlement platform, the 'Single Shared Platform' (SSP). Three Eurosystem central banks – Banca d'Italia, Banque de France and Deutsche Bundesbank – jointly provide the SSP for TARGET 2 and operate it on behalf of the Eurosystem.

6.5 TARGET2-Securities (T2S)

T2S is the new European securities settlement platform, to replace domestic and cross-border settlement through the harmonisation of post-trade services and standards, contributing to stronger financial integration and a true European single market.

The aims of T2S are to:

- cut settlement costs to one of the lowest levels in the world. It will bring down cross-border settlement fees by exploiting economies of scale using a single IT settlement platform, a single set of standards and a single operational framework;
- be a catalyst for harmonisation across Europe by creating a single, sound and competitive financial market in Europe;
- have a positive impact on financial stability, which, given recent financial turmoil, is crucial for the future of markets. T2S will settle exclusively in central bank money and offer the most advanced standards of resilience, availability, business continuity and security. It will enable banks to optimise their liquidity and collateral management, thereby providing greater diversification and sharing of risk; and
- foster competition, open new business opportunities and benefit European investors.

Stop and think 5.3

What are the problems with cross-border clearing and how may they improve?

7. Counterparties and clearing houses

Clearing houses have been part of market structures since trading began. They assume some of the risk in a trade, by acting as the counterparty between a buyer and seller in a transaction. As trading has grown over the centuries, the size and complexity of deals has increased, and with it, counterparty risks. Investment clearing houses have expanded their business as a result of the financial crises and now clear non-market trades, including OTCs and **currency swaps** (see Chapter 7). Clearing houses are an important part of the settlement process.

currency swaps
Financial instruments sometimes referred to as cross-currency swaps. They are contractual agreements between two parties swapping principal and fixed interest in one currency for principal and fixed interest in another currency. They are not derivative instruments.

7.1 Examples of clearing houses

LCH.Clearnet clears a range of asset classes, including equities, exchange-traded derivatives, interest rate swaps, bonds and repos (repurchases) for major international exchanges, and MTFs. It is positioned in the middle of a trade, accepting the counterparty risk, when two members of an exchange trade. When a trade is registered, LCH.Clearnet becomes the legal counterparty to the trade and if one of the parties to the trade defaults, LCH.Clearnet steps in. It underpins many financial markets through the mechanism of undertaking the counterparty risk to a trade. This helps trading and confidence within a market. As a result of providing this facility, LCH.Clearnet assesses its members and the market risk on a daily basis. It is the leading European equity CCP, clearing equity-based trades for LSE Turquoise, SWX Europe, Equiduct, NYSE, Euronext, BATS Chi-X Europe, and others.

Eurex Clearing is a CCP. It is fully owned by Eurex Frankfurt AG and jointly operated by Deutsche Börse and SIX Swiss Exchange. Eurex Clearing services over 114 clearing members spread over ten European countries. It provides full clearing and risk management services for leading exchanges and marketplaces, wholesale trading, post-trade management, risk control, delivery management and reporting.

Euroclear, founded in Brussels in 1968, provides a clearing and settlement service in many European countries. It has developed over the years, expanding its services from US$ bonds into domestic bonds and equities, and later, fund markets. It recently launched its single settlement and custody platform for Belgium, France and Holland, called ESES.

Euroclear
A multi-currency settlement system for European securities where securities are held in dematerialised (non-paper) form.

SIX x-clear AG clears trades for SIX Swiss Exchanges and the LSE by acting as an alternative CCP, offering clearing and risk-management services in the cash-equity and bond markets. By 2010, SIX x-clear will offer services to NYFIX, BATS Chi-X, BATS, NASDAQ OMX Europe, Turquoise and NASDAQ OMX, enabling members to access a single CCP with a pan-European clearing offering.

EuroCCP, owned by the Depository Trust and Clearing Corporation of the USA, offers competitive clearing and interoperating with other CCPs depending on a client's requirements. In fact, competitive clearing and interoperating with other CCPs is embedded in EuroCCP's agreements. Turquoise uses EuroCCP.

In the USA, most securities clearing is undertaken by the Depository Trust and Clearing Corporation (DTCC), also known as Fedwire. It was founded to enable buyers and sellers of securities in the USA to clear and settle their transactions. It also provides a custody facility. International transactions in the US are cleared mainly by LCH.Clearnet.

The European Multilateral Clearing Facility was founded in 2007 with the objective of providing CCP services for MTFs in Europe. It offers post-trade services to MTFs and regular exchanges including BATS Chi-X Europe and NASDAQ OMX Europe.

Test yourself 5.6

What are the four aims of T2S?

8. Data vendors

Data vendors specialise in obtaining, processing and providing financial information to end-users such as brokers, management houses, banks and other financial institutions.

8.1 Examples of data vendors

SIX Telekurs was founded in 1930 and its headquarters is in Zurich, Switzerland. SIX Telekurs (now known as SIX Financial Information) has a long history of partnership with financial solution providers and financial institutions.

Thomson Reuters (TR) was formed in April 2008, when Thomson purchased Reuters. TR provides information and trading in foreign exchange, fixed income, equities and commodities, information and support rolls for portfolio managers, as well as news and information from around the world. TR also provides an independent consolidated tape and an analytical tool called Equity Market Share Reporter (EMSR), which allows traders to see share prices offered across exchanges and MTFs in Europe.

The Interactive Data Corporation was founded in 1968 in the USA. It is a global provider of financial markets data, analytics and related services to financial institutions.

Bloomberg is a financial software, news and data company founded in 1981 in the USA. It is well known for its analytics and equity trading platform, data services and news to financial companies around the world through the Bloomberg Terminal. They are direct competitors with Thomson Reuters.

NextVIEW provides news and real-time financial market information in Asian markets including China, Hong Kong, India, Indonesia, Malaysia, Singapore, Thailand and Vietnam.

Fidessa provides clients who use its systems with a market data workstation, giving them access to a wide range of market information and news, equity prices, indices, foreign exchange rates and market commentaries. Clients can also access Fidessa's trading system.

Proquote International is a market data system providing coverage of over 100 markets, data sources and news. It includes real-time and delayed global market data, news feeds from multiple sources, analytics with Proquote Clearview, and company fundamentals, including broker forecasts and charting facilities.

Markit BOAT is a MiFID-compliant trade reporting platform, formed by a consortium of nine investment banks in 2006. The BOAT system enables market participants to publish pre-trade quotes and report OTC equity trades in equities.

Test yourself 5.7

Explain the function of data vendors.

Chapter summary

- In a quote-driven market, trades are conducted through market makers who receive orders directly from brokers. In an order-driven market, a stockbroker places an order to buy or sell a certain number of shares at a particular price on a matching-order system.

- Recognised investment exchanges are organised institutions for the trading (buying and selling) of shares (stocks) and bonds.
- The main international exchanges and MTFs are based in the USA and Europe, but this is changing with the growth in size and liquidity of exchanges around the world. For example, many overseas companies are traded on the Hong Kong exchange as well as Chinese and local companies.
- The main London exchange is the LSE (including AIM).
- MiFID II which took effect in January 2018 replaced MiFID I (The Markets in Financial Instruments Directive). The function of MiFID II is to improve the function of financial markets in the light of the financial crisis and to strengthen investor protection.
- The world of securities dealing and settlement is fast-moving. In Europe, trading through recognised investment exchanges has been accompanied, since the introduction of the MiFID in Europe, by trading through MTFs.
- Settlement process and counterparties are linked together as part of the system in place to handle the process after a deal has been undertaken.
- The role of clearing houses is explained and the importance of counter parties and their associated risks has been discussed. Trades not executed through clearing houses presented a major problem in settlement during the 2007 financial crisis.
- Markets depend on financial information to function efficiently, and the business of data vendors is an important service to this end.

Test yourself answers

Test yourself 5.1

a) In a quote-driven market, trades are conducted through market makers who receive orders directly from brokers. Two prices are quoted by the market maker, normally on a computer screen: a bid price for sellers and an offer price for buyers.

In an order-driven market, a stockbroker places an order to buy or sell a certain number of shares at a particular price on a matching-order system, again computer-based, like SETS. Many stock markets around the world operate an order-driven system.

b) Trades are undertaken on either a quote-driven basis or an order-driven basis.

In a quote-driven market, trades are conducted through market makers who receive orders directly from brokers. Two prices are quoted by the market maker, normally on a computer screen: a bid price for sellers and an offer price for buyers.

Different market makers will be listed on the screen page for the same share, usually showing slightly different bid and offer prices for deals of a particular size. The size refers to the number of shares at the bid or offer price.

All companies quoted on this type of dealing system have a normal market dealing size determined by the stock exchange. The screen quote will be at this size or larger, depending on the market maker's position – that is, how many shares the market maker owns or needs to buy to keep his or her position in balance.

The screen page for the company will normally have a band showing the highest bid price and the lowest offer price, and which market maker(s) is/are making these prices and at what size.

The highest bid and lowest offer is known as the touch price. The broker then contacts the market maker showing the best screen price, depending on whether their client is a seller or buyer of the shares in the quoted company at that price and size, and a deal is done.

In an order-driven market, a stockbroker places an order to buy or sell a certain number of shares at a particular price on a matching-order system, again computer-based, like SETS. Many stock markets around the world operate an order-driven system.

Test yourself 5.2

a) Recognised investment exchanges (RIEs) are organised institutions for the trading (buying and selling) of shares (stocks) and bonds.

b) Potential benefits for companies trading on AIM are as follows:

- It allows access to capital at flotation and for raising capital through further share issues.
- It creates a market for companies' shares.
- It broadens a shareholder base.
- It allows existing shareholders to sell or reduce their holding – this is important for family business and individual taxation purposes.
- It offers a market valuation of business.
- Share incentive schemes can be introduced for employees.
- Shares can be used for acquisition purposes.
- It provides access to institutional and private investors.
- International companies, trading for at least 18 months on an AIM Designated Market in another country, may use their existing annual report and accounts for a complementary listing.
- It raises the profile and increases the credibility of a company.

Test yourself 5.3

The Stock Exchange Electronic Trading System (SETS) is a computerised system used in the London Stock Exchange which posts buying and selling prices and also undertakes (executes) trades. The SETS system is mainly used for shares that are traded frequently.

The Stock Exchange Automated Quotations (SEAQ) is a market maker-based system showing prices and dealing sizes for major shares quoted on the LSE. It is a quote-driven dealing system.

Test yourself 5.4

a) MiFID II covers the following:

- Market structure framework – a new framework to ensure that trading, where possible, takes place on a regulated platform.
- Market transparency – transparency is increased for equity trading and introduced for non-equity instruments such as bonds and derivatives.
- Strengthened supervisory powers – to meet G20 commitments, new rules for commodity derivatives are introduced to prevent market abuse, and assist regulators and participants to obtain better information on these markets.
- Trading and clearing of financial instruments – a new framework for non-discriminatory access to trading and central counterparties (CCPs).
- Controls for algorithmic trading activities – introduction of controls to safeguard against systemic risk through properly regulated market making strategy.
- Stronger investor protection – strengthening of conduct rules and introduction of better organisational requirements for the benefit of clients. Also to enhance the distinction between independent and non-independent advice.
- Effective and harmonised administrative sanctions – the use of strengthened cooperation to improve the effective detection of breaches of MiFID.
- Third country firms – access to EU markets, depending on assessment, may be granted to third-country jurisdictions by the Commission.

b) The requirements for best execution include:

- cost;
- speed;
- size;
- likelihood of execution and settlement; and
- any other consideration relevant to the execution of an order to achieve the best overall result for the client.

Test yourself 5.5

a) The main European stock exchanges are:
- London Stock Exchange;
- Euronext; and
- Deutsche Börse.

b) Turquoise provides a fully risk-managed clearing solution using EuroCCP and offers:
- a displayed platform which is similar to existing exchanges;
- a public order book; and
- a 'dark pool' facility for its participants.

Test yourself 5.6

The four aims of T2S are as follows:

- To cut settlement costs to one of the lowest levels in the world.
- To be a catalyst for harmonisation across Europe by creating a single, sound and competitive financial market in Europe.
- To have a positive impact on financial stability, which, given recent financial turmoil, is crucial for the future of markets.
- To foster competition, open new business opportunities and benefit European investors.

Test yourself 5.7

Data vendors specialise in obtaining, processing and providing financial information to end-users such as brokers, management houses, banks and other financial institutions.

Chapter six
Derivative markets and derivative instruments

List of topics

1. The derivatives market and derivative instruments
2. Futures (futures contracts)
3. Options
4. Company warrants
5. Covered warrants
6. Interest rate swaps
7. Credit default swaps
8. Contracts for differences and turbos
9. Crypto-currency derivatives

Introduction

Before exploring the subject of the derivatives market and its inherent instruments it is of paramount importance to understand the meaning of a derivative per se.

First, let us consider the word derivative itself. A derivative is something that is derived from another source or product. Therefore, for a derivative to exist, another 'product' or source (underlying asset) must already exist prior to the existence or creation of a derivative. Consequently, if there is no underlying asset, there can be no derivative. Underlying assets are most usually referred to as the 'underlying'.

The range of pre-existing products upon which derivatives may be based is very diverse and includes equities, fixed interest securities (including UK gilts), commodities, foreign exchange products, indices even more recently crypto-currencies (Bitcoin and Etherium). More abstract derivatives – for example, futures based on weather forecasts – have been introduced and more will be developed as different underlying assets are themselves created. Additional examples will be provided throughout the chapter. The main uses of derivatives are hedging, speculation and arbitrage, and these will be discussed.

It is important to remember that it is the price of the particular derivative instrument that is derived from the underlying asset ('the underlying'). More often than not individual other characteristics of underlying assets are not derived. For instance, the aroma of a coffee bean would not be a derived characteristic. Derivatives allow more sophisticated investors the potential to benefit from the price movements of underlying assets, whether rising or falling, without ever having to own them. The price of a derivative itself will be very close to that of the underlying asset in the relevant spot market from which it is derived, and should usually move in the same direction as the price of that underlying. Underlying assets may be physical in the case of commodities or abstract in the case of indices and interest-rate swaps.

1. The derivatives market and derivative instruments

1.1 Derivative instruments

There is provided within the list of topics at the beginning of the chapter coverage of main derivative instruments which will now be discussed in greater depth. These are the most common types, however, there are others and new ones may be created and developed in the future. It is also important to note that a range of different derivative instruments can apply to the same underlying asset, perhaps an index such as the FTSE100.

Derivatives are used for three main purposes: hedging, speculation and arbitrage. Those who use them for these purposes are attracted to the leverage (gearing) that they provide, and the deferred payment that they allow.

Derivatives are leveraged in the sense that users, when trading them, only have to pay an initial margin which represents a small percentage of the price in the spot market. Thus if an investor had £1 million which he wished to invest in Barclays Bank ordinary shares he could either purchase the shares directly in the spot market at the prevailing market price. Alternatively by using futures he could gain the same degree of exposure to the shares that would have been purchased using the £1 million but for perhaps for an outlay of only £100,000 and invest £900,000 elsewhere. Another possibility would be to use the original £1 million to gain exposure to potentially 10 times the amount of Barclays Bank shares originally intended. Futures also allow deferred payment to the final settlement date. If the underlying assets were purchased outright in the spot market, then both payment and delivery must be made immediately.

There are two main categories of derivative instrument:

1. Financial derivatives are based on underlying assets such as equities (ordinary shares), indices, gilts, currencies and interest rates.
2. Commodity derivatives may be sub-categorised as hard or soft. Hard would include metals such as gold and platinum, whereas soft may include assets such as coffee, pork bellies or sugar.

1.2 The development of derivatives

It is generally accepted that the first rudimentary futures contracts were used in 1650 in the Yodoya rice market of Osaka, Japan. The Chicago Board of Trade (CBOT), now the largest derivatives exchange in the world, was established in 1848. In the early 1970s, the first **standardised** options contracts were introduced.

standardised
'Standardised' in this context refers to a situation where the specifications contained within any one contract will not vary from those specifications contained within any other contract in relation to the same underlying asset.

Derivatives were originally created to reduce or eliminate risk. However, they have evolved into products that not only fulfil this requirement but also are now used by speculators to maximise returns and also by arbitrageurs.

To be more precise, derivatives were created originally to protect farmers from potential falls in the prices paid for their crops. Farmers needed to know exactly how much they would receive for their grain prior to harvesting in order to justify their efforts in terms of labour and cost. Futures contracts provided a mechanism for such protection. They were now able to sell their crops at a locked-in fixed future price, agreed before they started producing the crops. The buyer needed to know precisely what assets, in terms of quantity and quality, they would receive, and how much they must pay. Thus certainty is required by both parties, not just the seller.

2. Futures (futures contracts)

Futures are absolute contractual agreements. They are traded exclusively on recognised futures exchange to either buy or sell underlying assets, whether financial, physical or abstract, at a price agreed today, but paid actually on the final expiry date. Only a margin payment (or fraction of the agreed price) is paid today for delivery of that underlying asset in the future. This is not a down-payment; it merely represents a commitment to fulfil the contract. It should be remembered that everything about a future indeed happens in the future, whether final settlement or delivery, and not the here and now. Only the agreement and initial margin occur immediately.

A definition of a future is now provided which is somewhat idealised and is from an academic perspective only, and it is probable that those who use futures to achieve their various aims and objectives would not be able to provide such a definition, and indeed may not even understand the technical aspects; however, it does at least contain the various contractual obligations and responsibilities. It also implies that buyers and sellers trade directly with each other; this is not the case, as futures are traded exclusively via specialised futures brokers who have been approved by recognised futures exchanges. It also important to note that it is contractual obligations that are being traded not underlying assets. In order to demonstrate a thorough understanding of the subject matter, the definition should be committed to memory, as there is a possibility that students may be asked to provide such a definition in a future ICSA investment examination.

> A future (futures contract) is a standardised legally binding contractual obligation between two parties (a buyer and a seller) where one party will agree to sell while the other party will agree to buy a predetermined

quantity of a specified asset of a specific quality. Both the delivery of the specific asset and final payment for the specific asset will take place simultaneously on the fixed future date, the final price of which will be agreed today.

2.1 Considerations

Both parties – the buyer and the seller of a future – must each make a payment to a futures broker. The exact amount of this payment will depend on the nature of the underlying asset, its price volatility, market volatility and contract size. This payment is referred to an initial margin and is determined by the relevant futures exchange/futures clearing house which trades the particular future.

Final cash settlement (agreed price less margins already paid) will be made on the final delivery date, not immediately.

All futures are absolutely standardised units; indeed the standard unit is one future, with each one being standardised in terms of the underlying asset in terms of quantity, quality and place of delivery. However, it must be borne in mind that for certain underlying assets there is a minimum number of futures that can be bought (minimum trading size) – for example, five futures.

Every aspect of a future is standardised in terms of quality, contract size and place of delivery. The one aspect that is not standardised is its price; however, this is agreed at the time of either buying or selling futures, thus providing both producers and consumers alike with control over the future prices of assets that they will buy or sell. Notably, they will fix today the price to be paid in the future by a purchaser and received by the seller. Final payment will be made on the delivery date and not before. The purchaser cannot require delivery of the underlying asset prior to that expiry date. Thus futures provide absolute certainty in terms of the underlying asset whether bought or sold or in terms of the amount of money to be paid or received. As soon as a future's position is opened, everything become crystallised.

The price of the underlying asset of which delivery will be taken in the future is agreed today but not paid today; only the initial margin is paid immediately. This affords today price certainty in the future for both the buyer and seller. The seller of an underlying asset knows precisely how much will be received, whereas the purchaser knows exactly how much has to be paid and precisely what will be received in terms in terms of quantity and quality in relation to an underlying asset.

It must be emphasised that futures can be derived from any number of underlying assets including UK gilts, Treasury bonds currencies, equities, commodities and even weather patterns and, more recently, crypto-currencies including Bitcoin and Etherium.

In the United Kingdom, ICE futures Europe provides exposure to a range of derivative instruments including not only futures but also options. The groupings as at the timing of writing are provided below, while other exchanges may have different groupings:

- credit;
- energy – including crude oil (Brent crude) and gas;
- equity derivatives;
- FX;
- freight;
- interest rates;
- metals;
- agricultural and softs – corn, wheat and cocoa; and
- emissions.

At the agreed expiry date, futures can either be physically delivered or alternatively, and most commonly, cash-settled (closed-out). This is done by creating an equal and opposite position to that already open. If futures for a specific expiry date have been bought, futures for the same delivery date will be sold subsequently in order to close that position.

As futures, like all derivatives, are highly leveraged financial instruments, they provide investors with the ability to gain exposure to a large amount of an underlying asset for an initial outlay which is only a fraction of trading the same underlying asset in the relevant spot market. However, it is necessary to be aware the asset will never actually be owned. Investors could lose all of their initial outlay or possibly multiples thereafter and considerably more in terms of multiple margin calls.

When a future has reached its expiry date, it is irrelevant how much the price of the relevant underlying asset has moved against any trader. Even if a price eventually recovers in the spot market, the future has expired. As nothing is owned when a futures is purchased, at expiry this is still the case. Another significant downside is that many multiples of an original outlay may have to be made, and a trader may still end up not owning any underlying asset. This would particularly be the case when futures are used speculatively.

2.2 Futures terminology

Standardised contracts

Futures are legally binding forward contracts in which both parties must fulfil their respective obligations (contrast with options, discussed in section 3 of this chapter, where there is an option to exercise). A traditional seller of a futures agrees ('contracts') to provide a predetermined quantity (specific amount) of an underlying asset of a specific quality on a specific future date, and the buyer contracts to buy this underlying asset, at a price agreed today, on a specific future date. Futures trades are made only in whole numbers. There is no immediate transfer of ownership of an underlying asset, as there would be in the spot market, where the purchaser would receive either the asset itself or documents of title relating to it and the seller would provide the underlying asset or documents of title.

standardised
The standard unit of futures trading is known as a futures contract.

In practice, the majority of futures will be closed out and cash-settled prior to expiry, while others will be for physical delivery. At the point of closing out, profits will be made or losses incurred. It might only possible to purchase a minimum of two or even ten futures, depending upon the specific underlying asset on which the future is based. This will be determined by the relevant futures exchange.

Contract specifications

All relevant information will be included within in the 'contract specifications', which itself is included within a detailed and extensive document: 'contract terms and administrative procedures'. For Robusta Coffee, for example, a futures contract is 29 pages in length.

The details that will be included in the contract specification are:

- the underlying asset, including a detailed description;
- the unit of trading;
- the fixed future date for delivery (settlement date);
- last trading day;
- the price agreed today; and
- contractual obligations.
- minimum trading size.

The underlying asset

Futures contracts are available for such diversified underlying assets as:

- commodities including corn, rice and wheat;
- currencies including the Swiss franc, United States dollar and Japanese yen;
- indices – Dow Jones, Standard & Poor's 500;
- government bonds – gilts;
- interest rates – Eurodollar three-month, US Treasury bond;
- equities – Post Office ordinary shares;
- livestock;
- metals including gold, silver and palladium; and
- crypto-currencies including Bitcoin, Etherium and Litecoin.

The unit of trading

The minimum unit of trading is one contract (and only in whole numbers). For example, it is not possible to buy or sell 1.5 futures contracts. The minimum size of each unit depends on the underlying asset in question.

- Feed futures: 1 contract = 50 tonnes;
- Robusta Coffee: 1 contract = 10 tonnes;
- Aegon NV ordinary shares: 1 contract = 100 shares;
- FTSE 100 Index: 1 contract = £10 per index point;
- Gold: 1 contract = 100 troy ounces;
- Silver: 1 contract = 5,000 ounces.

The size of the contract and the minimum trading unit are determined by the exchange where the futures are traded.

Making it work 6.1: Specification for the FTSE 100 Index future

Delivery months for a FTSE 100 Index future: March, June, September, December.

For example, when June 2018 futures expired, June 2019 futures were introduced.

Quotation for a FTSE 100 Index future is index points.

Minimum price movement will be given.

Last trading day: for FTSE 100 Index futures, this is the third Friday in the delivery month.

The applicable currency will always be given; in this case it is sterling.

Final settlement date: when all obligations have ceased.

Settlement: cash or physical. In this case it must be cash settlement, as the underlying asset is abstract.

Fixed future date

The fixed future date (also known as the delivery or last settlement date) is the final date or the date on which the counterparties must fulfil their outstanding obligations, whether the settlement is to be physical or in cash. There is no range of exercise dates as there is with options, discussed in section 3 of this chapter. In the case of physically delivered futures, those contracts with open positions on the final settlement date must finish with the actual delivery or acceptance of the underlying asset. There is no requirement to make final payment or to make or take delivery prior to this date.

Last trading day

Some authorities confuse the last trading day with the final delivery date or last settlement date. This is not the case. Although it is possible to close-out a position, there is no obligation to make payment or make delivery before this date. The last trading day occurs a few days before actual delivery date and affords the futures contract seller a period of time to make goods available for delivery. This is particularly pertinent in the case of physically delivered goods.

The price agreed today

The seller of the underlying asset wants price certainty, whereas the buyer wants to know how much they have to pay. The buyer also requires certainty in relation to the quantity and quality of the underlying assets that will be provided by the seller. Consequently, the price the buyer must pay in the future (on the settlement date) will be agreed today. When opening any futures position, whether buying or selling, only an initial margin will be required (5–20%). This margin is determined by the relevant futures exchange and settled through a futures clearing house.

Bid and offer prices for futures are readily available from approved brokers and futures exchanges. For example, in order to buy September futures for FTSE 100 Index futures, if the offer price were £7,450, it would cost an investor £74,500 (£10 per index point) to buy one futures contract.

Although the price is agreed today, money will only be exchanged simultaneously when the seller delivers the underlying asset on the fixed future date. However, as all futures are traded on regulated exchanges and have to go through a clearing house, both parties must provide an initial margin to the clearing house at the time of opening the position. Subsequent variation margins may also be called from either party. Margin levels are determined by the relevant exchanges. One reason why investors find futures contracts attractive is because had they bought the underlying asset directly in the relevant spot market, they would make full and immediate payment and sellers would have to deliver now when they might not be able to do so.

Worked example 6.1

Futures for hedging

We use the London Cocoa futures as an example and which are traded on the London ICE.

The margin figures provided are approximate. A 10% initial margin has been used for illustrative purposes, but the specific margin requirements may vary according to a number of factors.

The contract of one London Cocoa future is equivalent to ten tonnes; therefore the minimum amount of exposure that hedger could obtain is ten tonnes. If they were to buy or sell two cocoa futures, then they acquire exposure to 20 tonnes of cocoa.

Thus if a chocolate manufacturer requires 100 tonnes of cocoa in order for its chocolate production in three months' time and needs to take delivery in three months' time but needs to lock in the price today, it will be necessary to buy 10 London Cocoa futures.

In this instance, the chocolate manufacturer is hedging against a price rise of cocoa and thus will buy futures.

If the chocolate manufacturer were to buy the cocoa today in the relevant spot market, it would be necessary to pay the full spot price immediately, which is currently £1,000 per metric tonne. Thus the manufacturer would be obliged to make an immediate payment of £100,000. However, by using the London Cocoa futures instead by buying five futures (opening a long position), the chocolate manufacturer will only have to pay a 10% initial margin to the futures broker which will be paid into the margin account which will be equivalent to perhaps £10,000. There is the advantage not only of deferred payment, but also of not having to take delivery, as the cocoa manufacturer may not have storage facilities.

Thus the cocoa manufacturer has bought the right to buy cocoa at £1,000 per tonne. If the price in the spot market rises to perhaps £1,200 per metric tonne, the chocolate manufacturer will still only pay the agreed £1,000. The cocoa producer could obviously obtain £1,200 in the spot market, so why would this be sold to the chocolate manufacturer for only £1,000? It should be remembered that the cocoa producer, when opening a short futures position, would have provided an initial margin as the price in the spot market rises, thus affording a potential gain. This would be offset as there would be an equivalent loss on the short futures position of £200 per metric tonne. So the result is more or less the same.

Conversely, it could be questioned why the chocolate manufacturer would pay £1,000 per metric tonne if this could be bought in the spot market for perhaps £800. Once again, any potential gain in the spot market would be counter-balanced by a loss of £200 per metric tonne on the long futures position.

Contractual obligations

The buyer of a future enters into a contract to buy an underlying asset for which they will agree to provide payment while the seller of the future enters into an obligation to provide the underlying asset on a fixed future date. It is not an underlying asset being traded, merely the right to buy or sell; it is obligations/contracts being traded, not assets.

Although both parties are acquiring obligations, they are doing this for various reasons to suit their own requirements. The buyer will want either to make a profit (using futures speculatively) or to hedge a position, whereas the seller wants to obtain certainty in relation to the price of their goods, although again they may want to make a profit or hedge a position.

The buyer of a futures is acquiring an obligation to buy an underlying asset and is said to be 'long the future', whereas the seller of a future is acquiring an obligation to sell an underlying asset and is said to be 'short the future'. In practice, most futures will be cash-settled prior to the expiry date.

2.3 The futures market users and uses

It is very important not to confuse how futures are used (their purpose) with those who use them. Futures have three main purposes: hedging, speculation and arbitrage, all of which are employed by various users. They use futures because of the high degree of leverage they afford combined with the fact that they allow exposure to a an underlying asset without ever having to own that asset. They can also disassociate themselves from any of the inherent obligations of actually owning an underlying asset – for example, insurance, storage and transport costs. In addition, futures allow for deferred payment or deferred delivery to the final settlement date.

Uses of futures

Futures have three main purposes and they may be either bought or sold in pursuit of these purposes.

- **Hedging** – to reduce or eliminate risk. This is a type of insurance. Hedgers tend not to be profit-focused; they want to protect themselves from the price volatility of an underlying asset.
- **Speculation** – to make an investment in the hope of making a gain, but with the risk of loss. Those who use futures for this purpose are referred to as 'speculators'.
- **Arbitrage** – simultaneous buying and selling of assets in different markets (the spot market and the futures market) in order to take advantages of differing prices in these markets. For instance, differences in prices between the equities markets and the futures market based on the same underlying asset (equities). Those who use futures for this purpose are referred to as 'arbitrageurs'.

Users of futures

Those who use futures for the purposes included in the previous section include:

- financial institutions – including domestic, international and investment banks;
- insurance companies;
- manufacturers;
- airline companies;
- farmers;
- pension funds;
- hedge funds;
- trusts;
- local authorities;
- venture capital trusts; and
- **HNWI (high net worth individuals)** and UHNWI (ultra high net worth individuals) who are able to demonstrate an understanding of the product (futures) and are able to meet the initial margin and any subsequent margin requirements in relation to open positions.

high net worth individual (HNWI)
A classification used by the financial services industry to denote an individual or a family with high net worth. The figure associated with high net worth of liquid financial assets (after property assets) is $1 million.

2.5 Risks and rewards associated with futures

Those who buy futures (opening a long futures position) are expecting a price rise in an underlying asset and hope either to profit (speculation) from rising markets or to lock in a price for an asset (hedging) to be acquired in the future. Those who sell futures (open a short futures position) hope to profit from falling markets or are trying to lock in a price for an asset they are planning to sell in the future. It is often the case that matters do not go as these users anticipate, and huge sums of money are lost. However, considerable profits can also be made because of the leverage that futures afford. This also depends on whether the intended purpose of futures is hedging or speculation. Hedgers may also incur considerable losses in the event that they have a short futures position and are unable to provide the underlying asset on the final delivery date.

2.6 The futures process

Institutions and experienced individual futures traders who have signed a disclaimer either open long or short futures positions buying or selling one or more futures through a recognised futures broker.

The price of a future is derived/determined from a number of factors including the price of an underlying asset, the price volatility of that underlying asset, market volatility and also the demand for the future itself.

An initial margin will be set by the futures exchange (which has created the future and in which it trades). This is taken from both the buyer and seller.

The initial margin is taken from the buyer as a commitment to pay the agreed price on the final settlement date. It is taken from the seller as a commitment to deliver the underlying asset on the final settlement date.

The price of a future is determined by the exchange – for instance, a trader who wants to buy ('go long') a single futures contract based on HSBC ordinary shares might agree to pay £6.75 for each HSBC share on the final settlement date. The price in the equities spot market for an HSBC share may be £6.50 per share today; however, this particular trader may believe that the price of the HSBC shares will rise to £7.50 within a three-month period.

It should be noted that buying a single future (it is not possible to trade a fraction of a future) is buying exposure to a minimum of 100 HSBC shares. If two futures were being bought, there would be exposure to 200 shares, and so on. Having bought one or more futures, the trader is then obliged to take some form of action, as there are contractual obligations. In buying a single future, a commitment to buy 100 shares on the expiry date has been made. Additionally, the trader must pay the initial margin immediately to the broker, and meet any and subsequent margin calls – for instance, if the margin went below the maintenance margin.

If this same trader decides that he or she wants to gain exposure to 20,000 HSBC ordinary shares for delivery in three months' time, 200 futures must be purchased. In doing so, the trader has agreed today to pay £6.75 per share in three months' time. Thus the trader has agreed today to pay a total of £135,000 in three months' time to acquire 20,000 shares also in three months' time. This trader will not pay the full amount immediately and will not receive any shares today.

However, there is a cost to acquire this contractual right to buy (the futures contract itself). This cost is set by the futures exchange and is usually in the region of 10% of the agreed contract price (but can vary considerably). This is referred to as the initial margin, which in this case would be in the region of £13,500. This will be paid by the trader, via a futures broker, to the relevant exchange and will be retained by the exchange until final delivery date or alternatively the contract is closed out early by taking a contra position. The initial margin is not a down payment, as it may be returned to the trader depending on how prices move. Instead, it is a commitment to fulfil the contractual obligations.

From the point that the future is purchased (a long futures position is opened), the clock is ticking. The purchaser has agreed absolutely to pay £135,000 in three months' time to acquire the HSBC shares. This is not optional; some form of action must take place (contrast with options contracts, discussed later in this chapter). Either acceptance of the shares must take place on the delivery date, or the position must be closed out prior to the final delivery date by taking an opposite position by selling futures for the same delivery date.

This illustration demonstrates that futures are not appropriate for savers or investors with limited funds. Nor are they suitable for investors who are risk-averse, as in this example this investor would have to pay out £13,500 immediately. This money could be lost if prices do not move as anticipated by the final settlement date, and many more margin calls may be made. Consideration should be given to the fact that there is a possibility the entire margin could be lost.

Consequently, the trader's obligation does not cease after their original margin call, but can continue right up to the final settlement date.

It is necessary for traders to monitor their position daily and it may also be a requirement to top up a margin account if the price moves adversely. Sufficient funds must always be maintained in a margin account in order to prevent an account being closed out by the broker/futures exchange clearing house.

Most contracts are cash-settled rather than resulting in actual physical delivery. However, some contracts will result in ultimate physical delivery.

There is no acquisition of any rights whatsoever in relation to underlying assets such as attending AGMs, receipt of dividends, etc. These would only be acquired should delivery of the assets actually be taken.

Note also that if the same investor had actually bought the ordinary shares outright today in the spot market, he or she would have had to pay out today £135,000, and would not only actually own the shares but would also acquire the inherent risks and rewards. There would be no additional margin calls; this is not the case with futures and the maximum outlay would be limited to £135,000 plus commission and stamp duty in the spot market.

We have already referred to how futures may be used for hedging, speculation and arbitrage. Each of these will now be discussed in detail.

2.7 Hedging

Hedging is a strategy used as protection against potential financial loss. It is an insurance against price volatility.

Hedgers cannot prevent price rises or falls of an underlying asset. They want to use futures to offset the impact of any price volatility that may adversely affect them. However, in all cases, hedgers are protecting themselves against a potential negative price movement or financial loss related to an underlying asset.

Some want to hedge against a price rise while others want to protect against a price fall. Unlike speculators, hedgers are not profit-focused, but they want to achieve protection against unexpected developments such as sudden fall in the prices of crops, commodities or currencies. They use futures to manage, reduce or eliminate the risk of a price movement that would affect them negatively whether in the form of price falls or rises.

Hedgers will generally open a position that is 'opposite' to what they currently have. Thus if they are planning to buy an asset, they will buy futures – a long hedge. Conversely, if they have an asset to sell in the future or will have an asset in the future which they are planning to sell, they will sell futures.

There are two ways in which futures can be used to hedge against negative price movements:

1. **a long hedge –** the buying of futures (going long on futures); and
2. **a short hedge –** the selling of futures (going short on futures).

A long hedge is the buying of futures in order to protect the purchase price of an asset that the hedger is planning to buy in the future but does not have now but will require in perhaps three months' time. The hedger is anticipating a price rise in the underlying asset and thus tries to offset this risk by buying futures. Long hedges would typically be used by manufacturers perhaps planning to buy a raw material in the near future – say three months' time. This strategy is generally used when a hedger is trying to protect the price of an underlying asset he or she is planning to buy and thus offset the effects of any price rise in the spot market. This strategy would be used by those who need raw materials to produce their own final products. They are anticipating a price rise and want to hedge (insure) against this.

Examples include:

- industrial consumers – particularly those who require fuel in their own business, perhaps airline companies, – who have to protect themselves against oil price rises, so they will buy oil futures;
- chocolate manufactures, who need cocoa for chocolate production, so buy cocoa futures, whereas the cocoa producer would sell cocoa futures; and
- ice cream manufacturers concerned about price rises in vanilla, who would buy vanilla futures. In 2018, the price of vanilla rose to over $600 per kilogram, outstripping the price of silver.

A short hedge is the selling of futures contracts in order to protect the value of an underlying asset which the hedger already holds, or will acquire in the near future and then wishes to then sell. They are anticipating or concerned about a price fall in the value of an underlying asset. In this instance, the hedger will sell futures ('go short the future'). If the price of the assets they have falls, then so will the price of the future. This will enable the hedger to close out (cancel) their 'short' exposure in the futures market by buying a matching contract (the same size and specific settlement as the original futures sold), but at the cheaper price. The loss on the value of the asset will be offset by the profit on the futures contract. Thus the position is hedged, selling futures in order to protect against a price fall. The gain on the short futures position will offset any loss as a result of the falling price of an underlying asset.

To summarise, a short hedge would be used by a supplier or manufacturer concerned about falling prices in the stock they were planning to sell. Conversely, if the price of the underlying asset rose rather than fell, then extra profit that could have been made in the spot market will be cancelled by having to close out their futures' position at a higher price.

For example, imagine a cocoa producer who did not currently have a cocoa harvest but would have in three months' time, which would then be sold. The cocoa producer wishes to lock in a price today, thus crystallising now the amount to be received in the future. They are concerned that the price of cocoa in the spot market will fall between today and the delivery date, and that they would therefore only receive the market price on the delivery date, which may be far from what they wanted. However, if a short futures position is opened (short hedge), then the futures price movement will track that of the underlying asset. Consequently, if the price of cocoa does indeed fall, this loss of expected income will be offset by gains on the short futures position, because the futures can be sold at the price agreed today, yet be purchased at the much lower price, thus reducing the risk of loss.

If the producer has sold futures, any reduction in the amount they would receive in the spot market will be offset by the amount provided in the margin account by the buyer of the corresponding futures. However, the producer must be able to deliver the underlying asset. If the producer cannot deliver in harmony with the contractual obligations, they have to go into the spot market and buy to sell, therefore losing the difference between the agreed selling price and spot price. Alternatively they could close out and the buyer would take the amount in the margin account so the buyer's position is crystallised, as the buyer would have to pay more in the spot market. The amount in the margin account would mean it would be only the agreed price that was paid, not the current spot price. Hedgers can still lose money if they are unable to deliver the underlying asset.

2.8 Speculation

Speculators will buy futures ('go long the future') or sell futures ('go short the future') entirely for speculative purposes. They do not have any interest in owning an underlying asset or physical commodity whatsoever, and are not concerned about the responsibilities of ownership. They are entirely profit-focused and hope to gain from price movements in the underlying assets, whether up or down, and hence in the price of futures. They are attracted particularly by the high degree of leverage (gearing) that futures provide. As a result of this leverage the price movement will be far greater in percentage terms than buying the underlying asset directly and there is also the benefit of deferred payment. Speculators can have a long position in one market and short positions in other markets. Mindful of this, they will open a position based on how they believe the price of an underlying asset will move.

If speculators buy futures, they are anticipating a price rise in an underlying asset and they want to profit from this. Consequently they hope to profit from their exposure to the underlying asset. Some authorities say that the profit is infinite, but it is perhaps more accurately stated as potentially very considerable though unquantifiable, as the price can neither move up nor down after the future's expiry date. Thus maximum profit must therefore be restricted by the expiry date. If the price of the underlying asset and also the future falls rather than rises (as the speculator had anticipated), losses can be enormous yet quantifiable, as the price of the future can only fall to zero. Thus the maximum loss is the difference between the price agreed for the underlying asset less any margin payments and zero, multiplied of course by the number of open contracts. There may be a point when a speculator decides that his or her position is no longer tenable and will close out the position.

Alternatively, if speculators sell futures they are anticipating a price fall in an underlying asset, thus they will profit from price falls in relation to their exposure to the underlying asset. Speculators' maximum profit is known and can be huge but it is limited as the price of the future can only fall to zero. The maximum profit is the difference between the price agreed for the future and zero, multiplied of course by the number of open contracts. The maximum loss occurs if the price of the underlying asset/future rises rather than falls (as the speculator had anticipated); losses can be enormous as the price of the future can rise considerably.

2.9 Arbitrage

Futures may also be used for the purpose of arbitrage. This essentially involves locking in riskless profits by simultaneously entering into transactions in two or more different markets relating to the same underlying asset. This may happen if the price of a futures contact deviates considerably from that in the spot market. They are essentially looking at discrepancies in prices for the same asset in different markets. There is also the possibility that assets are mispriced in one market. Exchange rates may also impact on arbitrage opportunities, and it is likely that such opportunities will disappear as more traders become aware of them.

2.10 Summary of futures positions and potential losses or gains

When using futures, it is vital to understand the following key points.

Futures are used for three purposes:

1. hedging (by hedgers);
2. speculation (by speculators); and
3. arbitrage (by arbitrageurs).

Each of these users can use futures to achieve their own various aims and objectives; however, they only have two choices in how they use them:

1. buy futures (go long on futures/ open a long futures position/go long the future); or
2. sell futures (go short on futures/open a short futures position/go short the future).

Whether futures are being used for hedging or speculation, if futures are bought there is an expectation of a price rise in an underlying asset. If futures are sold, there is an anticipation of a price fall in an underlying asset.

Having bought or sold futures, these users then have two choices:

1. Wait until final settlement date and either make final payment in the case of a long position and take delivery (in the case of physically delivered futures). In the case of a short position, they will receive final payment and make delivery (in the case of physically delivered futures).
2. Close-out a futures position before final settlement date by taking an opposite position to that already held. Notably, if you had bought futures you would then sell futures for the same delivery date and if you had sold futures you would then have to buy futures for the same delivery date.

Losses and gains

If a speculator buys futures, the maximum profit is unquantifiable (yet finite) at the point of opening the long position, but potentially huge if the price rises as anticipated. However, the maximum profit is limited by the number of contracts and is restricted by the final settlement date after which the future will have expired. Some authorities suggest that profit is infinite but this is impossible and a speculator will decide when sufficient profit has been made and will close-out the position.

The maximum loss can be huge but known at the point of opening a long position – the difference between the agreed price of the underlying asset and zero – less any margin payments already made multiplied by the number of contracts.

Profits will start to be made as soon as the price of the underlying asset rises above the agreed price.

If a speculator sells futures, then assuming that the price of the underlying asset and hence that of the future falls as expected, the maximum profit is potentially huge but known at the point of opening a short position – the difference between the agreed price of the underlying asset and zero – less any margin payments already made multiplied by the number of contracts.

Assuming that the price of the underlying asset and hence that of the future rises contrary to expectations, the maximum loss is unquantifiable (yet finite) at the point of opening the short position, but potentially huge. However, the maximum profit is limited by the number of contracts and is restricted by the final settlement date after which the future will have expired. Some authorities suggest that profit is infinite but this is impossible and a speculator will decide when sufficient profit has been made and will close-out the position.

2.11 Futures margins

Margins are not down-payments on underlying assets (speculators do not want to own an underlying asset). It is possible that those trading futures could receive all of the initial margin back, depending on which way the price of underlying asset moves and hence the price of the future itself.

Initial margins are paid by both buyers and sellers. If a seller and buyer were trading with each other, both would make the same initial margin payment to the futures broker.

The initial margin

This will set by the relevant futures exchange and depends upon a number of factors including the underlying asset itself, the price volatility of the underlying asset, market volatility and a range of other relevant factors. The futures clearing house can raise or lower margins as required. The amount of the initial margin is usually 5–20% of the price that has been agreed to be paid on the agreed future date (final settlement date). This amount will be placed in both of the trader's margin accounts with the future's broker. The amount in the margin account is allowed to fall by 10–20% of the initial margin without there being any additional margin calls. This initial margin affords the traders the opportunity to keep open futures positions past a trading session's close, whether long or short.

Some key points are as follows:

- Traders should be mindful of margin requirements for the underlying asset to which they wish to gain exposure.
- Although margins are taken, futures are not traded on those margins.
- A small movement in the futures price can equate to a disproportionate move in the margin account.
- Margins are posted on the relevant futures exchanges websites.
- Derivatives including futures are a component of management strategies in relation to collective investment schemes including hedge funds where they are often used speculatively.

The maintenance margin

In the first instance, the trader must meet the initial margin requirement in full, which may subsequently be reduced to the maintenance margin. It must then be kept at least at the maintenance margin until the position is closed. However, the position cannot fall below this maintenance margin.

This is the absolute minimum amount that must be maintained in the futures broker's account. It is effectively the initial margin adjusted to take into account the maximum permitted fall in relation to the initial margin, so it could fall to 80% of the initial margin. If the amount falls below this maintenance margin, the margin account will have to be topped up to the amount of the initial margin. (Note that this is topped up to the original initial margin level rather than the maintenance margin.) This is done by a margin call.

The margin is a kind of performance bond. Every business day at settlement time the trader would have a number of choices if a margin call were made:

- To provide funds to meet margin requirements whether initial or maintenance.
- Close the position in full.
- Close the position partially – closing some futures positions while keeping others open.

Worked example 6.2

- The price of a single December gold future is $1,350 dollars per troy ounce.
- The future contract size is 100 troy ounces, therefore 1 gold future =100 troy ounces.
- If an investor wished to buy one December gold future, this would give exposure to 100 troy ounces of gold value of $135,000.
- In order to gain this exposure, the investor would have to pay an initial margin of 5% to the futures broker $6,750 per contract. This is only a fraction of buying this gold outright in the spot market. Note the seller also has to provide the same margin.
- Traders can of course put more than the initial margin into this account; however, the initial margin is allowed to fall to 80–90% of the initial margin. This is referred to the maintenance margin. In the event that the amount in the margin account falls below the maintenance margin, the trader will have to top up to the original margin not the maintenance margin. The trader will receive a margin call from a broker.
- Any amounts in excess of the initial margin can be withdrawn by the investor.
- If the price moves against you, margin calls may be made.
- Futures are marked to market and will be adjusted accordingly at the end of each trading day. Accounts adjusted on a daily basis and margin calls made.
- Margins may be returned – they are therefore not a down payment.

The two main uses of futures are hedging and speculation.

Both hedgers and speculators tend to be institutional rather than individual traders. However, HNWIs and UHNWIs may use futures if they can demonstrate that they have sufficient funding and an understanding of the product, and can service both the initial and maintenance margins as required by the futures clearing house.

2.12 Clearing house functions

Futures clearing houses are comprised of various members who will have placed money with the futures exchange. The members may be recognised futures brokers or not any broker that is not a member must deal through a recognised broker.

Each exchange will have its own affiliated clearing House and their functions will include:

- acting as counterparties to all futures transactions – effectively buyers to every seller and the sellers to every buyer;
- the elimination of counterparty risk;
- acting as guarantors to the fulfilment all contracts, ensuring that the number of contracts bought and sold are in equilibrium;
- recording and monitoring every transaction – notably acting as registrar;
- closing out contracts without the agreement of buyers or sellers in the event that a counterparty is unable to fulfil its obligations whether at final delivery or in relation to margin calls;
- setting a price barrier on maximum daily price movement;
- providing a settlement mechanism;
- calculating the net position of each of its members;
- maintaining margins of member brokers;
- facilitating and regulating the delivery of goods in the case of contracts that will ultimately result in physical delivery;
- ensuring that all parties meet their obligations under the futures contract – 'novaton';
- ensuring that traders meet margin requirements, notably the initial margin and potentially top-up calls.

Test yourself 6.1

a) **What are underlying assets?**

b) **Why are futures legally binding?**

3. Options

Options, like futures contracts, are leveraged derivative instruments, as their own prices are once again derived from (based on) the prices of various underlying assets including gilts, corporate bonds and even indices such as Standard & Poor's 500 and even crypto-currencies. Options are so-called because the holders have options as to what can and cannot be done. It must be emphasised that options contracts, like futures, tend to be for the more sophisticated investor and it may be very difficult to trade OTC options. Indeed in order to be able to trade OTC options it will usually be necessary to engage the services of specialist options brokers, which are few and far between.

There are two categories of option:

1. Traditional options are over-the-counter (OTC) bespoke financial products without exchanges, with their individual terms and conditions such as their strike price and expiry date being negotiated by the **writer** and the holder.
2. Exchange-traded options are traded on exchanges such as Euronext.liffe.

writer
The original seller of an options contract providing the purchaser with a right without any obligation to buy or sell an underlying asset.

Options are derivative contracts that are purchased by a party referred to as the 'holder' from another party referred to as the 'writer'. They give a holder the right (without any obligation) either to buy or to sell standard quantities of an underlying asset on or before a specified fixed future date (expiry date).

The price at which the underlying asset may be bought or sold is known as the strike price and will be agreed when an option is purchased. It is important to be mindful that an option holder is not under any obligation to exercise an option that would give the right to buy or sell. These are options and thus exercise is optional. If a holder cannot make a profit, exercise will not take place and the option will be abandoned. The amount that a holder will pay to either a writer or a broker for an option is referred to as the 'option premium'. This option premium will never be returned to the holder, and unlike futures contracts there are no additional margin calls.

There are two types of option:

1. **Call options** give the holder the right (without obligation) to buy an underlying asset.
2. **Put options** give the holder the right (without obligation) to sell an underlying asset.

call options
Provide the holder with the right (without obligation) to buy an underlying asset.

put options
Provide the holder with the right (without obligation) to sell an underlying asset.

At the point where the holder pays the option premium to the writer (or a broker in the secondary market), there is possession of an option without any obligation. However, a contractual obligation is created whereby in the event of exercise of the option by the holder, the writer *must* deliver in the case of call options and *must* buy in the case of put options. There are also obligations placed on the holder, including to pay the option premium as agreed and to pay the strike price if the option is exercised, or provide the underlying asset if a put option is exercised. When the option premium is purchased, no rights in relation to any underlying assets are acquired unless the option is actually exercised. The option aspect refers to the option to exercise.

3.1 Options terminology

Options writer
The writer is not only the creator of the option but also the first seller. When the option has been created and is in the possession of a holder it may be traded, usually through a broker, just like equities. A purchaser may buy or sell either call or put options in the secondary market without having to deal with the original writer. In addition, the writer must either provide the underlying asset to the current holder (call option) or buy it from the holder (put option) in the event of exercise. In practice, options are usually cash-settled.

Holder
The holder is the party in current possession of the option bought either from the option writer or through a broker.

Standard quantity
Options are traded only in whole numbers (as is the case with futures). For example, it is not possible to buy 1.25 options. For ordinary shares, the standard quantity is equal to 1,000 shares. Thus, two options represent 2,000 ordinary shares.

Underlying
'Underlying' is the asset upon which the option is based – for example, Barclays Bank plc ordinary shares.

Expiry date
The expiry date is the last day on which an option may be exercised. There are two main styles of exercise: American style and European style. American style may be exercised at any time up to and including the expiry date, whereas European style may be exercised *only* on the expiry date. Despite their names, European and American style options are available throughout international markets. In addition, there are Bermudan style options, which can be exercised at a number of pre-specified times before expiry. Bermudan options are thus a hybrid between American and European styles.

Strike price (also known as exercise price)
The strike price is the price at which the option holder may purchase from or sell to the underlying asset from/to the writer, should the holder decide to exercise the option. Conversely, this is the price at which the writer must provide the asset to (or buy it from) the holder.

The option premium
The option premium is the price that the holder must pay to the writer or broker for the option that is for the right to buy (or sell) an underlying asset. This premium is made up of two elements: **intrinsic value** and **time value** (referred to in section 3.6). Option premiums are upfront payments paid to the writers or brokers that will never be returned to the holder, and the holder must still pay the strike price in full.

intrinsic value
An inner value, a value contained within.

time value
The option premium price less intrinsic value

There are four options positions:

- a long position in a call option – the purchaser of a call option acquiring the option to buy an underlying asset;
- a long position in a put option – the purchaser of a put option acquiring the option to sell an underlying asset;
- a short position in a call option – the seller of a call option selling the right to buy an underlying asset; and
- a short position in a put option – the seller of a put option selling the right to sell an underlying asset.

3.2 Call options

Call options give holders the right (without obligation) to buy a standardised quantity of an underlying asset at the strike price. This means that the writer has a contractual obligation to sell the underlying asset to the holder in the event that the option is exercised by the holder.

Using ordinary shares as an example of underlying assets, it means that a purchaser of a call option believes that a particular share price will rise. We need to look at the situation as it is 'today' (at the point that the option premium is purchased).

Worked example 6.3

Call options

If today, Barclays Bank plc ordinary shares can be purchased for £2.79 in the equities market and the investor believes that the share price will rise to £4 before the expiry date of the option, they could purchase a call option at an option premium price of perhaps 42p. This would give them the right to buy the ordinary share at £3.

This means that the option writer now has a contractual obligation to sell a standardised quantity of shares to the holder, should the holder decide to exercise the call option. If the price were indeed to rise to £4, the writer would still be obliged to sell the shares to the holder at £3, which the holder could subsequently resell in the equities market for £4.

The profit for the option holder would be as follows.

Future market price of share	£4.00
Less strike price	–£3.00
Less option premium price	–£0.42
Profit per share	= £0.58

Therefore, the option holder has made a profit of 58p per share for an outlay of only 42p per share, which represents a 138% return. This can be contrasted with buying the ordinary shares directly in the equities market at £2.79 today and selling at £4, which would represent a 43% return. The exact profit will decide when a holder exercises, as it is not required to wait until the market price reaches £4.

There are a number of considerations in this example:

- The writer and holder will be viewing the situation from differing perspectives. The holder believes that the price of the underlying asset will rise sufficiently in the market so that they are able to exercise the option profitably. While the writer believes that the holder will not be able to exercise the option profitably (perhaps the share price would fall), this would mean that the option premium can be kept as profit by the writer.
- There are no further margin calls with options as is the case with futures; consequently the maximum loss to the holder is the option premium. This is also equal to the writer's maximum profit.
- These amounts may be colossal, depending on the number of contracts bought.
- Option holders will only exercise an option if it is profitable to do so, and they must take into account not only the strike price and option premiums, but also commissions when calculating any net profit.

3.3 Put options

Put options give the holder the right without obligation to sell a standardised quantity of an underlying asset to the writer at the strike price. This means that the writer has a contractual obligation to buy the underlying asset from the holder if the holder exercises the option.

If we again use ordinary shares as an example of underlying assets, it means that such a holder believes that the price of a particular share will fall. Again, we need to look at the situation as it is 'today'.

Worked example 6.4

Put options

If today, Barclays Bank plc ordinary shares could be sold for £2.79 in the spot market and an investor believes that the share price will fall to £1.50 before the expiry date of the option, they could purchase a put option at a premium price of perhaps 33p to sell the share at £2.40 to the options writer.

The options writer then has a contractual obligation to purchase a quantity of shares from the holder of the put option in the event of exercise. If the price does fall to as little as £1.50, as the put option holder anticipates, the writer still has to pay the holder £2.40 per share to the holder.

The put option holder can thus buy the underlying shares in the market at £1.50, knowing they can resell them to the writer at the strike price of £2.40.

The profit for the holder would be as follows.

Strike price	£2.40
Less market price of share	–£1.50
Less premium	–£0.33
Profit per share	= £0.57

Therefore, the holder has made a profit of 57p per share for an outlay of only 33p per share, which equates to 172% return. This can be contrasted with selling the shares directly in the equities market at £2.79.

3.4 Users and uses of options

Users tend to be institutional rather than individual investors, but there are individual options traders and writers. For individual investors, it might prove rather difficult if wanting to trade OTC options, but there are brokers to help with this. However, such brokers will probably require a minimum opening balance of £10,000.

One of the main advantages of options is the high degree of leverage ('gearing') they give. This degree of leverage affords investors the potential to make larger returns from a smaller initial outlay, which will be only a fraction of the amount required to gain the same degree of exposure as investing directly would require. There is still the possibility of losing the entire option premium.

Speculators

The focus for speculators is to increase their exposure to the markets. As such, they are attracted by the huge potential returns associated with options. As with futures, speculators do not actually want to take possession of the underlying asset.

In practice, the speculator will sell their put options through a broker and these will be cash-settled.

Hedgers

Hedgers, unlike speculators, attempt to reduce their exposure by covering existing positions, rather like taking out an insurance policy. They do not have to sell their currently held shares but can instead buy put options. Some or all of the losses of the underlying shares can be offset by an increase in value of the put options. Unlike futures, there are no additional margin calls.

3.5 The risks and rewards of options

Risks

Purchasers of either call or put options will always know their maximum potential downside. This risk is limited to the price paid for the option premium plus any transaction costs incurred. However, depending on the amount of options purchased, considerable losses can be incurred.

If the market does not move as anticipated, option holders may decide to abandon their options and thus lose their premiums.

Worked example 6.5

Abandoning an option

Let us suppose an investor (holder) purchased 100 call options equivalent to 100,000 ordinary shares, with the option premium price being 25p per share. If events did not move in line with an investor's expectations and the option were abandoned, the investor would lose 100% of this investment (that is, the premium paid, plus any applicable commissions).

The loss would be 100,000 × £0.25 = £25,000.00 plus any commission charges. This is a known downside, however it can still be very significant.

Matters could be worse. If, rather than buying the call options, the investor bought the 100,000 shares directly in the market at a cost of £3 per share (total cost £300,000) and the company went into liquidation, the loss would be greater by £275,000.

An option holder will not exercise a call option if the strike price is higher than the spot price. The market price must be higher in order for the holder to make a profit. If this were not the case, they could buy the underlying asset cheaper in the market. They will not exercise a put option if the strike price is lower than the market price, because again they can obtain a better price in the market.

For option writers, the risks vary depending on whether the writers create **covered options** or **naked options**. If the writers have covered themselves by perhaps already holding the security, then matters may not be so bad, and at least they still receive the option premium to offset any loss.

However, if writing naked options, the risks can be quite considerable. For call options, writers will have to go into the equities market to buy shares to sell to the holder (or, if cash-settled, pay the cash difference). With put options, writers will be committed to buying the underlying security and then can either sell at a loss in the market or hold and hope that the price will recover.

covered option
An option is written by a writer who already owns the underlying asset on which the option is based. Thus, the writer protects himself from adverse price movements.

naked (uncovered) option
Where a call option is written without the writer actually owning the underlying assets upon which the option is derived.

Rewards

Writers of call or put options will be hoping that matters will not go as the holders have anticipated, in which case they will keep the option premium as their profit. The option premium is the writer's reward. Losses can be enormous.

It is often stated that the rewards for call option holders are unlimited, but it is probably better to say 'considerable', because it is very unlikely that a share will change from £1 to £1,000 prior to the expiry date of the options.

3.6 The pricing of option premiums

Live prices for both call options and put options are available on www.euronext.com and also many specialised broker websites. There will be a range of prices for both call and put option premiums, and a range of exercise dates. Each premium will have both bid and offer prices, and there will be considerable **spreads** between them. Different brokers may offer varying prices for the same option.

spread
A range of selling and buying prices. The selling price will be shown on the left-hand side of the range and the buying price on the right-hand side.

The calculation of option premiums is based on two factors:

1. the price of the underlying asset; and
2. the period of time to expiry of the option.

The fine-tuning of premiums is calculated using relatively complicated formulae, which are outside the scope of the Investment syllabus. Options premiums cannot have negative values.

The premium price has two components: intrinsic value and time value. Intrinsic value is simply the profit that an option would realise if it were exercised immediately. Time value is equal to the option premium price minus intrinsic value, as outlined in Worked example 6.6.

It should be noted that option premiums will be more expensive the further away the expiry date is, as the option writer is exposed to risk for a longer period of time. In addition, the greater the amount the strike price is below the market price in the case of call options, the more expensive the premium will be.

Worked example 6.6

Intrinsic and time value

Rather than purchasing Barclays Bank plc ordinary shares directly in the equities market at £3 per share, an investor decides to purchase a call option for 77p, giving the right to buy shares at an exercise price of £2.50. The difference between £3 and the exercise price of £2.50 is 50p, meaning the option has an intrinsic value of 50p. In theory, the holder would be able to buy the shares for £2.50 and then sell for £3 in the market.

Intrinsic value therefore = current market price of the share minus exercise price £3.00 – £2.50 = 50p.

The option premium is 77p, and we know that this is made up of time value and intrinsic value.

Therefore, time value is equal to the option premium less intrinsic value 77p – 50p – that is, a time value of 27p.

However, if the exercise price is greater than the market price, there will be no intrinsic value. Consequently, the option premium will be made up of time value alone.

It is also necessary to be aware of the following terminology.

- In-the-money options: where an option has intrinsic value. The price of the underlying asset is higher than the strike price in the case of a call option and lower than the strike price in the case of a put option. Thus the option contract may be exercised profitably.
- At-the-money options: where the market price of an underlying asset equals the strike price of an options contract.
- Out-of-the-money options: where an option has no intrinsic value. Thus the price of the underlying asset is lower than the strike price in the case of a call option and higher than the strike price in the case of a put option. Thus the option contract cannot be profitably.

Test yourself 6.2

a) **Name the two types of options.**

b) **In an option premium price, how is time value calculated?**

4. Company warrants

Company **warrants** (also referred to as equity warrants or warrants) which are issued by companies and investment trusts are often compared to call options and although there are some similarities, they are stand-alone leveraged securities with both buying and selling prices being made available from brokers and stock exchanges. Company warrants should not be confused with **covered warrants;** these are discussed in section 5 of this chapter.

warrant
A security that entitles the holder to buy shares in the issuing company on a specific date or within a specific period and price.

covered warrants
Similar derivative instruments to 'ordinary' warrants. However, they differ in that they are issued by third parties rather than the original share-issuing company. There is now a 'put' version – that is, giving the right to sell the company's shares.

Covered warrants are fully negotiable (can be both bought and sold) securities issued by a company over its own shares to its existing shareholders. They are not shares in themselves but they give the holder the right, without obligation (as is also the case with call options), to buy new ordinary shares in the issuing company, which will be created by the company at some point in the future. Although a comparison to call options has been made, there are a number of significant differences – notably options are issued by third-party writers rather than the company itself. Additionally, warrants tend to be longer term (perhaps 5–10 years), whereas options generally have life-spans measured in terms of months.

Company warrants allow holders to purchase ordinary shares on or before a fixed date (expiry date) and at a fixed price (also referred to as the subscription price or exercise price).

Company warrants, when exercised, raise additional capital for the issuing company and result in new shares being created at a specified time in the future. The exercise of warrants is a form of share dilution as there will be more shares created. If an existing shareholder wishes to maintain an existing percentage stake-holding in the company, then additional capital must be provided by subscribing for the new shares in line with the terms and conditions of the warrants. The expiry date stated on the warrant is the last date on which it may be converted into new ordinary shares.

It must also be borne in mind that there would be two separate income streams for the issuing company:

- payment for the warrants (where they have not been issued free) from the existing shareholders; and
- payment for the new shares at the exercise price should the warrant holders decide to exercise the warrants which they will only do if it is profitable to do so.

The warrants are traded on recognised stock exchanges (the LSE, in the case of the UK). The issuing company sets the warrant price, which is derived from that of the company's own underlying share price. Warrants are deemed to be derivative instruments because their own price is derived from that of the underlying share price, although the fine-tuning of the price is actually calculated by the issuing company and its advisers. Once traded on the secondary market, the forces of supply and demand will determine the warrant price.

4.1 Warrant terminology

Warrant price

The warrant price is the price set by the issuing company and must be paid by an existing shareholder to that issuing company for a warrant that gives the right to buy new shares at the stated exercise price at some time in the future. Warrants may, however, be issued free as so-called 'sweeteners'. For example, warrants may be attached to a bond issued by a company to make the issue more attractive to potential investors. In addition to the bond, investors would also obtain the warrants free of charge (although they will have to pay the exercise price, detailed next, to the company if they wish to subscribe for the underlying shares).

Exercise price /strike price/subscription price

The exercise price is that price at which a warrant holder may purchase the new ordinary shares from the company by exercising the warrants.

Exercise date

The fixed date or specific period within which a shareholder must exercise a warrant to buy the new shares.

Underlying share price

The underlying share price is that for which the ordinary shares may be traded in the equities market by any investor.

Intrinsic value

The intrinsic value of a warrant is the difference between the current market price of the underlying share and the future exercise price of that same share. Investors will want the market price of the relevant equities to be higher than the stated exercise price at the time of exercise in order to make a profit.

Time value

Time value is equal to the warrant price minus the intrinsic value of that same warrant. This reflects the amount that investors are willing to pay for possible future share price rises.

Warrant premium

This essentially indicates the cost to the investor of two alternatives: buying a share directly in the equities market or paying for the warrant and subsequently exercising the warrant at the exercise price. The warrant premium is equal to the warrant price plus exercise price minus the current market price of the share. This is then exercised as a percentage of the current market price.

Worked example 6.7

Warrant pricing

We assume that the warrant basis is one new share for every existing share (one for one).

The price of the warrant is 40 pence.

The current market price of one ordinary share of XYZ LTD is £2.40.

The warrants carry the right to subscribe for new shares at £2.60.

At this point the warrant has no intrinsic value: The warrant holder would not exercise if the price is market price cheaper than strike price.

The warrant premium: £2.40 + 40p -£2.60 =20p = 20/2.40= 8.33%

If the market price of the share rises to £3.60 the warrant holder would be able to exercise profitably and the warrant would have an intrinsic value.

Intrinsic value = £3.60 (market price) -£2.60 (subscription price) = £1

It is important not to confuse intrinsic value with profit, and it is necessary to calculate the original cost of the warrant.

Warrant holders are not obliged to exercise their warrants: this is an option. Instead, they can, if they wish, sell their warrants on the secondary market or even allow them to expire.

Gearing

Gearing (also known as leverage) is where the performance of the warrant is magnified by that of the underlying share. The warrant price tracks that of the underlying share, but the price movement of the warrant in percentage terms can greatly exceed that of the underlying share.

4.2 Characteristics of warrants

Warrants tend to be instruments of bull markets (where investors believe the price of the underlying share will rise and will buy in the hope of being able to sell at a higher price). Warrants are considered to be high-risk investments; although there is potential for considerable gain, there is also the possibility of total loss if they are not exercised. The loss, however, is limited to the cost of the warrant itself.

Warrants have no income tax implications, as they produce no income, and so are suitable for higher-rate taxpayers.

There are considerable prospects of capital gains (and potential capital gains tax (CGT) liability). Warrant holders can sell in the secondary market or exercise warrants, or allow them to expire if there is no intrinsic value.

Stamp duty reserve tax and other commissions would be payable in the event that the warrants are exercised to acquire the shares.

Warrants are long-dated, and carry the right to subscribe for new shares in the company often many years after issue. They also carry much greater risk than ordinary shares as they have an expiry date. However, if they have been issued free by companies as so-called equity sweeteners, there is no risk at all, because no loss would be incurred even if allowed to expire. However, if they were bought in the secondary market, there obviously would be attached risks.

The Financial Conduct Authority (FCA) rules state that investors must sign a warrants' risk notice before trading in warrants, in order to confirm their understanding of the product and the inherent risks. Their potential downside is limited to the cost of the warrant rather than the full cost of purchasing the underlying ordinary shares.

4.3 Pricing and value of warrants

The price of a warrant will never be greater than the price of the underlying equities, because an investor will not pay £1 for the right to buy a share that can be purchased in the equities market at £0.90 any time in the near future. Nonetheless, a warrant can become worthless when it is obvious that there is little likelihood of an appropriate price rise in the underlying share and the exercise price is greater than the market price of the share.

4.4 Advantages and disadvantages of warrants

Advantages to the issuing company

- From the perspective of the issuer, warrants are inexpensive to issue.
- The company is obtaining money from existing shareholders.

- Warrants raise additional capital for the company: money raised from the warrant itself and potentially from the newly created shares, even if shareholders decide not to exercise them.

Advantages for an investor

- Warrants may be traded independently of the underlying shares.
- The initial outlay is only a fraction of the cost of the corresponding ordinary shares.
- They are leveraged investments and allow investors increased exposure to the shares of the company.
- Allocation is proportional to existing shareholding.
- They are suitable for higher-rate taxpayers as there is no income generated from warrants.
- The maximum loss is known – it is the cost of the warrant.

Disadvantages to the issuing company

- Reliance on existing shareholders for funds is necessary.
- The take-up for the warrants or indeed the new shares may be low.

Disadvantages for an investor

- New shares are created – this may result in the dilution of a shareholding in the event a warrant is not exercised.
- Purchasers will not have any voting rights until the warrants are converted into ordinary shares.
- Warrants produce no income and warrant holders are not entitled to dividends associated with the ordinary shares.
- The market tends to be rather illiquid.
- If not exercised prior to the expiry date, the warrants will expire worthless. This may result in a significant loss.
- There is a need to monitor warrants to ensure that they do not expire worthless.
- The price of the warrant in the secondary market is dependent upon investor confidence.

5. Covered warrants

Covered warrants are securitised derivative financial products. They are derivative in the sense that their value is derived from or linked to underlying assets such as equities, indices, commodities or even currencies. Covered warrants are referred to as 'covered' because the issuers or writers protect (or cover) themselves by buying the underlying securities in the market; alternatively issuers may already hold the underlying assets.

Covered warrants provide a holder with the right without obligation either to buy or to sell an underlying asset from or to the issuer, through a broker, at a predetermined price (known as the exercise price or strike price), on or before a certain future date (expiry date).

The price paid for this right is known as the premium, and this is usually a small fraction of the price of the underlying asset. However, there are circumstances when the premium can be close to the price of the market price of the underlying asset.

It is vital to understand the difference between 'ordinary' warrants and covered warrants. For example, Rolls-Royce would issue 'ordinary' warrants relating to its own shares and would subsequently create new shares resulting in a share dilution. Rolls-Royce would also receive the proceeds of these two income streams. Rolls-Royce equity covered warrants would be issued by an investment bank such as Société Générale or Goldman Sachs. There would be no new shares created with no share dilution, and Rolls-Royce would not be involved whatsoever.

Historically, covered warrants were purchased by institutional investors. However, they are also now increasingly being used by individual investors.

5.1 Types of covered warrants

There are two types of covered warrant: call and put.

Call covered warrants

A call covered warrant gives the holder (alternatively referred to as the purchaser or owner) the right – crucially without any obligation – to purchase underlying equities or other underlying assets at a pre-agreed price, referred to as the strike price. The price paid for this right is referred to as the covered warrant premium.

An investor is purchasing the right to buy an underlying asset believing that the price of that underlying security is going to rise. This is indicative of a bull market. This investor would profit from a price increase in the underlying asset.

Put covered warrants

A put covered warrant gives the holder (alternatively referred to as the purchaser or owner) the right – again, crucially without any obligation – to sell underlying equities or other underlying assets at a pre-agreed price which is referred to as the strike price. The price paid for this right is referred to as the premium.

An investor is buying the right to sell an underlying asset believing that the price of that underlying security is going to fall. This is indicative of a bear market, where investors sell the assets hoping to buy them back at a lower price in the future. This investor would profit from a price fall in the underlying asset.

5.2 Exercise styles: American versus European

There are two main exercise styles for covered warrants: American and European. These refer to how the covered warrants will be exercised, and each of these styles can be applicable to both call covered warrants and to put covered warrants.

American-style allows the holder of the covered warrant to exercise it at any time up to and including the expiry date. European-style allows the holder to exercise it only on the expiry date.

Each covered warrant will have a term sheet, which will cover generic information such as the:

- name of the issuer, usually an investment bank;
- details of the underlying security;
- strike price;
- expiry date;
- type, whether call or put; and
- style, whether American or European.

The investor will make a decision to buy either call or put covered warrants, depending on how they believe the market will move. However, the actual purchase of the covered warrant itself would be made through a stockbroker rather than the company on whose share the covered warrant is based. The purchaser would have already established a trading account with their stockbroker and would have indicated their intention to trade in covered warrants.

The investor will have to agree to a disclaimer and must indicate that they understand the product and the inherent risks in a combined risk/suitability questionnaire.

Settlement for the covered warrant is T+3 days and, in the UK, trading is on the LSE through CREST.

After three working days, the cost of the covered warrants will be debited (charged) to the purchaser's trading account, and the purchaser will receive the covered warrant electronically by way of an entry on an account with their stockbroker.

At this point, the holder has the right to buy (call) or sell (put) the underlying security up to the expiry date (in the case of an American-style covered warrant) or on the expiry date (in the case of a European-style covered warrant).

5.3 Choices for covered warrant holders

Holders of covered warrants have a number of choices:

1. They can exercise the covered warrant to buy or sell the underlying security. If this option is taken, then at the point of exercise, there is a legal obligation by the issuer to deliver (for calls) or receive (for puts) that security. If the covered warrant expires and is not exercised, there is no such obligation on the issuer to take any further action.
2. Alternatively, holders may abandon the covered warrant if it is not possible to exercise it profitably on or before the expiry date.
3. It is also possible to trade back – that is, to sell back to the issuer through the stockbroker – as the covered warrants are fully tradable securities. This is the most common option as this is really just buying and selling covered warrants as a product in its own right.

All buying and selling of covered warrants is executed through the investor's trading account maintained with a stockbroker.

The underlying assets are neither bought nor sold. Rather, covered warrants are cash-settled. If the warrant can be exercised profitably, the purchaser will receive cash profit rather than the underlying asset itself. The price of the current warrant moves in the same direction of the underlying asset.

5.4 Additional points relating to covered warrants

- The market in covered warrants is regulated by the FCA.
- There is no stamp duty to pay, but there may be a liability to tax on any capital gains.
- Each covered warrant has an underlying term-sheet.
- Investors need to be aware that there are many different competing covered warrants from different issuers in relation to the same shares or other underlying assets.
- Prices may vary considerably.
- When assessing profits or losses or making decisions to buy or sell, investors must also consider brokers' commissions and transaction charges.
- Their prices can be changed in certain circumstances – for instance, if the original issuer of the underlying assets announces a share split.
- There is a legally binding obligation on the issuer to make or to take delivery of the underlying assets or cash settle if the purchaser decides to exercise the warrant during its life.
- Covered warrants cannot have a negative value.
- There are no margin calls (in contrast with futures).
- There are two distinct income flows: payment for the covered warrant itself, followed by potential cash settlement by issuer.
- Covered warrants are 'wasting assets', as they have no value whatsoever after their expiry date.

5.5 Advantages and disadvantages of covered warrants

Advantages

- The initial outlay is only a fraction of that of the buying or selling underlying assets in the relevant spot market.
- Stamp duty (currently 0.5%) is not applicable, because trades are cash-settled.
- Covered warrants provide holders with the ability to hedge in either rising or falling markets.
- Investors do not need to monitor covered warrants on a daily basis, as exercise is automatic.
- As they are leveraged derivative instruments, they allow investors to obtain greater exposure than through direct investment.

Disadvantages

- They cannot be short sold (particularly important in times of financial crisis).
- After the expiry date has passed, the covered warrant is worthless.
- They cannot be bought or held in an individual savings account (ISA).
- They are considered to be higher-risk investments than others.

Profit/loss scenario

There is potential for considerable gains, given that the product is highly geared and they have a known maximum loss which is limited to the original investment (the premium plus commissions).

5.6 Settlement

In theory, settlement is by the delivery of the actual underlying asset. However, all covered warrants are cash-settled. There is in fact a legal obligation for the issuer of the covered warrant to make or take delivery of the underlying asset during the life of the covered warrant.

If the warrant is exercised, or indeed if it is exercised automatically, the trade usually has to be settled with the market within five working days of the covered warrant expiry. There will then be a further delay after the funds are received by the stockbroker. This will be outlined in their various terms and conditions.

Test yourself 6.3

a) What is intrinsic value in relation to company warrants?

b) Give three characteristics of covered warrants.

c) Give three advantages and three disadvantages of covered warrants.

6. Interest rate swaps

Interest rate swaps are bilateral over-the-counter (OTC) derivative products. There are no exchanges or clearing houses involved and they are the largest component of the international derivatives market.

interest rate swap
A contractual agreement between two counterparties where one agrees to swap with the other a stream of fixed-interest payments (cash flows) in return for a stream of floating-rate interest payments. Both interest streams are based on the same notional (hypothetical) amount over a specific period.

There are three main categories of interest rate swap:

1. fixed rate for floating rate;
2. floating rate for floating rate; and
3. fixed rate for fixed rate.

The most common type of interest rate swaps, and the ones we shall consider in detail, are fixed rate for floating rate, which are often referred to as 'plain vanilla swaps'. One party agrees to swap with a counterparty a fixed rate of interest based on a notional (hypothetical) amount in exchange for a floating rate of interest, based on the same notional amount.

This is why interest rate swaps are classed as derivatives, as their own existence is based on an underlying asset, be this hypothetical. Instead, the interest rates are based on the notional amount.

Exchanges of interest payments take place during an agreed period, perhaps over three years. These interest rates are usually established at the start of the contract period and settled at the end. As there is no exchange of a principal sum, they are also deemed to be off-balance-sheet transactions.

6.1 Fixed for floating (plain vanilla) interest rate swaps

An interest rate swap is a contractual agreement between two counterparties where one party agrees to swap with the other a stream of fixed-interest payments (cash flows) in return for a stream of floating-rate interest payments. Both streams are based on the same notional (hypothetical) amount over a specific period. The floating rate will be based on an index such as LIBOR, whereas the fixed-interest rate may be based on a different index.

This is a simplified explanation of what actually occurs. In practice, the transactions may be far more intricate and, where both parties are non-financial companies, there will also be a financial institution involved which will serve as an intermediary, charging for its services in the process.

The participants involved in an interest rate swap transaction are always referred to from the perspective of the payment of the fixed stream of interest payments.

The counterparty making the fixed interest payments while receiving the floating-rate stream of interest rate payments, after the start of the swap, is referred to as the 'payer', whereas the counterparty receiving the fixed stream of interest payments while making floating interest rate payments, after the inception of the swap, is referred to as the 'receiver'.

Making it work 6.2: Swap rates and coupon swaps

Counterparty A agrees to swap a fixed rate of interest with Counterparty B. (Counterparty A receives a floating-interest rate commitment.) This fixed interest rate payment is referred to as the 'swap rate'.

Counterparty B agrees to swap floating rate of interest with Counterparty A. (Counterparty B receives a fixed interest rate commitment.) The floating interest rate is referred to as the 'coupon swap'.

In relation to swaps, all interest payments are based on a notional amount because there has to be some reference amount (for example, £5 million). Although this is sometimes referred to as the principal amount, it is never exchanged by the counterparties; instead only the difference in interest payments is exchanged.

Making it work 6.3: Floating interest rate obligations and fixed interest rate obligations

Counterparty A (a financial institution) agrees to swap a fixed interest rate, perhaps 5% per annum based on a notional amount of £5m, and Counterparty B would swap a floating rate of interest which is based on an index such as LIBOR, so the interest rate for the floating rate may be 25 basis points above LIBOR. Again this would be based on the notional amount of £5 million.

Counterparty A would have, after the swap, a floating interest rate obligation, and Counterparty B would have a fixed interest rate obligation. In this instance, Counterparty B is the 'payer' while Counterparty is the 'receiver'.

We are assuming a fixed interest rate of 5% and variable interest rate of 5.75% (that is, LIBOR of 5.5% plus 25 basis points).

Mindful of what has been stated already, it is only interest rate differentials that are ever swapped between the parties. However, because of the large sizes of the notional amounts, such interest rate differentials can be quite significant.

Thus, Counterparty A (now in possession of a floating-rate obligation) will pay to Counterparty B:

£5,000,000 × 5.75% per annum = £287,500 per annum or £23,958.33 per month.

Counterparty B will pay to Counterparty A:

£5,000,000 × 5% per annum = £250,000 per annum or £20,833.33 per month.

These amounts would be netted. Thus, in our example, Counterparty A will pay to Counterparty B:

£23,958.33 – £20,833.33 = £3,125.00

In addition to the notional amount, there has to be a reference rate, such as LIBOR, for the floating-rate element. A set of predetermined dates when such payments are to take place must also be agreed between the two counterparties from the outset. It also depends upon which way the floating interest rate moves (up or down) as to which way the cash movement occurs (it could go in either direction).

6.2 Uses and users of interest rate swaps

Institutional investors (rather than individual investors) use interest rate swaps. Typical users may include:

- financial institutions such as investment and commercial banks;
- non-financial companies;
- local authorities;
- insurance companies; and
- pension funds.

Each of these user groups will employ different strategies to achieve their own objectives.

Hedgers will use interest rate swaps in order to manage their interest rate exposure and their fixed and floating assets and obligations.

Speculators will speculate on future interest rate movements. One who expects interest rates to fall would obtain a floating-rate obligation and swap this for a fixed rate (received the fixed rate). As the floating-rate obligation falls, the speculator will pay a lower floating rate in exchange for the same fixed rate.

Because of differing credit ratings between counterparties, there are opportunities for arbitrage by those who are therefore known as arbitrageurs.

6.3 Controlling interest rate risk

Companies use interest rate swaps to manage exposure to changes in interest rates. Financial institutions (particularly banks) make a considerable amount of their revenue from being involved in the swaps market.

It is also important to note that independent of the swap, there may be an underlying obligation that is the rationale for the swap in the first place. Such an obligation is completely outside of the swap arrangement.

Risks of using interest rate swaps

The two main risks are interest rate risk and counterparty risk.

Interest rate changes may affect the floating interest rate payer, as the rate is linked to an index such as LIBOR. If LIBOR increases considerably, this could cause anticipated profits to vanish or losses to be incurred. If interest rates rise, the fixed-interest rate payer benefits while the payer of floating rate loses out. Conversely, if interest rates fall, the payer of fixed-interest rate loses out while the payer of floating rate will benefit.

There is a chance that one of the counterparties may default on its obligations to make interest payments. The risk should be lower the higher the credit rating of the counterparty and in general, the counterparty making the fixed-rate payments is considered less creditworthy than the counterparty with the floating-rate obligation.

There is no credit risk in respect of the notional amount (as would be the case with a loan).

7. Credit default swaps

Credit default swaps (CDSs) are derivate instruments that are classed as credit derivatives – they are unregulated. They were first introduced by J P Morgan in 1995. They were originally created in order to allow financial institutions including banks a way of transferring their credit exposure as prior to this there was no means of transferring the risk of default or bankruptcy or other such credit event from one party to another. After their introduction, all of this changed. It has been suggested that credit default swaps made a significant contribution to the credit crisis of 2007/2008. However, this chapter will focus on what they are and how they work.

CDSs are derivative instruments that are used as vehicles for transferring the risk of default on a particular debt instrument such as a bond (whether corporate or local authority) from a lender such as a bank to an insurer – an insurance company or another entity which is prepared to take on the risk, such as a hedge fund. In exchange for taking on this risk, the insurer will charge a fee (a premium). The level of this will depend on the perceived risk of default. In transferring the risk to the insurer, the transferor does not transfer any of the benefits and is only liable to the extent of the premiums. The transferor of the risk still owns the credit asset. The terms and conditions of credit default swaps are determined when the specific contract is written. Essentially they are contractual agreements providing insurance against the likelihood of a particular entity defaulting on its debt obligations.

A company that is the subject of the loan is known as the reference entity. If there were to be a default by the reference entity, this would be referred to as a credit event.

The buyer of the insurance obtains the right to sell assets issued by the reference company for their full face value in the event that the reference company defaults. The total face value of the bonds that can be sold is referred to as the credit defaults swap's notional value. The buyer of the CDS will make periodic payments to the seller until either the end of life of the CDS or alternatively until a credit event occurs.

CDS transfer or swap the risk of default of a debt security from the lender to an insurer. In return for providing this insurance, the insurer will charge a premium; this will vary according to the level of perceived risk. If there is no default, the insurer will not have to pay and will keep all of the premiums as profit. If the reference company does default, it will depend when default ensues. The insurer will retain the premiums up to default but will generally have to honour the full outstanding commitment whether the full face value of a bond or full loan amount; however, this will of course depend on the terms and conditions. If default occurs, this will be deemed a credit event and the buyer may receive a lump sum payment.

7.1 Uses of credit default swaps

As with futures, the three main uses are hedging, speculation and arbitrage:

- Hedging – this is the main purpose. For example, if an investment bank loaned £10 million to corporate entity at 6%, and they bought a CDS costing 3%, the risk of default of the corporate bond has been transferred from the bank to an insurance company. Therefore the investment bank is guaranteed a risk-free investment of 3%. If the corporate entity defaults, the investment bank would at least have a return of capital.
- Speculation – a purchaser is hoping that the risk is under-priced and hopes that the reference company will actually default and thus they can call in the insurance. It is not actually a requirement to own debt in order to buy a credit default swap based on that debt.
- Arbitrage – this would be the case where dealers had not responded quickly enough to premium changes.

It should also be understood that CDS are unregulated.

Settlement is generally in the form of cash payment or exchanging bonds for their par value. Alternatively, it can be in the form of a cash payment which equates to the bonds market value and par value.

8. Contracts for differences and turbos

8.1 Contracts for differences (CFDs)

A CFD is a stand-alone leveraged derivative instrument that is in reality a contractual agreement between an investor (purchaser) and a broker (seller), whereby both parties agree to settle in cash the difference between the opening and closing position of a contract based on an opening and closing prices of a specific underlying asset. This difference is multiplied by the number of units (contracts) purchased or sold. CFDs are based and available on a wide range of different underlying assets including ordinary shares, fixed-interest securities and indices such as the FTSE 100 more recently cryptocurrencies.. Trading of CFDs is based on margin payments. Derivatives brokers must be authorised under the Financial Services and Markets Act 2000.

A CFD may be suitable for both institutional and experienced individual investors alike as it affords the price movement benefits whether up or down of owning an array of underlying assets but without actually owning them. They are traded on margins (as determined by the broker). This initial margin will be based on the market price of the underlying asset multiplied by the number of units either bought or sold. This margin must be maintained throughout the duration of the contract. If it falls below the initial margin, then additional margins payments will have to be made to the broker.

CFDs enable investors to earn returns associated with the underlying assets without actually owning them, and most importantly allow this to be done for a fraction of the price of the underlying asset (typically 10–25%). It is important to emphasise that investors are buying and selling CFDs as products in their own right, but the net result is that investors are either buying or selling prices of underlying assets that they hope will move to their advantage.

The CFD unit could be based on any number of ordinary shares or an index such as the FTSE 100 or S&P 500. If it were the latter, it would be passed on per point movement. There are no final settlement dates with CFDs (as there are with futures and options); consequently investors may maintain either long or short positions as long as they can afford to do so.

Investor choices are as follows.

Long position ('going long')

If an investor believes that the price of an underlying asset (for example, Tesco ordinary shares) will rise in the near future (perhaps because the investor considers them to be undervalued), they could buy these shares directly in the spot market. However, the investor has another choice to purchase CFDs based on the same Tesco ordinary shares opening a long position with a broker ('going long').

If the price of the underlying asset, such as Tesco equities, does rise as anticipated, the broker will credit the investor's account with profits.

Short position ('going short')

If the same investor believes that the prices of the ordinary shares will fall rather than rise, they could open a short position with the broker, whereby they will make a profit as long as the price falls.

In summary, an investor will open a long position by buying CFDs and will close the same position by selling CFDs at some time in the future. A short position will be opened by selling CFDs and an investor will close the same position by purchasing CFDs at some time in the future.

Additional considerations

- Positions must to be monitored on a day-to-day basis by investors.
- Investors should take a view as to how they believe the relevant market might move and thus endeavour to make a profit based on this particular view.
- CFDs track the performance of an underlying asset.
- It is a position or price that is owned, not an underlying asset.
- There is no standardisation as in the cases of futures and options.
- CFDs may be considered as speculative or quasi gambling products and there is not that much difference between these and spread-betting.

Margins

Initial margins tend to be 10–25% of the overall contract value. However, this will depend on the particular derivative broker, the client, price volatility of the underlying asset and overall market volatility. Initial margins and any subsequent calls will be credited to the investor's account maintained with the futures broker. If the price moves considerably in the investor's favour, they might be able to withdraw it without closing out the contract, while the initial margin is always maintained.

In the case of CFDs based on ordinary shares, an investor with a long position will be entitled to receive a sum that is equal to the net dividend payable on those shares. This dividend will be netted against the deposit in the investor's account. Conversely, an investor with a short position would have this amount deducted from their account.

It must be noted that before any CFD trading occurs, it is necessary to open an account with a specialist derivative broker, who will require the investor to be able to demonstrate an understanding of the inherent risks of CFDs and the trading of leveraged products generally.

Some authorities believe that CFD trading is akin to spread-betting and hence gambling, and so the lines become rather blurred.

Prices

Brokers will quote two-way prices for all CFDs in which they trade: both a selling and a buying price.

The prices quoted by many CFD brokers should mirror the market price of the underlying asset on which the CFD is based but this may vary between brokers. Prudent investors should check prices with a range of brokers.

Risks

As CFDs are leveraged (geared) products, both profits and losses are magnified and either of these could be significant. However, to mitigate this risk, a stop-loss could be placed.

CFDs are generally more suitable for short-term investors. The longer the position is open the greater the chance of something going wrong – for example, the price not moving in the direction anticipated.

Advantages

- There is no stamp duty to be paid, as there is no transfer of ownership of any asset.
- There is potential to profit from both rising and falling markets as there is ability to open short positions.
- Stop-losses may be established in order to limit losses and crystallise gains.
- There is no automatic expiry as in the case of futures and options.
- Margins are not automatically lost (as is the case with option premiums), but may returned to the investor.

Disadvantages

- There is a need for day-to-day monitoring in order to limit losses and meet margin calls. This could be limited by using a stop-loss arrangement. However, as soon as the stop-loss is reached the position is automatically closed-out.

- Commissions are calculated on the total position, and not the margin actually paid.

Examples
An investor is bullish and believes that BP (British Petroleum) ordinary shares will rise considerably over the next month. He could buy the shares outright from a broker at 502p per share. Rather than buy 50,000 shares outright which would cost £251,000 plus commission and stamp duty, the investor could obtain the same degree of exposure to the price movement of 50,000 BP shares by using CFDs. This exposure would cost only a fraction, perhaps 10–20% (the margin as determined by the broker) of buying the shares outright.

If the above investor decides to open a long position with his broker in relation to 50,000 BP shares, and assuming the market price of the share is 502p, the situation could be as follows.

The broker's spread may be 500–504 and the broker would open the position for the investor by selling the contract at 500p per share and the margin has been set at 15%. The opening price of the position is thus 500p per share.

The cost to the investor is: selling price of spread × exposure (number of shares) × broker's margin.

$$500 \times 250{,}000 \times 15\% = £37{,}500$$

In addition to the above cost, there will be the broker's commission (typically 0.20% of the total contract value). In this case, it would be:

$$500 \times 50{,}000 \times 0.20\% = £500$$

It can be seen that the investor now has an exposure to 50,000 BP ordinary shares, but for a fraction of the cost of buying outright in the equities market.

If, in two weeks' time, BP's shares have risen, as expected by the investor, to perhaps 516p per share and the brokers spread has moved to 514–518, and the investor wishes to close their position by selling CFDs, the position would be:

- Opening price = 500p
- Closing price = 518p
- Difference = 18p
- Investor's profit =£9,000

The investors overall profit will be:

- Investor's profit = £9,000
- Less commission = £500
- Net profit = £8,500

This represents a return of $\dfrac{£7{,}018}{£36{,}632}$ = 19.15% return over a very short period of time

In addition, financing charges have to be factored in, which are added in the case of long positions and deducted in the case of short positions.

Example of a short position

In this instance, the investor believes the price of Legal and General shares will fall in the near future and would like to open a short CFD position. Remember, it is not always possible to short-sell physical shares, particularly in times of economic instability.

The price of the underlying Legal and General shares in the market is 241p per share, while the broker's spread is 240–242 for CFDs based on the shares.

The investor wants to open a short CFD position for 20,000 Legal and General shares which would cost £48,200 in the spot market.

However, if the investor opens a short CFD position, this will cost:

$$240 \times 20{,}000 \times 15\% = £7{,}200$$

In addition to the cost, there will be the broker's commission (typically 0.20% of contract value). In this case it would be:

$$240 \times 20{,}000 \times 0.20\% = £96$$

If, in one week's time, the shares fall to 228p per share and the broker's spread is quoted at 227–229, the investor can now close out his short position by buying CFDs.

The profit will be:

- Opening price = 240p
- Closing price = 229p
- Difference = 11p
- Investor's profit = £2,200

However, in the case of short positions, broker's commissions have to be deducted while financing charges are added.

Important

CFDs are highly leveraged instruments, because brokers only take 10–20% of the market price of the underlying asset. This allows investors to gain exposure of five to ten times of an underlying asset than they would otherwise be able to do in the relevant spot market. We have also seen that one of the key criteria when setting margins is price volatility. Mindful of this, the price volatility of some crypto-currencies has been particularly significant. The financial regulators are particularly concerned in this respect, and the ESMA (European Securities and Markets Authority) and the FCA have stated that CFDs can only have a leveraged limit of 2:1 based on crypto currencies. CFDs are already considered high risk based on higher risk. This essentially means that investors would have to pay a 50% initial margin of the value of the underlying contract.

8.2 Turbos

Turbos are very similar instruments to traditional CFDs in that they are leveraged derivate instruments that are traded on margins. This again means that investors need only provide a percentage, which is typically 10–15% of the amount of the underlying asset to which they wish to have exposure. In reality, it is the price movement of the underlying asset that investors will gain exposure to, rather than the underlying asset itself. Investors are buying and selling turbos, not any underlying asset.

Turbos have a much lower risk profile than traditional CFDs, as they include an in-built stop-loss facility for which no extra charge is made. This results in the investor having all the benefits of CFDs, but without having to monitor day-to-day price movements, and no additional margin calls will be required throughout the life of the turbo. This in turn means that the investor is in control of their own total loss being the initial margin as determined by the broker plus the in-built commissions and finance charges.

In this respect, investment in turbos should be avoided unless the investor is prepared to lose their total initial margin.

Turbos may be either long or short. Long turbos allow you to gain exposure to the price movement of an underlying asset which you hope you will be able to sell at a higher price. Short turbos allow you to open a short position by selling the exposure at a high price and then buying it back at a lower price. The investor is in reality either buying or selling exposure to a price that they hope to buy or sell at a price advantageous to themselves.

Advantages

- Turbos carry a lower risk than traditional CFDs.
- They are available on a range of underlying assets including ordinary shares and indices and can be used by individuals and institutions.
- Investors have full exposure to the underlying asset price movement, but for a far smaller initial outlay than buying the asset in the market.
- There are no additional margin calls as with ordinary CFDs.
- Investors are able to gain exposure to a greater portfolio through leverage than by buying in the spot market.
- Both long and short positions may be opened, affording investors to make profits in both rising and falling markets.
- All costs, including financing fees and dividend payments, will be included in the initial price, therefore investors know the total cost and indeed total exposure from the outset.
- In common with CFDs, no stamp duty is payable, as underlying assets are being neither bought or sold.
- The purchaser dictates the opening position price they will deal at, as this is based on the prevailing market price of the underlying asset rather than being set by the broker.
- For every one penny or cent that the underlying asset moves upwards, so too will the turbo; however, this will be greater in percentage terms.

Disadvantages

- Investors can still lose a considerable amount of money, including their initial margin, commissions and built-in finance charges.
- No ownership of the underlying will occur and the holder has no rights in relation to any underlying asset.
- Even though there will be no additional margin calls, once the investor's stop-loss position has been reached, the position is closed out, which may result in significant losses.
- For every one penny or cent that the underlying asset moves, so too will the turbo. If the price moves down, so will the turbo price; however, this will be far greater in percentage terms.

9. Crypto-currency derivatives

The Financial Conduct Authority (FCA) stated in April 2018 that it was aware that there was an increase in the number of UK firms offering crypto-currencies and crypto-currency related assets. The FCA emphasised that it does not regulate them and they are not part of other regulated products or services. It did, however, acknowledge that crypto-currency derivatives are capable of being financial instruments under MIFID II, although they are considered to be neither currencies nor commodities for regulatory purposes under MIFID II, and firms conducting regulated activities in derivatives based on them must comply with rules in the FCA's Handbook and any relevant provisions directly applicable to EU regulations.

It is important to be mindful of the following definitions.

- Crypto-currency future: a derivative contract where each party buyer and seller agrees to exchange cryptocurrency at an agreed future date at a price agreed today.
- Crypto-currency options: the right to buy or sell crypto currencies.
- Crypto-currency CFD: a cash-settled derivative contract where the parties agree to settle the difference in price between the value of the CFD contract at inception and closure.

Chapter summary

- The derivatives market is based on a variety of underlying assets. The prices of the derivatives instruments will move in line with the prices of those underlying assets. However, there will be a magnification because of the effects of gearing (leverage), which means that for a relatively small initial outlay, an investor obtains the same exposure to the underlying assets that direct ownership of that same asset would give.
- The main derivative instruments discussed within this chapter are futures, options, warrants, covered warrants and interest rate swaps.
- Although futures traditionally began with physical delivery, nowadays most tend to be cash-settled.

- Futures are contractual obligations that are considered to be high-risk investments. Today all futures contracts are traded on recognised exchanges, therefore they are classed as exchange-traded derivative products.
- A distinction must be made between trading a futures contract, which involves either buying or selling a contract, or exercising a contract, which would involve providing or taking delivery of the underlying asset. If you buy an underlying asset directly in the market, you own it; by contrast, if you buy a futures contract, you only acquire a right to obtain the underlying asset.
- Being short on futures is not the same as short-selling underlying assets themselves.
- Warrants are issued by a company to its existing shareholders, giving them the right to subscribe for additional shares in the company. In contrast, covered warrants are issued by third parties such as investment banks and no new shares are issued; instead existing shares are redistributed.
- An interest rate swap is a contractual agreement between two counterparties where one of the counterparties agrees to swap with the other a stream of fixed interest payments (cash flows) in return for a stream of floating-rate interest payments. Both streams are based on the same notional (hypothetical) amount over a specific period. The floating rate will be based on an index such as LIBOR, whereas the fixed-interest rate may be based on a different index. Interest rate swaps are very illiquid over-the-counter (OTC) derivative products.
- There are no exchanges or clearing houses involved, and they are the largest component of the international derivatives market.
- Contracts for differences and turbos are available on a range of underlying assets.
- Contracts for differences are stand-alone leveraged products that allow investors exposure to the price movement of a range of underlying assets without actually owning the asset. Investors can open either long or short positions, depending on how they anticipate prices will move.
- Turbos are similar to CFDs. However, they have embedded stop-loss arrangements which afford an investor a degree of protection and negate the necessity of having to monitor day-to-day price movements.

Test yourself answers

Test yourself 6.1

a) Underlying assets are those from which other classes of asset may be derived or created. Such underlying assets may be either physical as in the case of ordinary shares or commodities or alternatively abstract in the case of indices such as the FTSE 100.

b) Futures are legally binding as the buyer and seller are entering into a contract. The buyer is contractually obliged to provide payment and the seller is obliged to provide the underlying asset at a fixed future date.

Test yourself 6.2

a) The two types of option are call options and put options.

b) Time value is equal to the option premium price minus intrinsic value.

Test yourself 6.3

a) The intrinsic value of a warrant is the difference between the market price of the underlying share and the future exercise price of that same share. Investors will want the market price of the relevant equities to be higher than the stated exercise price at the time of exercise, in order to make a profit.

b) Characteristics of covered warrants include the following.

- The market in covered warrants is regulated by the FCA.
- There is no stamp duty to pay, but there may be a liability to tax on any capital gains.
- There is a legally binding obligation on the issuer to make or to take delivery of the underlying assets or cash settle if the purchaser decides to exercise the warrant during its life.
- Covered warrants cannot have a negative value.
- There are no margin calls (in contrast with futures).
- Covered warrants are 'wasting assets', as they have no value whatsoever after their expiry date.

c) Advantages of covered warrants:

- The initial outlay is only a fraction of that of the underlying assets.
- Stamp duty (currently 0.5%) is not applicable, because trades are cash-settled.
- They provide holders with the ability to hedge in either rising or falling markets.
- Investors do not need to monitor covered warrants on a daily basis, as exercise is automatic.

Disadvantages:

- They cannot be short sold (particularly important in times of financial crisis).
- After the expiry date has passed, the covered warrant is worthless.
- They cannot be bought or held in an individual savings account (ISA).
- They are considered to be higher-risk investments than others.

Chapter seven
Money markets and foreign exchange

List of topics

1. Money markets
2. The main users of money market instruments
3. Money market instruments (MMIs)
4. Foreign exchange (FX) contracts
5. Currency futures
6. Currency swaps
7. Carry trade

Introduction

This chapter focuses on a number of key areas of the investment environment. First, the money markets and their inherent instruments, together with their key participants, are discussed. Second, the foreign exchange market and its associated products are explained. This is followed by an introduction to currency futures and currency swaps. The chapter concludes with an explanation of carry trade.

Money market instruments fall into two distinct categories: those that make interest payments, in the form of coupons, and those that are issued at a discount to their face (par) value. The short-term nature and immense size of the individual transactions cannot be overemphasised.

The foreign exchange market is comprised of both spot and forward exchange contracts (FECs), which are unregistered and mostly unregulated. (It is envisaged that future legislation will be implemented in order to discourage and eliminate some of the bad practices which have prevailed – these are described later in this chapter.) They are over-the-counter (OTC) obligations with physical delivery of the currencies ultimately taking place. It should also be stressed that forward exchange rates are not expectations of future spot rates.

Currency futures differ from forward exchange contracts (FECs) in that they are standardised, exchange-traded products where physical delivery of the currencies will not generally occur, and in common with ordinary futures contracts, margin requirements will be required.

Carry trade is a foreign exchange strategy employed by speculators relying on interest rate differentials between two currencies in order to make profits.

1. Money markets

The money markets are essential components of any country's financial system. It is important to refer to the money markets in the plural rather than 'the' money market in the singular. There are a number of individual money markets, each of which is defined by its own respective instrument. The money markets derive their name because they are wholesale financial markets that deal with the buying and selling of money or near-money instruments, which can be converted into cash at very short notice. The money markets are considered to be a group of individual sub-markets, each of which is characterised by its own inherent financial instruments with their own unique features. However, all money market instruments do have a number of common characteristics, which are given in section 3 of this chapter. All of the individual markets, without exception, trade in low-risk unsecured debt instruments which facilitate or act as mechanisms for the movement of short-term finance from those parties with an excess of liquidity to those parties with a short-term need for liquidity. Different issue and settlement methods will apply to each of the instruments. The movement of these short-term funds is facilitated by the markets' key participants, which are a network of banks, including central and overseas banks, institutional investors, and government bodies which borrow and lend among themselves. All of the individual markets are highly organised, however, no formal exchanges are involved and there are no central locations. Participants may be lenders in one market while being borrowers in others, depending on their particular short-term funding requirements.

The main money markets are:

- deposit (cash) market;
- **Treasury Bill (T-Bill)** market;
- commercial paper (CP) market; and
- certificates of deposit (CD) market.

Treasury Bills (T-Bills)
Registered, redeemable and unconditional short-term (less than one year) obligations of a government issued by a central bank at a discount to face value. They are used to finance a government's short-term funding requirements.

2. The main users of money market instruments

The main users of money market instruments include:

- governments;
- central banks;
- commercial banks, including overseas banks; and
- large national and multinational corporations insurance companies and pension funds.

2.1 Governments

Governments usually act via their central banks. In the UK this role is executed through the Debt Management Office (DMO).

2.2 Central banks

Central banks in some countries have the words 'Central Bank' in their name. In the case of other countries, however, the name does not instantly tell us that the entity in question is the country's central bank. For example, in the UK, this role is carried out by the Bank of England.

2.3 Commercial banks

Commercial banks supply and utilise money market funds, and can also act as intermediaries between other participants. Banks with a surplus of funds may wish to utilise the funds to their best advantage. Other banks might well be short of funds. By using MMIs, commercial banks can thus ensure that excesses and shortages are reallocated.

2.4 Large companies including insurance companies and pension funds

Companies can be both borrowers and providers of finance in the money markets. Those with cash surpluses may invest in these short-term instruments while those who need to borrow for short-term periods can do so. Larger corporations will participate in the market either directly or through brokers, whereas smaller companies will invest in money market funds consisting of only short-term instruments.

2.5 Institutional investors

It is essential for institutional investors to maintain a proportion of their funds in the form of safe, cash and near-cash instruments in order to meet short-term liabilities as they fall due. MMIs allow fulfilment of this requirement. Therefore, investors such as pension funds and insurance companies utilise MMIs extensively.

Test yourself 7.1

a) **What is the function of money markets?**

b) **List the key money market participants.**

3. Money market instruments (MMIs)

Money market instruments (MMIs), also referred to as cash instruments, fall into two broad categories: those with coupons (those paying interest) and those without coupons (those not paying interest). The latter are issued at a discount to their par value (face value), which means that any purchaser will pay less than the par value of the instrument. However, they will still receive their face value at maturity.

All MMIs are debt instruments used by its key participants in order to facilitate the movement of large amounts (wholesale) of short-term money between themselves. Under usual circumstances, MMIs they have maturities of less than one year, although potentially may be for longer periods. The amounts traded each working day tend to be for many billions of pounds or dollars. The two key considerations are the short-term nature of the market together with the vast sizes of the individual trades.

The returns on MMIs generally tend to be low, as they are considered exceptionally safe and hence the degree of risk is deemed low. They are shown as cash on a lender's balance sheet.

Money markets have no central trading venue with dealing in MMIs taking place by telephone and also via computer terminals rather than on any formal exchange. This involves a network of dealers and brokers and, within the money markets, there are sub-markets for each of the individual instruments.

As MMIs tend to be traded in very high denominations, they are used by institutional rather than individual investors. The participants may be lenders or borrowers, or both. Those participants providing the finance for the instruments require securities that are both low-risk and liquid.

It is important to understand the relationships of the participants. Issuers of MMIs are borrowers, while purchasers are lenders.

All money market instruments have their own set of unique characteristics, which will vary from country to country. However, they will all have the following core characteristics.

- All are debt instruments of short-tenor (short-term to maturity from one to 360 days), and are unsecured.
- No security is provided by borrowers to lenders. The reputation of the issuer (borrower) is deemed sufficient.
- There is no public register, although they are recorded by issuers.
- There is a perception of low risk.
- Instruments are of large denominations.
- They are predominately, although not exclusively, used by institutional rather than individual investors.
- They are always OTC (over-the-counter).
- They are unregulated yet sophisticated.
- They have no central trading location.
- They are used as mechanisms for the absorption and redistribution of cash surpluses.

3.1 Deposits

Interbank deposits are the simplest and most liquid of all MMIs, and are available for varying maturities, with the majority being for three months' maturity or less. They are unsecured and are usually for a minimum amount of £500,000.

interbank deposits
The simplest and most liquid of all MMIs; they are available for varying maturities. The majority of interbank deposits are for three months or less. They are unsecured and are usually for a minimum amount of £500,000.

Interest on such deposits is calculated on a simple-interest rather than a compound-interest basis.

Worked example 7.1

For example, on a three-month (91 days) £500,000 interbank deposit paying interest at 2% pa, the return would be: £500,000 × 2/100 × 91/365 = £2,493.15.

In the case of sterling and domestic Japanese yen, interest rates are based on a 365-day year (366 days in the case of a leap year), whereas for many currencies, including the US dollar, they are calculated using 360 days. This is known as **bank basis** (also referred to as cash basis and money market basis).

bank basis
A convention where interest rates are based on a 365-day year in the case of sterling and Japanese yen, whereas a 360-day year is used for US dollars and many other currencies.

3.2 Treasury Bills (T-Bills)

Treasury Bills (T-Bills) are registered, unconditional, short-term money market debt instruments issued at a discount to face value. They are issued exclusively by governments including those of the UK, the USA and Japan in order to finance their short-term funding requirements. Although our discussion will be from the perspective of the UK, the principles, characteristics and methods of issue will be similar for any government issuing Treasury Bills.

In the UK, HM Treasury provides an annual remit to the DMO regarding the issuance and annual targets for T-Bills funding. UK T-Bills are essential components of the cash management operations of the DMO and indeed they will become liabilities of the DMO after issue.

The Chancellor of the Exchequer's cash flow is subject to a great deal of uncertainty as a result of the unpredictability in the timing of tax inflows and expenditure outflows. The DMO will deal with this by taking a pragmatic and 'big picture' approach via the mechanism of the weekly issuance of T-Bills with varying maturities and also in conjunction with other MMIs.

In the UK, T-Bills are obligations of the government, issued by the DMO on its behalf (in this respect, the DMO has recourse to both the National Loans fund and the consolidated fund). T-Bills are deemed to be zero-coupon eligible debt securities, as they are issued at a discount to their face value, which means that they are a class of security that is dematerialised, issued and held in CREST and Euroclear, thus creating rights and obligations corresponding to those in relation to paper and negotiable MMIs.

Characteristics

T-Bills neither pay interest nor have any coupons, as they are issued at a discount to their face value. They are fully marketable instruments tradable both in the primary and secondary markets. Their 'reward' is the difference between their face value (receivable at maturity) by the final holder and the price paid in either the primary or the secondary market.

maturity date
The same as the redemption date. The date when the bond is redeemed and cancelled. The bond holder will receive the principal amount from the issuer.

T-Bills have as their reference point a **maturity date** (see Table 7.1 on page 193). Subsequent issues with the same maturity date will be seen as a further issue of the original bills for that date. At redemption date, the government will pay the final holder the full face value. Essentially, their interest is their face value minus the discounted price paid by the purchaser. Consequently, if there is no income in the form of interest, there can be no income tax.

mutual fund
An investment vehicle made up of a pool of funds collected from many investors for the purpose of investing in securities on their behalf by a manager and structured to match the investment objectives as stated in the prospectus.

T-Bills are held, issued and settled electronically in CREST, the settlement system of Euroclear UK and Ireland (the Central Securities Depository of the UK). In the UK, the minimum purchase is £500,000, which then increases by amounts of £50,000. They may be purchased by commercial banks, corporations and **mutual funds** rather than individuals, although they can be purchased by individuals through primary participants (described later in this section).

Primary participants (not to be confused with main users) are banks that have agreed to bid at Treasury Bill tenders on behalf of investors. These banks are registered by the FCA (Financial Conduct Authority) and the Prudential Regulatory Authority (PRA).

Maturities in the UK

UK T-Bills are issued with varying maturities, and in theory may be issued for as little as one day. In practice, however, maturities are issued for:

- one month: approximately 28 days;
- three months: approximately 91 days; or
- six months: approximately 182 days.

It is possible that T-Bills with maturities of 12 months could be issued; to date none have been issued.

In addition to weekly tenders, the DMO can hold ad-hoc tenders with maturities of up to 28 days. These will vary from standard tenders in two ways:

1. Bids will only be accepted by telephone.
2. Bids must be for a minimum of £5 million and thereafter in multiples of £1 million.

Primary participants

Primary participants (different from main users) are financial institutions that have agreed, subject to their own due diligence to bid at Treasury Bill tenders on behalf of investors. They are registered financial institutions that are regulated by the FCA and the PRA, and obviously subject to their rules and guidance. These firms also provide secondary market dealing levels for Treasury Bills. As of July 2018 there were 28 primary participants, including:

- Barclays Bank plc;
- Deutsche Bank (London branch);
- Goldman Sachs International;
- J.P. Morgan Securities plc; and
- Société Générale.

Method of issue

In the primary market, T-Bills are issued by the DMO on a weekly basis to market makers through a competitive tender process, which takes place on the last business day of each week. Settlement is T+1 (that is, on the next business day). An announcement is made each Monday in the *Financial Times* with the details of the previous week's tender.

When the bills have been acquired by in the primary market, they become fully tradable securities and specialist brokers will quote two-way prices to subsequent buyers and sellers in the secondary market.

Tenders are usually oversubscribed, with the minimum accepted bids being the lowest made that is sufficient to dispose of the entire offer. Such bids must be lower than face value in order for a holder to make a profit. The tender process means that all successful tenderers will pay the same price; this is in contrast with auctions, where bidders will pay different prices.

All bids must specify the maturity (for example, one month or three months) of bills being bid for which must be made on a money market yield basis and there is no limit to the number of bids that can be submitted by any one tenderer. The DMO ranks all received bids for each maturity on offer by yield and all bids must be received by 11 a.m. on the day of tender.

While the tender process is underway for the current week's issue, the DMO will announce details of the following week's issues, including tender size and the maturities of the bills on offer. Announcements are available on the DMO's wire service and also Reuters Registration.

CREST constitutes the central register of T-Bill ownership with the legal title being evidenced by the entry of a given number of units against a holder's name in the relevant CREST record, which may also be held in Euroclear.

Returns

There are no coupons or interest payments on T-Bills. Instead, T-Bills are issued at a discount to their face value. Returns may be calculated as the difference between their face value and the price actually paid by the purchaser. The resulting figure may then be annualised (expressed as if it were measured over one year). The majority of Treasury Bills are for three or six months. In the UK, this is typically six months from the original issue date.

Methods used to evaluate returns

These methods include:

- the discount rate; and
- the interest rate (or yield).

Worked example 7.2

Discount rate

The discount rate is the par value ('face value') minus the price paid for the bill. The discount is based on the face amount of the Treasury Bills.

For instance, a successful bidder might pay £997,500 now for £1 million nominal of three-month T-Bills (that is, purchased at a £2,500 discount to the face amount). The bills will be redeemed at maturity for £1 million in 91 days' time. This represents a 0.25% discount of the nominal value, however, calculated over 91 days. This must now be annualised.

Annualised, this is:
(£1m-997,500)/£1M X365/91 x100% = 1.00274% pa.

The interest rate or yield

The interest rate or yield can also be calculated. This is based on the price actually paid by the holder rather than on the face value.

Worked example 7.3

(£1m-997,500)/£997,500 X365/91 x100% = 1.00526% pa.

It is conventional for T-Bills to trade on the discount rate. If, however, investors wish to compare the return on T-Bills with other types of investment, they should use the interest rate (yield) formula, which will make this possible.

Care must be taken when calculating either of these rates, as a common error in the investment examination is to multiply by 91/365 rather than 365/91. At the time of writing, the returns on T-Bills are extremely low.

Credit rating

In relation to credit ratings, T-Bills are similar to cash and in the UK have the same credit status as gilts: AAA (often pronounced 'triple-A') rated by Standard & Poor's and Aaa by Moody's. T-Bills are backed by the governments. Although UK government default is not impossible, it is unlikely. Due to this low risk, returns are relatively low when compared to other investments.

Table 7.1: Outstanding Treasury Bills in the UK

Maturity Date	Original Issue Date	Original Nominal Amount (£ million)	First Re-opening Date	First Re-issue Amount (£ million)	Second Re-opening Date)	Second Re-issue Amount (£ million)	
29 May 2018	27 November 2017	£2,000	26 February 2018	£500	30 April 2018	£500	
04 June 2018	04 December 2017	£1,500	5 March 2018	£2,000	08 May 2018	£500	
11 June 2018	11 December 2017	£1,500	12 March 2018	£1,000	14 May 2018	£500	
18 June 2018	18 December 2017	£2,000	19 March 2018	£1,000	21 May 2018	£500	
25 June 2018	27 December 2017	£1,500	26 March 2018	£1,000			
02 July 2018	03 April 2018	£1,500					
09 July 2018	08 January 2018	£2,000	9 April 2018	£1,000			
16 July 2018	15 January 2018	£2,000	16 April 2018	£1,000			
23 July 2018	22 January 2018	£2,000	23 April 2018	£500			
30 July 2018	29 January 2018	£2,000	30 April 2018	£500			
06 August	05 February 2018	£2,000	8 May 2018	£500			
13 August 2018	12 February 2018	£2,000	14 May 2018	£500			
20 August 2018	19 February 2018	£2,000	21 May 2018	£1,000			
28 August 2018	26 February 2018	£2,000					
03 September 2018	05 March 2018	£2,000					
10 September 2018	12 March 2018	£2,000					
17 September 2018	19 March 2018	£2,000					
24 September 2018	26 March 2018	£2,000					
01 October 2018	03 April 2018	£2,000					
08 October 2018	09 April 2018	£2,000					
15 October 2018	16 April 2018	£1,500					
22 October 2018	23 April 2018	£1,500					
29 October 2018	30 April 2018	£1,500					
05 November 2018	08 May 2018	£1,500					
12 November 2018	14 May 2018	£1,500					
19 November 2018	21 May 2018	£1,500					
Totals		£46,500		£10,500		£2,000	£59,000

It may be observed as a snapshot on 25 May 2018 that there was a total outstanding amount of £59 billion. Most Treasury Bills now tend to be to be of six months' tenor. We may elicit a number of factors from the information contained within Table 7.1, notably:

- there is a weekly issuance pattern;
- tenders tend to be £1 billion, £1.5 billion and 2 billion;

- the tenor period is currently six months; and
- subsequent issues of the same maturity date tend to be issued with either three months' or one month's maturity.

Test yourself 7.2

How are Treasury Bills issued?

3.3 Commercial paper

Commercial paper (CP), often referred to as a 'corporate IOU', is a short-term money market instrument issued and used by large companies as a cheaper alternative to bank borrowing. It is a method of raising short-term and unsecured finance. The funds raised through the issuance of CP are used to fund daily operations such as the payment of wages and the purchasing of stock. However, it would not be used to purchase fixed assets, such as plant and machinery, or to provide finance for long-term capital projects.

CP maturities range from one to 270 days. In practice, maturities tend to be for one or two months. A CP is usually held to maturity, as there is virtually no secondary market.

CP is unsecured debt and it is the 'good name' of the borrower (issuing company) combined with the credit rating of the CP itself, as assigned, by credit ratings agencies that are the key components of any CP.

Most companies issuing CP have excellent credit ratings, provided by the main credit ratings agencies. Moody's provides ratings P1 to P3, whereas Standard & Poor's provides ratings from A1 to A3. The highest ratings are A1 and P1, but A2 and P2 are still considered high-quality CP, indicating a smaller company or one having a larger debt portfolio.

From an investor's perspective, CP is considered a safe investment, but not as safe as government-backed T-Bills. Therefore, the rate of return will be slightly higher on CP in order to compensate for the additional risk. Borrowing by way of CP is not very different from bank borrowing, except that CP issues are for larger amounts and there is no security provided to lenders (investors).

The company will set the rate of return, not a financial institution, and companies will issue CP directly to investors rather than banks acting as intermediaries.

Market size

This is a vast market and by way of an example, at the peak of the USD commercial paper ($CP) market in August 2016, there was US$ 1 trillion outstanding. However, in recent years in the UK this has fallen from a peak of over £6 billion in 2016 to less than £140 million in 2017.

Process

If a company issues CP with a term of, for example, 180 days then at maturity, the holder must be paid the full face value. In common with T-Bills, CP is sold at a discount to face value, thus the reward is the difference between the face value and the amount originally paid.

It can be a perpetual cycle: as paper matures, new paper is issued.

Making it work 7.1: Quantitative easing

In May 2009, the Bank of England bought £50 million of CP in order to help companies raise working capital. This was part of the Bank's quantitative easing (QE) scheme. The Bank advised that it would purchase private-sector debt with a credit rating as low as BBB but, crucially, it would only buy such paper from those companies making an important contribution to the UK economy.

In the USA, CP with a maturity of fewer than 270 days does not have to be registered with the Securities and Exchange Commission.

3.4 Certificates of deposit

Certificates of deposit (CDs) are fully negotiable short-term MMIs that are in effect acknowledgements of indebtedness issued by banks and other financial organisations to other institutional investors (purchasers of CDs rank as unsecured creditors). They have specific maturity dates ranging from three months to one year. Theoretically, certificates with longer maturities could be issued, but to date, none have been.

In the UK, CDs can only be issued by those institutions that have been authorised to accept deposits in possession of a Part-IV permission under the Financial Services and Markets Act 2000. Unlike T-Bills and CP, CDs are not issued at a discount; instead, coupons payments are made.

The issuer will acknowledge that in relation to the value of certificates issued, a sum has been deposited with it on terms that the principal amount is repayable together with interest on the maturity date payable at the rate and under the terms and conditions set out.

At the end of the fixed term, the deposit is returned to the investor together with interest. Although the term is fixed, the coupon can be either fixed or floating.

In the UK, CDs are issued with a minimum denomination of £100,000. The minimum transfer value above this amount is one penny, although some issuers specify a minimum trading value.

As there is a perception of higher risk, interest rates tend to be higher than on T-Bills.

Nowadays, CDs are predominately issued in dematerialised form and held in CREST, but they can also be issued in paper form, if they keep to conditions laid down by the British Bankers' Association. All CD payments are made through CREST including interest and it is necessary for both issuers and purchasers to be CREST members.

Yields depend on the:

- credit rating of the issue;
- amount invested; and
- level of interest rates for the currency in which the CD is denominated.

Test yourself 7.3

a) For what purposes would a company issue CP?

b) Give three factors that may affect yields on CDs.

4. Foreign exchange (FX) contracts

Foreign exchange is often abbreviated to 'FX', 'Forex' or 'FE'. 'FX' will be used throughout this study text.

A range of different FX instruments is available to investors who may use them for a variety of reasons, including:

- speculation;
- hedging;
- the settlement of imminent or future liabilities denominated in a foreign currency and in order to lock in a receipt; or
- to maintain funds on a foreign currency-denominated account.

Prior to discussing foreign exchange contracts, it is first necessary to understand how to calculate exchange rates.

Exchange rates

An exchange rate is the price of one currency expressed in terms of another currency for the purpose of conversion.

To state this in simple language: 'How much of one currency (A) can be purchased with a set amount of currency (B)?'

There will be many exchange rates quoted: for instance, sterling against the United States dollar, the United States dollar against Japanese yen, the euro against the Swiss franc. These rates will change, second by second, throughout the course of the business day while markets are open. They may vary considerably over time and in particular during periods of economic instability. For instance, when the UK decided to leave the EU in June 2016, the exchange rate between the British pound and all other currencies fell by as much as 30%, meaning that the pound became worth less in relation to other currencies. There may also be a considerable variation in rates provided by different financial institutions for the same pair of currencies.

Factors that may affect currency rates are discussed later in this chapter (section 4.5).

When calculating exchange rates, the most important consideration is to understand which is the more valuable currency of the two currencies involved in the exchange. Students need to know whether a particular currency should be multiplied or divided by the exchange rate. If the rate were multiplied rather than divided or vice versa, this could have serious implications. Significant losses might be incurred, whether in terms of actual financial loss, reputational risk or damage to customer relationships if they were overcharged.

You will always receive less of the more valuable currency in exchange for more of the less valuable currency. Sometimes it is difficult to know which is the more valuable currency.

4.1 Spot FX contract

A **spot FX contract** is a binding obligation between two parties, a bank and its customer, where one party agrees to sell a currency to another party in exchange for a different currency. Exchange of the currencies will take place on T+2 (the transaction day plus two working days). Therefore, two days after the deal is struck, the investor will receive one currency while paying in another. Most spot FX contracts are concluded either on the telephone with currency dealers or via the internet.

The rate used is referred to as the current spot FX market rate.

spot FX contract
A binding obligation between two parties where one party agrees to sell a currency to another party in exchange for a different currency. The deal is immediate with the exchange of the currencies taking place on T+2 (transaction day plus two working days).

Worked example 7.4

Party A (a trading company) might wish to purchase US$20,000 from Party B (a bank).

Party A has sterling, which it will use to pay for the US$20,000.

Let us suppose that the spot selling rate is US$1.32 = £1.00.

US$20,000 / 1.32 = £15.151.15

It follows, therefore two working days after the contract is entered into, Party A will either receive in cash US$20,000 or, more usually, have this amount credited to a US$ account (alternatively the US$ may be used to pay a third-party obligation, by telegraphic transfer). The sterling amount (£15,151.15 in our example) will be debited to Party A's sterling account.

In general, the British pound is more valuable than most international currencies. However, there are exceptions and in this example, the United States dollar is less valuable than sterling as more units of the dollar have to be given in order to receive one pound. There are some currencies that are more valuable than the pound, where you would have to give more than one pound to obtain one unit of a particular currency.

For example, the Bahraini dinar (BHD) where the quoted exchange rate as at 26 May 2018 was GBP 1 = BHD 0.50. Therefore, to obtain one Bahraini dinar would cost £2. If this rate were multiplied rather than divided, it could result in only paying 50p rather than £2. If this were based on, for example, BHD 1 million, significant losses could be incurred. If a customer who should pay £2 million could pay only £500,000, this would result in a loss of £1,500,000 for the financial institution.

FX rate spread

This spread is the range between bid and offer prices.

An institution such as a bank will quote both buying and selling rates for each currency in which it deals. These rates are in the form of a 'spread', and are more commonly referred to as 'bid' and 'offer' prices. The bid rate is the buying price – that is, what the bank will bid (give you) for what you are selling. The offer price is the bank's selling price – that is, what the bank will charge you for the currency that you are buying (how much of a currency it is prepared to offer/give to you).

By convention, most currencies are quoted against the US dollar (this being known as the fixed currency). The main exception to this is sterling, where the US dollar is quoted against UK pound where sterling is the fixed currency. Traditionally, the USD/GBP spot rate is referred to as 'cable'.

When a bank is quoting its rates (in the form of a spread), it will always state those rates that are most advantageous to it, known as 'sell low, buy high'. This means that, by selling low, it will give you as little as possible of the currency you are buying for your money. Conversely, when you are buying a currency, a bank will buy high – that is, the bank will take as much of one currency from you as it can in exchange for the currency it sells to you.

By convention, selling rates are quoted on the left-hand side of the specified spread, and buying rates are given on the right-hand side of the quoted spread. One way of remembering this is to memorise: 'Hello, Bye Bye' (i.e. sell low comes first, followed by buy high).

The mid-rate is the rate at which the bank will break even. The greater the amounts being traded, the more close the buying and selling rates will be to the mid-rate.

Banks will only use rates that are advantageous to themselves. However, the larger the amounts of currency, the more preferential rates will be offered to a customer.

Worked example 7.5

Let us use, for example, the USD/GBP rate with a spread of 1.32–1.34.

The bank will sell dollars at 1.32. In other words, the bank will give you US$1.32 for each pound that you provide. (Note: If you were selling dollars, the bank would want US$1.34 for every pound that it would be prepared to give you.)

If you were to buy US$20,000 from a bank, it would cost you £15,151.51 (US$20,000 / 1.32).

If you were selling US$20,000 to a bank, you would receive £14,925.37 (that is, US$20,000 / 1.34).

So, if a customer were to buy the US$20,000 at 1.32 and immediately sell back at 1.34, you would lose –226.15 (£15,151.51 – £14,925.37). This may not seem like a huge amount. However, if, rather than $20,000, the amount were US$2 million, this would equate to £22,615.00 which is significant.

Frequently, spreads are considerably wider than the two cents used in Worked example 7.5. In addition, banks' commissions, if applicable, should always be considered. However, commissions are not usually applied to commercial transactions, profits being earned via the spread.

Foreign exchange spot contracts can be made between any tradable currency, for instance, the Euro (EUR) against Japanese Yen (JPY) or Thai baht (THB) against Australian dollar (AUD).

Many bureaux de change that do not charge any commissions, including those contained in household name stores, make their profits through very wide spreads.

4.2 Forward exchange contracts (FECs)

A forward exchange contract (FEC) is a legally binding obligation where two parties enter into a contract; one party (a financial institution) agrees to sell a currency to another party (customer) in exchange for another currency where the forward exchange rate is agreed today. However, physical delivery of the currencies takes place at an agreed future date, perhaps one month. Typical terms are one month, two months, three months and six months. Generally, the maximum is one year, but may be even two to five years in the most widely traded currencies.

FECs are considered OTC transactions as there is no central trading location and transactions are conducted between various parties using telephones or the internet. FECs are not tradable in their own right as is the case with currency futures. An FEC eliminates the risk of fluctuating exchange rates because the price (exchange rate) is locked in today for future delivery. Physical delivery of the currency will not take place until the agreed date, and despite what happens in the FX markets in the intervening period, the rate is fixed today.

FECs are usually for a whole number of months. However, there is no reason why an FEC cannot be for a 'broken period', for example, six weeks, or 57 days forward, subject to agreement between the bank and its counterparty. A forward exchange rate is not an expectation of what future 'FX' spot rates will be. Rather, it is calculated using the interest rate differential (IRD) between the two currencies concerned, which will vary according to the length of the contract.

Many banks will take a deposit (typically 5–10% of the amount due), generally payable at T+2. This affords the bank some degree of protection in case the customer fails to honour the contract at maturity. If 'closing out' the contract, the bank might incur a loss by having to buy or sell the currency in question at a now-unfavourable rate resulting in a financial loss to a bank. Prior to agreeing to any 'FX' contract, a bank would consider the creditworthiness of its customer.

FECs are legally binding contracts and, even if rates and circumstances change in the intervening period, there is still an obligation to deliver at maturity at the agreed rate. If rates improve in the market afterwards, there will be no benefit, as the rate is locked in.

Reasons to use an FEC

FECs are a hedge when a customer has an obligation to receive or make a foreign currency payment. They are also used to protect against market fluctuations. In addition they may be used as speculative instruments; unlike currency futures, amounts traded can be small and contracts are not standardised with ultimate delivery of currency occurring.

Worked example 7.6

If a trading company had a US$100,000 liability due in three months' time from today, and if the current spot exchange rate were US$2 = £1.00, at today's rate $100,000 could be obtained for £50,000. (This exchange rate is exaggerated in order to make understanding easy.)

However, as the liability is not due for three months, the company would not wish to settle the deal today, but, at the same time, is concerned that the USD rate may move against them in the intervening period (three months' time). For example, the spot rate might then be US$1.50:£1, which means that $100,000 will now cost £66,666.

This risk can be eliminated using an FEC.

Alternatively, FECs can be used by speculators believing the exchange rate will move in their favour. They could buy currency spot today and place it in an interest-bearing currency account, and perhaps sell in three or six months' time – hopefully at a profit.

FECs are useful for importers and exporters as all profits could conceivably be wiped out if they had not arranged an FEC.

4.3 Quotation and calculation of forward exchange rates

Forward exchange rates are not an expectation of what currency spot rates will be in the future. Nonetheless, the present spot rate, together with the two countries' interest rates, is required as a component of our calculation of the applicable premium (pm) or discount (dis) or very occasionally at par in those cases where there is no IRD.

It should be noted that the forward exchange rate and delivery date is agreed today, whereas the actual exchange of currencies will take place at the agreed delivery date.

Worked example 7.7

For example, using sterling and the US dollar as the relevant currencies, assuming today's mid-rate is quoted as US$1.3350 = £1.00 and the quoted spread as US$1.3250 – 1.3450. If an investor were to buy USD today using the bank's spot selling rate, it would cost £75,471.70 (100,000 / 1.3250).

If an investor has sterling and wishes to receive US$100,000 in one month's time and the one-month forward rate is quoted 42–40 premium; the spread is now 1.3208–1.3410.

The forward exchange rate would be the selling rate of 1.3250 minus the premium of 0.42 cents, thus, at 1.3208 = £75,711.70

It is important to note that premiums and discounts are quoted in cents (or centavos, etc.) or fractions of currencies.

There is a rule ('discount add, premium subtract' or DAPS) regardless of which currencies are involved. Discounts are always added, whereas premiums are always deducted.

Referring to the example, if our spot rate were quoted at US$1.3250–1.3450, how do we calculate the six-month forward rate?

If sterling (annual) interest rates were 5% then the six-month rate = 5% × 6/12

If USD interest rates (annual) were 2% then the six-month rate = 2% × 6/12

Thus, buying US$100,000 at today's spot rate 1.3250, it would cost £75,471.70

If you invested £75,471.70 at 2.5% (5% × 6/12) = £77,357.78

If you invested US$100,000 at 1% (2% × 6/12) = US$101,000.00

$$\frac{\$101{,}000}{£77{,}357.78} = 1.3056$$

Therefore, the new exchange rate = US$1.3056

This relationship has to hold good in order that arbitrage profits cannot be made.

We can also observe that the USD would need to be quoted at a premium of 1.94 cents, which (by the rule 'premium subtract') would be deducted from 1.3250, giving 1.3056.

4.4 Interest rate parity (IRP)

The interest rate parity (IRP) theory shows the link between exchange rates and interest rates. In essence, it shows how forward exchange rates may be determined using the IRD (interest rate differential) between two currencies and their current spot rates.

The formula is as follows.

$$\text{Forward rate} = \frac{1+r\$}{1+r£} \times \text{spot rate}$$

Where:

- r£ = sterling (fixed currency) interest rate for the relevant period; and
- r$ = dollar (counter currency) interest rate for the relevant period.

The specific manner in which r$ and r£ are calculated should be noted. They should be based on the number of days in the period. For example, if dollar interest rates for a three-month (91-day) period are 8% pa, the relevant value for r$ is (8% × 91/360) 2.02%. If sterling interest rates for a three-month (91-day) period are 10% pa, then the relevant value for r£ is (10% × 91/365) 2.49%.

The use of a 360-day year for USD interest and a 365-day year for sterling is market convention. When banks work out the yield that they wish to pay or receive, they take this convention into account when quoting rates.

Worked example 7.8

Suppose that the current spot rate is £1 = $1.4275 and three-month forward rate (using the formula) is:

- r$ = 1 + (8% ´ 91/360) = 1.02022
- r£ = 1 + (10% ´ 91/365) = 1.02493

Therefore, the three-month forward rate would be 1.4209 (that is, 1.02022/1.02493) × 1.4275.

4.5 Factors influencing currency rates

Many factors influence the way in which exchange rates may fluctuate. All exchange rates are influenced to some extent by the forces of demand and supply.

Yield differential

A country's interest rate will affect the demand for and supply of its currency by influencing its capital flows. The yield differential is the difference between interest rates in various countries and how it affects currency values. Higher domestic interest rates contrasted to other countries' interest rates will tend to make the domestic currency more attractive to overseas investors, causing the value of the domestic currency to increase, all other things being equal. Likewise, lowering domestic interest rates will tend to make the currency less attractive.

As an example, the yield on British government securities (gilts) is increased relative to that of Japanese government securities. This should not only increase the inflow into GBP but should also reduce the outflow of GBP into Japanese securities. The increased inflow into British securities should increase the value of the pound and reduce the value of the Japanese yen.

Government budget surplus or deficit

If a government has a large budget surplus, the market will generally react positively, causing a currency's value to rise. Conversely, if there is a large budget deficit, it is often because a government has miscalculated its figures, thus failing to inspire market confidence and causing a currency to go down in value.

Balance of payments

Surpluses and deficits in the export-import trade of a country's goods and services are indicative of that country's competitiveness. If a country has a balance of payments surplus, the value of its exported goods and services exceeds the value of those imported. This will have a positive effect on a country's exchange rate relative to other currencies. By contrast, if the value of a country's imports is greater than the value of the goods it exports, it will have a balance of payments deficit. This, in turn, will have a negative effect on its currency.

Economic conditions

The economic condition of a country will determine the likely direction of a country's exchange rate. The brighter the economic outlook for a country, the stronger its currency will tend to be. Economic factors such as unemployment levels, retail sales, GDP and industrial output will also affect currency rates.

Economic growth will stimulate demand for a currency both through capital flows into the country, because of attractive investment opportunities, and through current account flows, because of increased supply of and demand for the country's traded goods and services.

A credit boom may cause demand for overseas goods and services, and may cause a currency to weaken.

Political considerations

A country's currency is inextricably linked with its country (for example, the USD in the case of the United States), and events inside the country in question will influence how the currency moves. Government policies may have considerable impact on a country's economic performance and therefore the value of its currency. Where an economy is overheating, a government may increase taxes to reduce spending.

Historically, in times of political instability, the Swiss franc and Japanese Yen have been refuge currencies, causing the value of these currencies to rise relative to other currencies. An unstable or corrupt political regime will have a negative effect on a country's currency, as would the outbreak of civil war.

Inflation rates

Higher rates of inflation reduce a country's competitiveness in international markets.

Consumers will try to avoid the effects of inflation, which is the process of rising prices eroding purchasing power. Where one country has a high inflation rate in contrast to another country's rate, this will reduce the purchasing power of the country with the higher level of inflation. This in turn will cause the value of its currency to fall.

Consumers will tend to buy goods and services from countries with lower inflation rates, as they appear more attractive. Therefore, the demand for the currencies of countries with the lower inflation rates will increase, causing their values to increase. Conversely, the currency where there is a higher inflation rate will tend to weaken.

Natural resources

The discovery or existence of valuable natural resources such as oil or gas can cause a currency to strengthen.

Non-political events

Natural disasters such as earthquakes or tsunamis can negatively affect a currency, either by reducing demand for a currency (for example, a decline in tourism) or because the country's financial system is unable to function.

Making it work 7.2: Natural disasters

Natural disasters can adversely affect the value of a currency. However, sometimes events do not turn out as expected. The earthquake and tsunami in Japan in March 2011 caused billions of yen worth of damage to Japan's economy and infrastructure. It might have been expected therefore that the Japanese Yen would have depreciated. Remember, however, that the Japanese yen is a 'safe haven' currency and as a result of political turmoil in the European markets at that time, the yen continued to be in demand and did in fact appreciate in value.

Government controls

The introduction of exchange controls may prevent the panic outflow of capital. An alternative may be to devalue a country's currency, which could reduce confidence in the currency and have a negative effect on exchange rates.

Central bank intervention

Occasionally a central bank may intervene in the markets by buying its own currency in attempt to support demand or defend exchange rates. This can only ever be a short-term measure.

Test yourself 7.4

a) What are spot FX contracts?

b) List four factors that may affect foreign currency exchange rates.

Making it work 7.3: FX 'fixes'

The international foreign currency exchange markets operate 24 hours a day and for 365 days a year with a daily turnover reported to be in excess of US$5 trillion.

The nature of operation of these FX markets means that there is no one universal or official exchange rate applicable to any pair of currencies or applicable to any cross rates. Indeed, any exchange rates quoted will vary considerably from bank to bank, trade size, time of day, country and relative importance of their customer. However, fund managers and major companies do need to have a daily reference rate (a benchmark) in order that they can evaluate their own portfolios, assets and liabilities that are denominated in foreign currencies. Notably, fund managers want to be able to mark to market, meaning that they need to ascertain or provide a realistic and fair appraisal of a fund's current value based on the daily losses or gains as a consequence of currency movements which may impact the value of foreign currency denominated assets.

In order to meet such fund managers' needs, an FX benchmark was created from within the FX markets. This benchmark is known as the 4:00 p.m. London fix.

A definition

FX 'fixes' are global exchange rate benchmarks that have been created from within the FX markets and which are used by multinational corporations, fund managers and institutional investors to provide global reference points (exchange rates) between any pair of currencies at a particular time or times during the day. The relevant fix rate will be the mid-rate of the selling and buying rates at the 'fix' time.

The relevant exchange rates that subsist at these 'fix' times in relation to any pairs of currencies are those that fund managers, pension funds and large companies will use as their reference point.

By way of example, the 4:00 p.m. 'fix' rate for United States dollars against sterling may be established thus.

The quoted rate spread is US$1.3600–1.3650. The fix rate will be the mid-point between these two figures: US$1.3625. Consequently, US$1.3625 would be the reference rate used by fund managers at the 'fix time', 4:00 pm. London time.

There would be applicable fix rates for the Japanese yen against the United States dollar, or the Swiss franc against the euro.

Fraudulent manipulations of the FX 'fix' rates

The director of the Serious Fraud Office (SFO, www.sfo.gov.uk), an independent government department that has the responsibility for investigating and prosecuting serious and complex fraud, bribery and corruption, launched a criminal investigation on 21 July 2014 into allegations of fraudulent activities in the foreign exchange market. These investigations were prompted by the observation of suspicious activity around the 'fix' time.

The SFO's investigations centred on whether or not foreign currency dealers at banks and other financial institutions colluded to manipulate the benchmark foreign exchange 4:00 p.m. 'fix' to the detriment of clients and/or their own benefit (making significant additional profits). It is suggested that if this were the case, then such fraudulent activity might have been facilitated by internet chat rooms and instant messaging, with dealers using their own jargon to carry out such alleged abuse.

It has been further suggested that because FX dealers knew that their clients wanted to deal at the 4:00 p.m. fix rate and also knew the amounts that their clients wished to buy or sell many hours ahead of the 'fix' rate' time, there was a possibility that dealers could have colluded to manipulate the rates to their own advantage. They would have done this by pushing through the clients' deals earlier in the day at exchange rates preferential to themselves, thus making additional profit.

5. Currency futures

currency futures contracts
Exchange-traded derivative products traded in exactly the same manner as ordinary futures contracts. However, they are based on foreign currencies rather than commodities or indices.

Currency futures contracts are exclusively exchange-traded derivative instruments traded in exactly the same manner as ordinary futures contracts. However, they are based on foreign currencies rather than commodities or indices. Unlike ordinary FECs, they are standardised, and are fully binding obligations to buy or sell a particular currency against another currency at a future date at an agreed exchange rate determined by the market. This exchange rate is fixed at the time the contract is made.

After the currency future has been created, it becomes a fully tradable instrument in its own right, with both buying and selling prices quoted on recognised futures exchanges. It is important to understand that it is the currency futures contracts being traded, and not the underlying currencies. This is in contrast to FECs, where actual physical exchange of currencies themselves will ultimately occur.

The main exchanges for currency futures are the Chicago Mercantile Exchange, Tokyo Financial Exchange, Philadelphia Stock Exchange and Euronext.liffe.

The currency futures contract specification will include:

- relevant currencies, such as JPY/GBP;
- exchange rate, such as JPY145 = GBP1;
- contract size, such as minimum sterling = £62,500; and
- minimum trading value, such as three future contracts = £187,500.

If a company is buying three sterling future contracts with yen, they will cost a total of JPY27,187,500. Settlements are in March, June, September and December.

Standard FECs can be transacted for any amount and there is no standardisation.

5.1 Users of currency futures

Hedgers
Hedgers use currency futures in order to reduce risks and to hedge against FX risks by locking in an exchange rate. They wish to protect the positions from currency fluctuations. Hedgers tend to be large companies intending to minimise their exchange-rate exposure; this is particularly important for multinational corporations as exchange fluctuations can turn profits into losses.

Speculators
Speculators tend to take on more risk, hoping to make a profit by predicting currency movements. They take a more short-term view of the markets, their focus being trade currency futures, hoping to profit from exchange-rate differentials between currencies. Speculators incur added risk by attempting to profit from either rising or falling exchange rates.

5.2 Additional points

Currency futures are cash-settled without exchange of currencies. They are 'marked to market' daily, with margin requirements both initial and maintenance.

Secondary dealing can take place – this is not the case with FECs.

Stop and think 7.1

Make sure you understand the main differences between forward exchange contracts (FECs) and currency futures contracts.

6. Currency swaps

Currency swaps, sometimes referred to as cross-currency swaps are contractual agreements between two parties exchanging both principal and fixed interest in one currency for principal and fixed interest in another currency. Unlike interest rate swaps, which are in the same currency, they are in different currencies and they are not categorized as derivative instruments.

swap bank
A bank that is either directly or indirectly involved in a currency swap. If directly involved, it will be the counterparty to the swap. If indirectly involved, it will facilitate the relevant aspects of the currency swaps between corporate counterparties.

Furthermore, there are exchanges of principal amounts at both the start and the finish of the currency swap. This is in contrast to interest rate swaps, where there is no exchange of principal amounts (they are notional). Maturities may be up to 10 years. Although, technically, currency swaps are between two parties and can be between a corporate and a swap bank or a corporate and a corporate. In corporate-to-corporate swaps, there is a need to find a corporate with equal but opposite requirements and they will also involve a **swap bank.**

6.1 Uses

Currency swaps were initially devised to circumvent exchange-control regulations. However, other uses have evolved since, including:

- to hedge against potential exchange-rate losses;
- to exploit inefficiencies in international debt markets; and
- to be important sources of income for financial institutions.

Worked example 7.9

A US corporate needs to finance a project in Europe costing €100 million. In order to obtain the necessary finance it decides to issue loan stock, for €100 million repayable in two years' time with a coupon of 5% pa, payable in semi-annual instalments.

At this point, the US corporate has cash €100 million (obtained via its loan stock issue), to finance the European project, The corporate must service the € interest payments of 5% pa, payable semi-annually for the two-year period.

However, the company could enter into a swap agreement with another party (a bank) whereby it swaps its €100 million obligation at 5% pa for a US$ obligation at 3% pa. This fixed interest rate will be based on a specified index.

At the start of the swap, the US corporate swaps the €100 million (raised through the loan stock) with the bank, which assumes responsibility for the 5% coupon obligation (payable in Euros); this is paid to the company and in turn to the € loan-stock holders. The dates will be lined up so the repayment of the coupons by the bank to the corporate will coincide with the due date of the obligation of the company to the loan-stock holders.

if an exchange rate of US$1.40 = €1, this €100m is converted to US$ and the corporate receives US$140 million in exchange for € and agrees to pay to the bank a fixed 3% pa interest payment on the dollar obligation throughout the period to maturity.

At this point, from the perspective of the corporate, the obligation has been converted from a € obligation (paying 5% pa) into a US$ obligation (paying 3% pa).

The corporate will now use its US$140 million to generate US$ revenue, which it will need in order to repay its US$ loan at the end of the two-year period. At which time the corporate must repay the US$140 million to the bank, which is obliged to convert back to € at the pre-agreed rate of 1.40. The corporate will receive the € and will then repay its € loan stock. In effect, the corporate has entered into an FEC to buy €100 million at 1.40.

6.2 Additional points

A currency swap is considered an FX transaction rather than a loan. As a result, it does not appear on the balance sheet and as the principal amounts and interest payments are in different currencies, they cannot be netted.

Banks can tailor the terms of currency swaps to the needs of their customers.

6.3 Risks

There are two main risks associated with currency swaps:

1. credit risk: the risk that the corporate will not be able to deliver the principal at the end of the period; and
2. sovereign risk: a country may impose exchange-control restrictions that may affect the swap.

7. Carry trade

Carry trade is an FX strategy where investors hope to profit from the interest rate differential (IRD) between two currencies. An investor or speculator will borrow a currency incurring a low interest rate and then use the proceeds of that loan to purchase another currency yielding a higher rate of interest. Investors hope that the exchange rates will not move against them throughout the tenor of the loan; this could cancel out any profits that may have been gained through the IRD.

carry trade
An FX strategy where investors hope to profit from interest rate differentials (IRD) between currencies.

The 'carry' is the difference on the return on an investment product minus the rate of interest paid on the loan.

7.1 Methodology

An investor will borrow currency A incurring a low interest rate and convert the proceeds into another currency B, which is then invested in higher-yielding assets denominated in currency B.

A currency such as JPY is borrowed, incurring a low interest rate perhaps as low as, for example, 1% pa. This JPY loan is used to purchase Australian dollars (AUD). The AUD is then used to purchase an AUD-denominated bond yielding 6% pa. The hope is that the exchange rate between the two currencies will not move against the investor during the period of the yen loan, which must ultimately be repaid.

Assuming that there is no negative movement in the JPY/AUD exchange rates during (or, rather, at the end of) the period, the investor will receive the difference between 6% and 1% = 5% ('the carry').

Eventually the JPY loan must be repaid. Therefore, the maturity date of the overseas bond should be harmonised with the loan repayment.

Worked example 7.10

The following assumes the Japanese yen is the borrowed currency, and the British pound is the invested currency, and also supposes that an investor borrows JPY100 million at 1% pa and the exchange rate is JPY130 = GBP1.

The JPY100 million are converted to £769,230.77, which is subsequently invested in UK government gilts.

Assuming that the sterling bonds (gilts) pay 3% p.a. they would yield £23,076.92 per annum. The carry is therefore 3% – 1% = 2%.

If the exchange rate has not changed by the time the loan repayment is due, then interest charges will be JPY1 million at an exchange rate of 130 = £7,692.31. The profit is therefore £15,384.61 pa (£23,076.92 – £7,692.31).

Carry trade tends to weaken the currency that is borrowed, because it is sold to buy another currency.

If the JPY rate fell to JPY160:GBP1, there would be additional profit on the exchange rate in that the investor would only have to pay back £625,000 plus interest of £6,250.

Conversely, if the rate changed to JPY100:GBP1, the investor would have to pay £1 million plus £10,000, thus cancelling out any carry-trade profit.

Worked example 7.10 shows that an investor can profit in two ways:

1. from the carry, as stated in the example; and
2. if the exchange rates move in their favour with currency borrowed depreciating considerably by the time the Yen loan becomes repayable. When the sterling bond matures, they can sell at an exchange profit.

7.2 Risks

There are two main risks in relation to carry trade:

1. If the borrowed currency appreciates considerably, this could cancel out any carry trade profits, as the investor still has to pay back the borrowed currency, which may now cost considerably more of the invested currency.
2. The carry margin may narrow.

Historically the three main currencies borrowed were the CHF, USD and JPY. The currencies purchased were the AUD, NZD and GBP. Nowadays the currencies offering higher yields are those of the emerging markets, but higher returns are linked to greater risks. However, there are still opportunities available in riskier currencies offering over 10%, such as the South African rand (ZAR).

Chapter summary

- The money market may be considered as a mechanism by which its main users are able to move around large amounts of money from those institutions with cash surpluses to those institutions requiring short-term funds, in contrast to the capital markets (consisting of shares and bonds) which allow institutions to raise capital for long-term purposes, usually in excess of a year.
- It is essentially that area of the financial markets where instruments with high liquidity and short-term maturities are traded. It is the arena where large financial institutions and governments resolve their short-term funding requirements and excesses. As a result of the highly liquid nature of the inherent money market instruments combined with their short-term maturities, the money market is regarded as very safe. MMIs cannot be issued by individuals.
- There are a number of money market instruments that facilitate this process which fall into two broad categories: those issued at a discount to face value and those paying coupons. The short-term nature and the vast size of money market transactions cannot be overemphasised.
- Spot and forward exchange contracts have their own unique characteristics. Both are considered as OTC products, as there are no central exchanges.
- Numerous factors may affect exchange rates including political and economic considerations together with inflation and balance of payments surplus or deficit.

- Currency futures are exchange-traded products in contrast with spot and forward exchange contracts.
- Currency swaps are contractual agreements between two parties swapping principal and fixed interest in one currency for principal and fixed interest in another currency. Unlike interest rate swaps (which are in the same currency), currency swaps are in different currencies.
- Currency swaps are not derivative instruments.
- Carry trade is an FX strategy where speculators hope to profit from interest rate differentials (IRDs) between two currencies. A speculator borrows a currency incurring a low interest rate and then uses the proceeds of that loan to purchase another currency yielding a higher rate of interest. The hope is that exchange rates will not move against them and cancel out any profits that may have been gained via the IRD. Carry trade may be summarised thus:
  - An investor will borrow a currency that incurs a low rate of interest, currency **A.**
  - Currency **A** is converted into currency **B**.
  - Invest the converted currency **B** into a product, perhaps a government bond or another fixed-interest security, which is itself denominated in currency **B** and crucially earning a higher rate of return than the interest being charged on the loan denominated in currency **A**.
  - At the end of maturity period for the fixed interest security the investor will receive both capital and interest in currency **B** and convert back into currency **A**, using the proceeds to pay off loan in currency **A**.

  The investor will hope to profit on the interest rate differential between currencies **A** and **B**.

Test yourself answers

Test yourself 7.1

a) The money market may be considered as a mechanism by which its key participants can move around large amounts of money from those institutions with cash surpluses to those institutions requiring short-term funds.

There are a number of money market instruments that facilitate this mechanism. The instruments fall into two broad categories: those issued at a discount to face value and those paying coupons.

The short-term nature and the vast size of money market transactions cannot be overemphasised.

b) The key participants in the money markets include:
- governments;
- central banks;
- commercial banks, including overseas banks; and
- large national and multinational corporations insurance companies and pension funds.

Test yourself 7.2

In the primary market, T-Bills are issued by the DMO on a weekly basis to market makers through a competitive tender process, which takes place on the last business day of each week. Settlement is T+1 (that is, on the next business day). An announcement is made each Monday in the *Financial Times* with the details of the previous week's tender.

When the bills have been acquired in the primary market, they become fully tradable securities and specialist brokers will quote two-way prices to subsequent buyers and sellers in the secondary market.

Tenders are usually oversubscribed, with the minimum accepted bids being the lowest made that is sufficient to dispose of the entire offer. Such bids must be lower than face value in order for a holder to make a profit. The tender process means that all successful tenderers will pay the same price; this is in contrast with auctions, where bidders will pay different prices.

All bids must specify the maturity (for example, one month or three months) of bills being bid for which must be made on a money market yield basis and there is no limit to the number of bids that can be submitted by any one tenderer. The DMO ranks all received bids for each maturity on offer by yield and all bids must be received by 11 a.m. on the day of tender.

While the tender process is underway for the current week's issue, the DMO will announce details of the following week's issues, including tender size and the maturities of the bills on offer. Announcements are available on the DMO's wire service and also Reuters Registration.

CREST constitutes the central register of T-Bill ownership with the legal title being evidenced by the entry of a given number of units against a holder's name in the relevant CREST record, which may also be held in Euroclear.

Test yourself 7.3

a) Commercial paper (CP), which is often nicknamed 'corporate IOUs', is a short-term money market instrument that is issued and used by large companies as a cheaper alternative to bank borrowing. It is issued as a method of raising short-term unsecured finance. Finance raised through the issuance of CP is used to fund daily operations such as the payment of wages and the purchasing of stock. However, it would be used neither to purchase fixed assets, such as plant and machinery, nor to provide finance for long-term capital projects.

Companies can issue CP directly to investors rather than have banks acting as intermediaries.

b) CD yields are dependent upon the:

- credit rating of the issue;
- amount invested; and
- level of interest rates for the currency in which the currency is denominated.

Test yourself 7.4

a) A spot FX contract is a binding obligation between two parties where one party agrees to sell a currency to another party in exchange for a different currency.

b) Many factors influence the way in which exchange rates may fluctuate. In reality, all exchange rates are influenced to some extent by the forces of demand and supply.

Factors include:

- yield differential;
- government budget surplus or deficit;
- balance of payments;
- economic conditions;
- political considerations;
- inflation rates;
- natural resources; and
- non-political events.

Part four

Chapter 8
Fixed-interest securities

Chapter 9
Collective investment schemes

Bonds and collective investments

Overview

This Part covers fixed-interest securities (also known as fixed-income securities) such as bonds, corporate bonds and eurobonds.

It then looks at the various types of collective investment schemes available to investors, both open-ended and closed-ended, including an explanation of their similarities and differences, and concludes with an assessment of these schemes.

Learning outcomes

At the end of this Part, you will:

- know about fixed-interest securities;
- understand the characteristics of different types of bonds;
- understand the risks involved in investing in bonds; and
- understand collective schemes and their inherent features.

Chapter eight
Fixed-interest securities

List of topics

1. Fixed-interest securities
2. Bonds
3. UK government bonds (gilts)
4. Corporate bonds
5. Eurobonds
6. Methods of eliminating or reducing bond-related risks

Introduction

This chapter introduces the very important topic of fixed-interest, or fixed-income, securities. These securities usually pay an annual fixed rate of interest, known as a coupon, which does not vary with any external factor, for example an increase or decrease in external market interest rates (LIBOR). The coupon values are known from the outset (the time of purchase), and are usually for the same amount and paid at regular intervals, usually semi-annually.

There are a number of exceptions to the coupon payments, most notably zero-coupon bonds which, although classed as fixed interest securities, do not actually pay coupons or fixed interest. The most important of all fixed-interest securities are bonds. This includes government bonds (whether domestic or overseas), corporate bonds, and eurobonds. Each of these instruments will be discussed in turn. The nature of the bond market tends to be longer term, compared, with the shorter-term nature of money markets instruments. From the perspective of the bond issuer, they will not need to repay the principal for many years hence. This does not preclude bonds being actively traded in the secondary market.

1. Fixed-interest securities

The main group of fixed-interest securities are bonds. This includes:

- government bonds (domestic or overseas);
- corporate bonds; and
- **Eurobonds**.

Eurobond
A bond which is issued and traded outside the jurisdiction of the country in whose currency the bond is denominated.

2. Bonds

The most common and most significant of all fixed-interest security instruments are bonds, and in contrast to certain other financial markets, such as derivatives, the bond market is rather less complicated. However, derivatives based on fixed interest investments do exist and are actively traded in the derivatives markets. Before providing a definition of a bond, it is perhaps pertinent to consider the relevant participants involved in this market.

*Note that premium bonds are not classed as fixed interest securities; rather they are savings products, issued by NS&I (National Savings and Investments).

2.1 The parties to a bond

Bond issuer (also referred to as the borrower or debtor)
This is the party that issues the bond to a purchaser, in exchange for a capital sum. The bond may be issued directly to a purchaser, or indirectly through a third-party intermediary. Issuers include national governments, local authorities and companies, and other supranational entities (those having power that transcends national boundaries or governments).

Initial purchaser (also referred to as the lender, creditor, or investor)
This is the party supplying the initial capital sum to the issuer in exchange for the bond. Again, a third-party intermediary may be involved.

The bondholder (or current owner)
This is the party that has current ownership of the bond, which may have been purchased in the primary market, or through the secondary market, probably through a broker.

The bondholder may or may not be the initial purchaser. Indeed, a bond may have a number of different holders up to its final maturity date, given that bonds may be purchased and sold any number of times in the secondary market, and the fact that the maturity date may be many years from the date of issue. At maturity, the bond issuer has a contractual obligation to pay the principal amount and final coupon, if applicable, to the final holder.

2.2 Types of bonds

As stated in the introduction to this chapter, all bonds are categorised as fixed-interest securities, even though there are certain types of bond that do not actually pay any interest at all. However, all bonds could be considered as being of a similar nature to IOUs, even though some are irredeemable (see section 2.5). All bonds will contain some, or all, of the characteristics of straight bonds, which are discussed next.

Straight bonds

Bonds have many different styles and forms, with the simplest form of bond being referred to as a straight bond. This is the basic 'model', paying a fixed coupon for a specified period. A straight bond will be redeemed at face value at maturity, when the issuer cancels the bond. Although there are many variations of bond, all are based on straight bonds, and indeed the vast majority of bonds still tend to be of this nature.

A straight bond is a long-term, negotiable, fixed-interest debt security, containing absolute contractual obligations whereby the issuer borrows a fixed amount of capital (referred to as the principal amount or face value) from another party, referred to as the purchaser, for a specific period. The straight bond is redeemed on a predetermined date, known as the redemption date or maturity date. Fixed-interest payments (usually paid annually or semi-annually – there are some anomalies), known as coupons, will be made to the current holder throughout the life of the bond.

An issuer of a straight bond has two distinct and absolute contractual obligations (the specific details being contained within the bond's original offering notice/prospectus, which investors should study before making any investment):

1. to repay the principal amount to the current bondholder on a specific future date (redemption date or maturity date); and
2. to make regular fixed-interest rate payments (coupons) to the holder at predetermined intervals throughout the bond's life, up to and including the redemption date.

* Issuers are not obliged to return the principal amount until the final maturity date.

This definition of a straight bond includes, as one of its contractual obligations, the regular payment of interest. However, there are certain bonds that do not make any coupon payments at all (these are referred to as zero-coupon bonds and are outlined in section 2.4).

All bonds promise some form of return, whether in the form of the coupon, or alternatively, in the case of zero-coupon bonds, the promise of enhanced capital growth.

It should be emphasised that, although the issuer has made a contractual obligation to return the principal amount to the final holder at maturity, the amount received by the holder will only be the principal amount and not the price paid. The price paid could be at a discount or premium to the principal amount, so the true return may be more or less than the coupon rate. It should also be borne in mind that if bonds are issued at a premium or discount, the borrower is only committed to paying the principal amount at maturity. If, at first issue, bonds are issued at a premium, issuers will receive more than the principal amount, and thus their cost of borrowing will be reduced. However, if bonds are issued at a discount to the principal amount, their cost of borrowing will increase. Once in the secondary market, the issuer will not benefit nor be adversely affected by a price movement of their bonds.

Making it work 8.1: The users and uses of bonds

Bonds are issued by various parties as long-term debt securities. Bonds are used to finance long-term capital projects, in the case of companies, and to part-finance government deficits, in the case of gilts. This is in contrast to money-market instruments, where the focus is short term.

For example, when this book was last updated in 2014, the price of oil reached in excess of US$140 a barrel, and a number of Gulf countries had vast budget surpluses. The price of oil in 2018 is now in the region of US$75 a barrel. The same countries now have to rely on the issue of debt securities, including government bonds and eurobonds, to finance their huge infrastructure projects, as their oil income will be insufficient. Remember that, unlike companies, sovereign states cannot issue ordinary or preference shares.

The UK government issues gilts (a type of bond) to part-finance the deficit (gap) between its revenue and its expenditure. Local authorities issue bonds to finance long-term local capital projects, while companies issue bonds to raise long-term finance, without giving up equity or taking out bank borrowing. Countries may issue eurobonds to raise debt in international markets.

2.3 Features of bonds

All bonds have a number of generic features, which include the following.

Negotiability

Bonds are bought and sold in both the primary and the secondary markets. Negotiability will depend on the credit rating of the particular bond issue, as assigned by various rating agencies.

Historically, bonds were issued in paper form and some bonds are still issued in this form. However, most are now 'dematerialised' (held and traded electronically).

Nominal amount

The bond nominal amount is a unit amount. It is not the same as the principal amount, or face value (which is in fact a multiple of the nominal amount). Typically, but not exclusively, in the UK the bond nominal amount is £100, whereas in the USA this tends to be $1,000. This needs to be checked in the particular bond's prospectus.

The nominal amount is also the figure upon which coupon rates are based.

All bonds, whether redeemable or irredeemable, must have a stated fixed nominal amount. This is necessary in order that:

1. coupons can be set where applicable (not applicable to zero-coupon bonds); and
2. investors will know exactly how much will be received at maturity (not applicable to **irredeemable bonds**). There are, at the time of writing (June 2018), no irredeemable gilts in circulation; however, this does not preclude their reintroduction In the future.

irredeemable bonds
Bonds which may be redeemed at the discretion of the issuer, but for which no redemption date has actually been specified.

Principal amount

The principal amount is the face value of the bond – that is, the total amount of money the holder will receive at maturity. It is a multiple of the nominal amount (the purchaser may pay a premium or discount to acquire a bond, but will only be entitled to receive the principal amount at maturity).

A bond may, for example, be for a principal amount of £50,000, but this is still based on £100 nominal. It is important to remember that an investor may actually pay more (a premium) or less (a discount) than the face value of the bond in the relevant bond market. This will depend on a number of factors including:

- prevailing market interest rates; and
- supply and demand for the bonds per se.

Principal amount (Face value) = Bond nominal amount × Number of units purchased or sold

Bond price

The bond price is the amount a purchaser must actually pay in order to acquire the bond, whether at first issue in the primary market or in the secondary market. The price paid may be the same as the face value, but this is not necessarily the case. Even at first issue date, the bond price may be at a premium or at a discount to face value.

Maturity date (redemption date)

The period to maturity (also referred to as its tenor) can be any length of time. It can even be irredeemable in the case of perpetual (everlasting) bonds.

The maturity date is the future date when the principal amount must be returned to the final holder by the issuer, and when the bond will be redeemed and cancelled by the issuer. The failure to return principal and/or the final coupon at maturity will be deemed to be default by the issuer.

* Issuers are not obliged to return the principal to a holder any time before final maturity date. They are only concerned with the payment of coupons, if applicable.

2.4 Coupons

The coupon, also referred to as the interest payment, is shown as an annual percentage of the nominal amount. It is the monetary amount that the issuer must pay annually (usually paid in semi-annual instalments) to the holder throughout the life of the bond. Historically, all bonds were issued in paper form, with coupons that could be torn off and presented to the issuer for payment of interest as it became due. This is no longer the case.

As bonds are categorised as fixed-interest securities, the coupon rate tends also to be fixed (straight bonds) until maturity. However, the rate can also be linked to an index such as LIBOR (London Interbank Offered Rate). Although the coupon represents the annual interest rate, the physical payment may be made annually; alternatively it may be split into semi-annual, or even quarterly payments.

Coupons are categorised into two distinct groups: predetermined and variable.

The coupon rate, set at the time of first issue, is decided by many factors, including prevailing market interest rates and the credit rating of the particular bond issue, and also the bond's period to maturity.

From the purchaser's point of view, there is absolute preservation of capital; that is, it is not lost (unless of course the issuer becomes insolvent).

Coupon types

- Straight bonds (also known as fixed-coupon bonds): this applies to the vast majority of bonds, where coupons are fixed throughout the life of the bond.
- Stepped coupon bonds: the coupon rate increases in steps to pre-stated amounts throughout the duration of the bond.

Zero-coupon bonds

As the name implies, zero-coupon bonds neither have coupons nor provide interest payments of any kind, being redeemed at face value at maturity. The final holder realises a capital gain when the bond is redeemed, as the bonds are sold at a substantial discount to their face value. There are obviously no income tax implications (given that there are no coupons and hence no income), but there may well be implications relating to capital gains tax (CGT), depending on a particular investor's tax position.

The advantage to the issuer of zero-coupon bonds is that coupon payments do not have to be made when cash flow may be low. By way of an example, at the conclusion of an infrastructure project, when cash flow may be healthier, issuers may redeem the bond, even though at maturity its redemption price is at a significant premium to the original issue price. This might be preferable to making regular interest payments, if a straight bond had been issued. It will also reduce the administrative burden and associated costs in this respect.

Variable coupons

Floating-rate bonds have a coupon linked to an interest rate index, for example LIBOR. The coupons could be 0.25% above LIBOR, or alternatively might be linked to a Treasury bill rate.

index-linked gilts
Gilts where both coupons and the final redemption payment are related to movements in the retail prices index. IGs should extinguish the impact of inflation; however, at the time of writing interest rates are historically low.

Index-linked bonds have both the coupon and the maturity proceeds linked to an index. The coupons and redemption values of UK **index-linked gilts**, for example, are linked to the UK Retail Prices Index (RPI).

2.5 Redeemable and irredeemable bonds

Traditionally, all bonds were issued with a specific redemption date. Nowadays, however, there are a number of variations, which are considered later in this chapter. Bonds fall into two broad sub-categories: redeemable and irredeemable (the latter are also referred to as perpetual bonds, or 'perpetuals').

Redeemable bonds

As the name suggests, these are bonds that will be redeemed, and will have a specific maturity date or a range of maturity dates when the principal will be repaid to the bondholder.

Redeemable bonds include:

- single-dated bonds: bonds maturing on one pre-stated future date only; and
- double-dated bonds: bonds that may be redeemed by the bond issuer any time between the two dates specified in the prospectus/offering letter.

With double-dated bonds, the earlier date is the date when the issuer *may* redeem, and the later date is when the issuer *must* redeem. The choice of redemption date is the issuer's, not the holder's. If the issuer fails to redeem by the later date, this will be deemed to be default.

Irredeemable bonds

Irredeemable bonds are so-called because they do not have a stated maturity date, and there is no obligation for issuers to redeem the bonds (although they are able to do so, should they so wish). Coupons will be paid in perpetuity (forever). Consequently, bondholders must sell in the secondary market in order to realise any capital sum, whether making a profit or incurring a loss.

The most famous of all irredeemable bonds were 2½% Consolidated Stock and 3½% War Loan, which were both UK government bonds (gilts). Both of these were redeemed in 2015 because market rates were lower than the coupon rates payable on these gilts; consequently the UK government could borrow more cheaply by issuing gilts with lower coupons.

It was interesting to note that the closing price of 3½% War Loan, on 22 August 2014, was 90.88 pence. However, the price varied throughout the course of the year, between a high of 92.26 pence, and a low of 78.65 pence per share, representing a 17.3% increase between the high and low. Astute investors with large holdings could have profited considerably.

2.6 Callable bonds

Callable bonds effectively contain an embedded call facility, where the bond issuer has the right, but not the obligation, to redeem the bond before its specified maturity date, under certain criteria that will obviously be advantageous to the issuer. The issuer will call in the bond and pay the face value to the current holder.

callable bond
A bond which has the potential to be 'called' by its issuer under certain circumstances which are advantageous to that issuer (contrast with 'puttable' bonds).

The decision to call a bond rests with the bond issuer, not the holder. This must be contrasted with puttable bonds discussed subsequently. Coupons on callable bonds tend to be higher than for straight bonds, in order to compensate the holder for the possibility of the bond being called early by the issuer.

If an investor were to purchase a callable bond, with a coupon of perhaps 5%, while interest rates for similar securities in the market were 4.95%, there would probably be little chance of the bond being called by the issuer. If market rates were 6%, there would be no likelihood of the bond being called. If, on the other hand, rates in the market were 2%, which would allow the bond issuer to borrow more cheaply elsewhere, the issuer would almost certainly call in the bond, and perhaps issue new bonds at, say, 2.25%. At the time of issue of the bond, the terms and times under which a bond can be called will be outlined in the prospectus.

Callable bonds will include **call protection**, giving a specific time after issue when the bonds cannot be called.

call protection
A period of time after a callable bond has been issued during which it will not be 'called'. This is to afford the investor a certain degree of protection.

Risks of callable bonds

Investors are exposed to what is termed 'reinvestment risk' because they are expecting a fixed coupon for a fixed period. If, however, the bond is called, this expectation will not be met, and the investor may have to reinvest elsewhere at a far lower rate. Alternatively, in order to obtain a similar coupon, the investor may have to purchase a bond with a higher risk, perhaps a junk bond, rather than an investment grade bond.

2.7 Puttable bonds

Puttable bonds are those containing an embedded put facility, giving the holder a right, without any obligation, to force the issuer to redeem the bond before the official maturity date. In other words, the holder can 'put' their bond to the issuer for repayment before the bond's maturity date. The put price that the issuer must pay to the holder is usually 100% of the face value. The decision to redeem rests with the bondholder and not the issuer.

In this case, the price of a puttable bond will be somewhat higher than for a straight bond, given that it is a form of protection for a purchaser. If an investor purchases a puttable bond and market rates then rise, making the bond coupons worth less in real terms, this provides the holder with an option to sell the bond and reinvest the proceeds elsewhere for a higher coupon. For this reason, the price of a puttable bond will be higher than a straight bond because of the additional cost of providing the embedded put facility and, as a result of this increased price, the yield on a puttable bond is lower than for a straight bond.

Crucially, the investor cannot exercise the put facility on any date prior to maturity, but only on particular dates as specified in the original offering letter.

2.8 Bond credit ratings

The lower the credit rating of the bond, the higher the coupon rate will tend to be. This is because of the perception of increased risk. Whereas a triple-A rated bond may have a coupon of, say, 1%, issuers with poor bond credit ratings may have to agree to, say, 3%, or 4% for a particular issue.

Test yourself 8.1

a) **Who are the main parties to a bond?**

b) **What is a straight bond?**

c) **What is the difference between a redeemable and an irredeemable bond?**

d) **Explain both callable and puttable bonds.**

e) **What are the obligations of bond issuers?**

3. UK government bonds (gilts)

Gilts are fully marketable and registered UK government, sterling-denominated bonds. They are issued by the Debt Management Office (DMO), on behalf of HM Treasury, as part of its debt management responsibilities. They are UK government liabilities, issued in sterling, and listed on the London Stock Exchange.

Today, their primary characteristic is security. They are called gilts because, historically, they were certificates with gold-leaf (gilding) around their borders. They have been issued by the DMO since 1998. Previously this function had been undertaken by the Bank of England. The market for government bonds (gilts) is a mature market. Indeed, the first marketable UK government debt security was issued in the eighteenth century. A mature market is one where the rate of growth has slowed, but the market still functions, however, it is characterised by the lack of innovation. Effectively, supply and demand are equal.

Central Government Net Cash Requirement (CGNCR)
This is the measurement of the annual cash requirements of central government. It is essentially the difference between central government's income and expenditure, in cash terms.

Gilts are issued in order to part finance the:

1. **Central Government Net Cash Requirement (CGNCR)**, which is the difference between the government's expenditure and income;
2. the annual repayment of maturing gilts; and
3. the payment of existing gilt coupons.

Gilts are deemed to be extremely safe investments, because it is widely thought that the UK government will not default on its obligations in relation to either principal or interest payments. To date, the UK government has neither defaulted on principal amounts, nor interest payments as they have fallen due. However, this is not impossible. Reference should be made to the Greek crisis in 2016, where there was a possibility the Greek government would default on its debt.

In 1980, the total size of the gilts market was £71 billion, rising to £478 billion in 2008. As of March 2018, this had risen to £1,547 billion, nominal. This is an indication of the vast size of the UK government deficit. It must be noted that gilt coupon payments must be serviced at regular intervals, representing a cash outflow from the government; therefore it is imperative that the UK government maintains its high credit rating for gilts, in order that it may continue to issue new gilts, which effectively results in it not having to redeem its imminent gilts.

Even if coupon rates are as low as 1%, based on £1,547 billion nominal outstanding, this still represents annual interest payments of over £15.47 billion. There are, however, gilts with coupon payments far in excess of 1%. These include 6% Treasury stock, first Issued in 1998, and 8% Treasury stock 2021, which was first issued in February 1996. This particular gilt was a long-term one when issued, but now would be classed as short-term.

The gilt market is now composed of only two types of gilt: Conventional and Index linked. There are no longer any double dated or irredeemable gilts in issue.

Gilts are suitable for private investors seeking low risk and also for institutional investors such as pension funds and insurance companies, which use gilts to match their known future liabilities. Pension funds tend to use long-dated gilts.

It is important to observe the relationship: the investor buying gilts is the creditor, whereas the party selling gilts, the UK government, is the debtor, because it has an increased liability.

The UK gilts market is composed entirely of two types of securities: **conventional gilts** and index-linked gilts.

The vast majority of dealing in gilts takes place over-the-counter (OTC), either on the telephone or through electronic trading platforms, which are neither operated nor controlled by the LSE. However, gilts are deemed to be 'on exchange' products; as such they are listed securities on the LSE.

3.1 The participants in the UK gilt market

The key participants in the UK gilts market are:

- dealers/traders who buy and sell Gilts for their own purposes;
- the Debt Management Office (DMO);
- **gilt-edged market makers (GEMMs)**; and
- **inter-dealer brokers (IDBs)**.

conventional gilts
Gilts where both the principal repayments and coupons are fixed in nominal terms.

gilt-edged market makers (GEMMs)
These are firms that have been recognised by the DMO as primary dealers in conventional gilts. There are also IL GEMMs specialising in index-linked gilts. They are prepared to make prices (at all times the market is open) to investors.

inter-dealer brokers (IDBs)
Firms, authorised by the DMO and LSE, providing facilities for dealing in gilts exclusively between GEMMs.

The Debt Management Office (DMO)

The DMO is an executive agency of HM Treasury and, as its name suggests, it has responsibility for the management of government debt, which it achieves through its participation in the gilt market. It has as its main objective the reduction, over the longer term, of the cost of meeting the government's financing needs, while also considering the risks involved in achieving this. It must be emphasised that the DMO's objective is not necessarily reducing the size of the debt, but reducing the cost of financing the debt.

The DMO is the issuer of gilts, operating in both the primary and the secondary markets. It not only controls the issue of gilts but also ensures that the market remains solvent. Its functions include maintaining an orderly and regulated environment, and ensuring investor protection. It also confers or revokes primary dealer status, and controls the entry and exit of GEMMs, and indeed holds gilts itself in order to help manage the market.

While the DMO has a mandate (an official order) to maintain the health of the market as a whole by keeping it liquid and orderly, it is actually the FCA that has the responsibility for the overseeing of individual GEMMs' operations in the gilt market, in terms of risks and balance sheet capabilities.

Gilt-edged market makers (GEMMs)

GEMMs are primary dealers in the UK gilt market, trading in conventional gilts, indexed gilts, or both. As of 1 May 2018, there were 21 GEMMs, three of which deal from a retail perspective, while only one deals solely in conventional gilts.

Examples of GEMMs include:

- Abbey National Treasury Services;
- Barclays Bank plc;
- Citigroup Global Markets;
- Deutsche Bank AG (London Branch);
- HSBC Bank plc;
- JP Morgan Securities plc; and
- Nomura International plc.

They are competing market makers, providing liquidity in the primary market, and are comprised of banks or securities firms that have been endorsed by the DMO as primary dealers in UK government bonds. They must be registered as market makers on an RIE (recognised investment exchange), and authorised by the FCA, either directly, or under the terms of an EEA passport, and must also satisfy certain obligations if they want to retain their primary dealer status. Wholesale GEMMs specialise in market making to institutional investors, whereas retail GEMMs service clients dealing in smaller amounts. In the primary market, in which they are granted special privileges, GEMMs are the only institutions that are able to bid directly in the DMO gilt auctions. This means that all other market participants wishing to bid at gilt auctions must do so through a GEMM. In the gilt secondary market, the DMO will only deal with GEMMs.

GEMMs are expected to make two-way prices (buying and selling) on demand to any of their clients and at all times, and in any market conditions, in all gilt-edged securities in which they have been recognised as a primary dealer. Additionally, they will provide the DMO with market intelligence, make possible gilt transfers from the DMO to other investors, and will also provide the figures for the overall daily turnover to the DMO.

Inter-dealer brokers (IDBs)

IDBs are broking firms, endorsed by the DMO, that are committed to deal exclusively with GEMMs. They act as principal to all gilt trades, and are intermediaries for anonymous trading between GEMMs, allowing them to unwind any unwanted long or short gilt positions. As all trades are conducted anonymously, any relevant information is retained within GEMMs and not distributed to the wider market. IDBs are not permitted to offer their services outside of this community, or to take principal positions on their own account, except where they are dealing on a matched principal basis with corresponding buying and selling counterparties.

Examples of IDBs in the UK include:

- BGC Brokers LP;
- BrokerTec Europe Limited;
- Dowgate;
- GFI Securities Limited;
- ICAP WCLK Limited; and
- Tullet Prebon Gilts.

Test yourself 8.2

a) Why are gilts issued?

b) What are the two main types of gilt?

c) Explain the functions of GEMMs.

d) What are the functions of the DMO?

3.2 The purchase and sale of gilts

All gilts are fully marketable securities, and as such, their prices are liable to fluctuate throughout each business day.

Most gilt sales (over 80%) are by pre-announced auctions. However, they may also be executed by methods including syndicated offerings and mini-tenders. These two additional methods have been used to enhance the sale of long-dated conventional and index-linked gilts. Since 2007, gilt auctions have been conducted using electronic bidding.

The relatively new Post Auction Option Facility (PAOF) allows those bidders who were successful at auctions to buy up to an additional 10% of the gilts they purchased earlier. The purchase price of the additional gilts will be the average accepted, or strike price, at the auction, and this option is only available between 12 noon and 2 p.m. on the day of the auction.

Gilts can be purchased directly through the DMO at its outright auctions. In this case, there are two methods of purchase:

1. Bidders at auctions may bid via a GEMM that deals directly with the DMO and has direct electronic bidding links via the Bloomberg bond auction system and additionally by telephone. Successful competitive bidders in conventional gilt auctions are allotted gilts on a bid-price basis, which means actually paying the price they bid.
2. Alternatively, investors may complete an application form, on the condition that they are members of the DMO's approved group of investors.

Gilts are also traded in the secondary market, where prices will fluctuate according to short-term interest rates, expectations for inflation, and indeed the supply and demand for gilts themselves. All of these factors will exert a significant influence on the price movement of gilts.

Investors may buy and sell gilts in the secondary market through a stockbroker, bank, or the DMO's purchase and sale service, operated by **Computershare**, which also has the responsibility for maintaining the register of gilt holdings.

There are many different names for gilts, including Annuities, Exchequer, Conversion, and Treasury. Their names are, in many ways, irrelevant, and are used only to denote which government department issued the gilts. All gilts rank equally, given that they are all government debt. Since 2005–06, all new gilts have been named Treasury gilts.

The different ways in which gilts are classified are outlined below.

3.3 Conventional gilts

Conventional gilts are the least complex of all government bonds, make up the largest share in the UK government's liability portfolio and, in fact, make up about 75% of the overall gilt portfolio. They are government bonds with an absolute guarantee given by the UK government to pay the holder a coupon every six months until maturity. At maturity, the holder will receive not only the original principal but also the final coupon.

Pricing of conventional gilts

The prices of conventional gilts are quoted in terms of £100 nominal, and can be traded in units as small as one penny. It is possible to buy a specific nominal amount of gilts at a discount or premium on face value.

The minimum amount of gilts that can be purchased is £1,000 even though gilts are priced in terms of £100 nominal. However, it is still possible to buy a specific amount perhaps £1000.01 as long as the minimum purchase is made.

Worked example 8.1

An investor wishes to purchase a specific amount of a particular gilt: £10,000 worth of £100 nominal of Treasury 8% 2021.

If the market price of the gilt were £133.33 per £100 nominal, then the investor's outlay would be £13,333.00.

Alternatively, it is possible to invest a specific capital amount: £21,211.01, for instance, would equate to 159.08 gilts.

Conventional gilts are denoted by their coupon rates, for example:

4% Treasury gilts 2060, issued in October 2009.

6% Treasury stock 2028.

The coupon rate specified before the name of the gilt is a reflection of the prevailing market interest rates at the time the gilt was first issued, combined with the period to maturity at the time of the first issue.

4% Treasury 2060 indicates that for every £100 nominal, the holder will receive £4 interest per annum, paid as two semi-annual payments of £2, whereas the nominal amount of £100 will be paid in 2060. These particular coupons are paid in January and July.

6% Treasury 2028 indicates that for every £100 nominal, the holder will receive £6 interest per annum, which will be made as two semi-annual payments of £3 each, whereas the nominal amount of £100 will be paid in 2028. These particular coupons are paid in June and December.

The coupon payments are made on fixed dates six months apart. However, where payment falls due on a non-business day, it will be made on the following business day.

If an investor had a holding of £100,000 nominal of Treasury 4% 2060, they would be entitled to an annual coupon of 4% per annum (£4,000 pa); that is, two payments of £2,000 each, paid every 22 January and 22 July, up to final maturity in 2060.

Traditionally, gilts have been issued with maturities of 5, 10 and 30 years, but in June 2013 the UK government issued a conventional gilt with a maturity date in 2068: 3½% Treasury 2068; and in September of the same year, the government issued 1/8% indexed linked Treasury Gilt 2068.The price of a gilt will gravitate towards the nominal value as it approaches its maturity date.

Irrespective of how much an investor pays for a conventional gilt (premium or discount), and whether purchased in the primary or secondary markets, they will only ever receive the principal amount at maturity.

3.4 Gilt maturities

Gilts are classified according to their maturity dates.

- **Shorts** are those gilts with less than seven years to maturity (sometimes split into shorts and ultra-shorts).
- **Mediums** are gilts with between seven and 15 years to maturity.
- **Longs** are gilts with more than 15 years to maturity (note the 2068 gilt issued in June 2013).

This classification of maturity is not based on the first issue date, rather it is the amount of time remaining until redemption, taken from the date of purchase (which can of course be when first issued), or the date of purchase in the secondary market. Consequently, a long-dated gilt will become a medium-dated gilt, then a short-dated gilt, up to redemption. Prices of short-dated gilts tend to be relatively close to par value as the redemption date approaches.

3.5 Index-linked gilts (IGs)

Index-linked gilts (IGs) ensure a return above the rate of inflation throughout their duration.

They are second only to conventional gilts as part of the government's overall gilt portfolio, and were first issued to institutional investors in 1981. The coupons on IGs, as with those of conventional gilts, reflect market rates at the time of issue. The secondary market in IGs is very illiquid, because most holders will retain them until their maturity dates.

The important point to note is that index-linked coupons reflect the real rate for the government borrowing contrasted with the nominal borrowing rate, so there is much smaller variation in real yields over time. The amount of interest will be lower than for conventional gilts because of the index linking of the capital.

In contrast to conventional gilts, both the principal and the coupons are altered in line with the RPI (Retail Prices Index). Coupons, and the principal paid on redemption, are adjusted to take into account accrued (built-up) inflation since the first issue of the IG. The rationale underpinning indexed-linked gilts is that an investor ought to be able to purchase the same amount of goods and services with the capital sum at redemption, as they could have done at the time of first issue.

clean price
In relation to bonds, this is the price without taking into account the accrued interest since the last coupon payment.

IGs trade on what is known as the real **clean price**, which means that the inflation element is stripped out of the price of new gilts for trading purposes (although it is included when the trades are settled). Effectively the government borrowing rate is more or less equal to the investor's rate of return. Furthermore, in relation to the index-linked coupon, the uplift is based on the uplifted principal. There are formulae available for calculating these and, although they are straightforward, they are rather detailed and are outside the scope of the Investment syllabus.

3.6 Other types of gilts

Double-dated conventional gilts

Double-dated conventional gilts are as standard conventional gilts, however, rather than a single redemption date, they have two. As of August 2014, there were no double-dated conventional gilts outstanding. However, this does not preclude the UK government from issuing them in the future if it considers this to be appropriate. The government can redeem **double-dated gilts** at any time between the first redemption date and the last redemption date, and would obviously only do so at the earlier date or before the final maturity date if it were advantageous.

double-dated gilts
Gilts having two redemption dates. The UK government has the option to redeem the gilts anywhere between the two specified dates. It is assumed that gilts will be redeemed on the earlier date if not specified.

Double-dated gilts can be redeemed, either in part or in full, any day between the two dates, but to do this the government must give at least three months' notice in the *London Gazette*. If it does not redeem until the final maturity, it will continue to pay the fixed coupon to the holder. The choice of redemption date is the government's, not the investor's, and it is assumed that double-dated gilts will be called on their first redemption date.

The oldest outstanding **undated gilts** were 2½% Annuities issued on 17 October 1853. There was, however, only £1 million nominal outstanding.

undated gilts
Gilts that do not have a redemption date. They are sometimes referred to as 'irredeemables' or perpetual gilts. However, should the government wish to do so, it may redeem them. There are now no undated gilts in issue, all having been redeemed.

Rump gilts

Rump gilts are those where the nominal amount outstanding is considered to be relatively small. There are now none of these in issue.

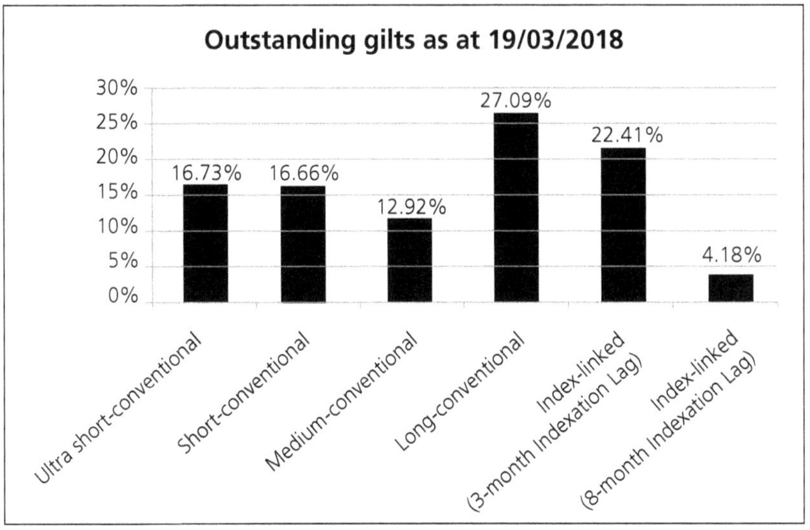

Figure 8.1: Outstanding gilts as at 19 March 2018

flat yield
The gross annual coupon expressed as a percentage of the nominal amount.

3.7 Gilt yields

The **flat yield** rate (also known as the coupon rate) is the annual coupon rate, expressed as a percentage of the bond's nominal value.

Worked example 8.2

$$\text{Flat yield} = \frac{\text{Gross coupon (annual)}}{\text{Nominal amount}} \times 100$$

Treasury 8% 2021 nominal value = £100

$$\text{Flat yield} = \frac{8}{100} \times 100 = 8\% \text{ pa}$$

- This assumes that the purchaser pays exactly the nominal value, therefore in this instance the purchase price = the nominal price.
- The gilt is held for exactly one year from the date of purchase.
- Inflation is not considered.
- At maturity, the purchaser will receive the principal amount, being a multiple of the nominal amount; in this case the price actually paid.

The interest yield (also known as the running yield)
This figure progresses a stage further than the flat yield, as noted in example 8.2.

This coupon rate of 8%, at first glance, would appear to be very generous indeed, mindful of today's historically low interest rates, which are generally in the region of (0.25% to 1%). This, combined with the high degree of security attributed to gilts, would mean the purchaser would expect to pay a significant premium for these gilts, bringing the real rate of return closer to the market rates.

The interest yield is the gross annual coupon divided by the price that the investor actually pays, whether in the primary or secondary market. It is not the same as the flat yield, and it indicates the annual return based on the price actually paid, not the nominal amount. Some authorities use flat yield and running yield interchangeably, but they are in fact different. The price paid may be more (a premium) or less than (a discount to) the face value.

The true interest yield could be higher or lower depending on the price actually paid, whether a premium or discount. In this case the price paid is £133.38 per £100.00 nominal, representing the payment of a premium of £33.38 per £100.00 nominal.

Worked example 8.3

$$\text{Interest yield} = \frac{\text{Gross coupon (annual)}}{\text{Price paid}} \times 100$$

Treasury 8% 2021 price paid = £133.38

$$\text{Interest yield} = \frac{8}{133.38} \times 100 = 5.9979\% \text{ pa}$$

- The interest yield assumes that the purchase price of the gilts is more or less than the nominal value, but not the same.
- As with the example in 8.2 the investment is held for exactly one year.
- Inflation is not considered.
- An investor would receive, annually, coupon payments of exactly 8% of the nominal value in monetary terms.
- At maturity the purchaser would receive the principal amount of the gilt, which could be more or less than the purchase price.

Gross redemption yield (yield to maturity)

The **gross redemption yield (GRY)** is the total yield on a bond, including coupon payments, allowing for any gains or losses over the whole life of the bond, up to and including final repayment. This annual return of 5.9979% still appears to be rather generous. However, in our worked example 8.3, the purchaser has paid a premium of (£33.38) per £100 nominal. It is very important not to confuse percentage terms with actual cash returns.

gross redemption yield (GRY)
The interest yield adjusted to take in to account gains or losses to redemption.

The starting point, when calculating the GRY, is to calculate the interest yield (see above), which is based on the actual price paid by the purchaser.

This is then adjusted to take into account any gains or losses over the life of the bond, and any such capital gain or loss is then divided by the number of years, or part-year, to maturity in order to show the true yield to maturity. This is added, in the case of a capital gain (bought at a discount), or subtracted in the case of a capital loss (premium paid), to show the GRY.

It is necessary to make the following assumptions when calculating the GRY.

- All coupon payments and the repayment of principal will be made promptly.
- Calculations are made without making any adjustments for tax liabilities.
- Dealing costs incurred by either the seller or the purchaser are not considered.

The GRY's purpose is to show the total real return on a gilt, assuming that it is held to its final maturity. It is important to be aware of how many years the gilt still has to run to redemption from the point of purchase, and then use either the discount or premium to calculate capital gain or loss to redemption.

Worked example 8.4

If we use the same figures as in the interest yield calculation – worked example 8.3, we can see that, if an investor were to purchase a Treasury 8% 2021 gilt, there is a £33.38. premium paid over nominal value (£100), as the holder will only ever receive the nominal amount (£100) at maturity. This capital loss, however, must be spread over the total period to maturity. If there were 11 years to maturity, this represents an annual capital loss of £3.0345 nominal. This is not the same as the percentage loss (£33.38/11).

Thus, the annual GRY may be calculated as follows:

Interest yield figure: 5.9979%

Less annual capital loss: £3.0345 (£33.38 / 11 years)

£3.0345/ £133.38 =2.275%

Annual GRY is therefore 5.9979 - 2.275% = 3.7229%.

This is significantly lower than the gilt coupon rate (flat rate).

If there is a capital gain, the GRY will be higher than the interest yield. If there is a capital loss (as in our example 8.4), the GRY will be lower than the interest yield.

This will necessarily involve a two-stage process:

1. calculation of all interest payments received to redemption; and
2. the amount that will be received at redemption.

3.8 Prices and pricing of gilts

Clean and dirty prices

The price of a gilt is comprised of two distinct components: the capital amount of the gilt and the **accrued interest** since the last coupon payment.

accrued interest
Interest accumulated since the payment of the last coupon.

dirty price
This is the clean price of a gilt plus accrued interest since the last coupon payment.

In the UK, gilt coupons are, without exception, paid semi-annually, with interest accruing on a daily basis and payment being made on the next dividend-payment date. This situation gives rise to the following pricing terms: clean price and **dirty price**.

The clean price is the price that is quoted in the financial press and does not include any accrued interest. If an investor were to purchase a gilt some days, weeks or even months after the last coupon payment date, there would obviously be an element of accrued interest. An investor would, therefore, pay the 'dirty price' – that is, the clean price plus accrued interest.

The dirty price is thus equal to the clean price plus interest accrued since the payment of the last coupon. This is the price a purchaser will pay.

3.9 Ex-dividend and cum dividend

Gilt coupon payments are, without exception, made semi-annually to the registered holder. (This is also the case with equities.) There must, however, be a cut-off date when gilts become ex-dividend and are, as such, designated 'XD'.

Gilts become 'XD' seven working days prior to the due date of the next coupon payment. If an investor purchases a gilt on or after the XD date, the coupon will be paid to the previous holder (the registered holder on the XD date). As a result, the price paid for the gilt in the secondary market will be lower. An **ex-dividend period** must exist in order to allow the registrar to ensure that coupon payments are made to the entitled party.

Interest on gilts accrues on a daily basis, and so a purchaser is entitled to any accrued interest for the previous six-month period. Hence, the gilt is referred to as being **cum dividend**. However, the XD date is the last day on which transfers will be accepted. This means an investor who buys gilts prior to the XD date is entitled to accrued interest for the six-month period. On or after this date, the investor would not be entitled to the interest payments.

If an investor buys a gilt between the XD date and the coupon payment date, they are still rewarded in lieu of interest for the intervening period. This is reflected in a lower selling price.

ex-dividend period
This is a period of seven business days prior to coupon payment date. A seller of a bond within the ex-dividend period will receive the entire future interest payment, but effectively pays back a portion to the purchaser by receiving a lower amount for the bond. A purchaser of a bond will not have entitlement to the forthcoming coupon payment.

cum dividend
The purchaser of a bond or gilt 'cum dividend' is entitled to receive interest accrued since the payment of the previous coupon.

3.10 Gilt STRIPS

In the gilt strip market (**Separate Trading of Registered Interest and Principal of Securities)** a gilt is broken down – that is, stripped of its semi-annual coupons. The principal and coupons are then traded separately. For instance, a five-year gilt will have 11 cash flows: 10 coupon payments (paid at six-monthly intervals) and the principal repayment at maturity. The original gilt can be traded as though it were a zero-coupon gilt. Gilts may also be reconstituted from all of the individual strips.

Strippable gilts are conventional fixed coupon gilts and all issues of new conventional gilts will be strippable. There are two series of strippable gilts: those paying coupons in June and December, and those paying coupons in March and September. However, not all gilts are strippable; in March 2018, there were 28 strippable gilts, which are all conventional.

Separate Trading of Registered Interest and Principal Securities (STRIPS)
This is where the gilts are 'strippable', allowing the coupons and principal to be traded separately.

3.11 Gilt settlement

The settlement of gilts takes place electronically through the Euroclear settlement system, where they are held in dematerialised form. Thus, an investor will not have a paper certificate. Approximately 99% of the total values of gilts within CREST are held in dematerialised form. Gilt settlement is T+1.

3.12 Taxation of gilts

All gilts are registered securities and interest/coupon payments are paid gross, without any deduction of tax. This is applicable to both conventional and index-linked gilts. Holders on the register, which is held by computershare, may opt to have income tax deducted at source by applying to them.

All interest/coupons are classed as income, and must be declared on tax returns. This will include any interest uplift on index-linked gilts, however, the uplift in principal as a result of index-linking is not deemed to be interest and therefore is not taxable.

An individual UK investor, selling or otherwise transferring gilts, could be liable to income tax on any interest which has accrued up to the transfer, under the accrued income scheme. Similarly, the scheme relieves an investor from tax on interest/coupons which accrued before the investor's acquisition of the gilt or after the investor's disposal of it. It must be noted that investors, whose holdings of all securities within the accrued investment scheme have not exceeded £5,000 nominal during the relevant year of assessment or the previous one, are outside these rules.

Profits or losses made on the disposal of gilts, including on maturity/redemption, are not taxable and do not even have to be included on an investor's tax return as either capital or income. By contrast, gilt coupons are taxable and must be declared on tax returns. This will include interest uplift on index-linked gilts, but it does not apply to any uplift in principal as a result of index linking, which is not taxable.

Interest on all registered gilts is payable gross, without deduction of any taxes. This is particularly useful for non-taxpayers. However, it is possible to have tax deducted at source by making an application to the Gilt Registry – Computershare Investment Services, which has been the registrar since December 2004.

Neither stamp duty nor stamp duty reserve tax is payable on the purchase or sale of gilts.

3.13 Gilts: additional points

- Gilts are appropriate for investors requiring a guaranteed return of capital combined with a known level of income.
- There is no penalty for selling gilts before their redemption date (that is, there is no penalty applied by the government. However, investors may suffer from negative changes in interest rates).
- The coupon is set at the time of issue, consequently it will not rise or fall in line with market rates.
- Where an investor uses a buy-and-hold strategy until redemption, there is absolute certainty in relation to both income flows and capital.
- There is no stamp duty of any description to pay.
- Gilts are settled electronically through CREST on the following business

day after the transaction (T+1). Settlement on T+3 is possible by special negotiation. CREST is the depository and settlement system for gilts in dematerialised form, and is owned and operated by Euroclear UK and Ireland.

Test yourself 8.3

a) What are index-linked gilts?

b) Explain the terms clean price and dirty price in relation to gilts.

c) Explain the terms cum dividend and ex-dividend in relation to gilts.

4. Corporate bonds

Companies, whether established or start-ups, may need to raise long-term debt capital for any number of reasons, and may achieve this in a number of ways:

- issuing ordinary shares – this will mean the company will relinquish a degree of control of the company;
- issuing preference shares; or
- bank borrowing by way of loans – they will be subject to the banks terms and conditions, interest rates set by the bank, and the possibility of a loan being recalled.

An additional method of raising (long-term) debt finance is by the issuance of corporate bonds. When investors purchase corporate bonds, they are in effect making a long-term loan to a company. This market is now vast, with many household names raising huge sums of capital by issuing bonds. Companies from any business sector may issue bonds.

In the UK, corporate bonds are issued in nominal amounts of £1,000, whereas in the USA they are issued in nominal amounts of $1,000. Other countries will have their own conventions, and there may also be a minimum initial investment of, perhaps, £10,000.

Examples of corporate bond issuance:

- In 2002, the Vodafone group issued corporate bonds to the value of £450 million, paying an annual coupon of 5.9%.
- In 2013, bookmakers William Hill Plc issued a corporate bond which will mature in 2020: the coupon was 4.25% – the nominal value was £100, the minimum trading unit was £1000, and the minimum amount that could be purchased was £100,000. This was to raise £375 million.

It is essential to look at the specific bond prospectus in relation to each issue and it must be remembered that an issuer may have many issues simultaneously.

4.1 Suitability profile

For investors, corporate bonds are an attractive proposition, as they provide fixed coupons and the promise of return of capital, although they are more speculative than government-backed gilts. They are now more accessible than they used to be and can be both bought and sold through stockbrokers via online trading platforms. Note that neither income nor capital is guaranteed. Corporate bonds may not be suitable for all, although they are available to both individual and institutional investors, with the level of skill and understanding required not on a par with that for derivatives.

There is less risk than with ordinary shares in the same company; however, investors will not receive any equity in the company. Coupon rates tend to be higher than for gilts because of the perception of increased risk. Even well-established and famous companies can go bankrupt and both their shares and bonds become worthless.

The corporate borrower will issue the bond in order to obtain long-term finance for a specific purpose. This will be at a par value of £1,000 nominal, with an interest rate of perhaps 5%. There will be a specific maturity date, which may be anything from 1 year to 30 years, and coupons will usually be split into two semi-annual payments.

Unlike holders of equities, bondholders have only a right to receive regular coupon payments and a return of capital at maturity; they have no rights in relation to the company and have no control over it.

Corporate bonds are loans to the company by the investor, who is the lender or creditor, while the company is the borrower or debtor.

After the bond has been issued, the company is only concerned with making coupon payments as and when they fall due, and the repayment of capital at maturity (which may be many years away). The company may receive more or less than the face value of the bond. Less, if it issues its bonds at a discount.

Correspondingly, the rewards to the investor are the periodic payments of coupons, usually biannually but may be annually, until the bond's maturity date, and the promise of the repayment of capital at maturity. Within the class of corporate bonds, the coupons on blue-chip corporate bonds will tend to be lower than on riskier high-yield ('junk') bonds (see section 4.2).

It is important to remember that the credit rating is applicable to a particular bond issue and not the issuer. Some bonds have no rating (in which case, they are annotated 'NR'), and such ratings are only provided at the request of the issuer, in order to market the particular issue.

4.2 Classification of corporate bonds

There are two main grades of corporate bond: investment-grade bonds and high-yield bonds (often referred to as 'junk bonds').

Investment-grade bonds

Investment-grade bonds, by implication, have less risk of default by the corporate issuer, and offer less risk to the investor.

High-yield bonds/non-investment grade ('junk bonds')

'Junk bond' coupons tend to be higher than investment-grade coupons, because of the greater risk of default by the riskier corporate issuer.

However, even though the perceived credit risk of such bonds is far greater, it does not necessarily follow that the issuer will actually default, and there are prospects of good returns for prudent investors. A start-up company's bond issue may have a high credit risk rating, while a famous blue-chip bond issue may have a low credit-risk rating.

In the UK there are two main credit rating agencies for corporate bonds: Standard & Poor's (S&P), and Moody's. These agencies assign credit ratings based on a company's ability to repay its particular bond debt at maturity, relevant to the particular bond issue, and also the ability to service interest payments as they fall due. Junk bonds tend to be rated lower than BBB (see Table 8.1).

The term credit rating is now analogous to credit quality, which is a measure of the issuer's ability to service its liabilities, in terms of interest payments, coupons and repayment at maturity. In addition to their own personal knowledge and skill, potential investors can use the ratings assigned by the main credit rating agencies, Standard & Poor's (S&P) and Moody's. Credit rating agencies have vast resources at their disposal, and they assess not only the bond per se, but also the issuer.

It should be noted that it is the issuing company that pays these rating agencies to rate their bonds, so this does create a potential conflict of interest. The ratings, which are applied by the two main agencies, are used by banks and the managers of investment funds when determining whether to include such a bond within a portfolio. The up-to-date ratings of most bond issuers can be found on the websites of the rating agencies. It is also worth noting that a downgrade in rating will probably cause a fall in the price of the bond.

Table 8.1 summarises the ratings applied by these agencies.

Table 8.1: Credit rating agency ratings

	S&P	**Moody's**
Highest rating for investment-grade bonds	AAA	Aaa
Lowest rating for investment-grade bonds	BBB-	Baa3
Highest rating for high-yield bonds	BB+	Ba1
Lowest rating for high-yield bonds	C	C

Note: 'D' indicates that a company is in default.

4.3 Liquidation profile

If a company enters into liquidation, bondholders are, in theory, paid out before ordinary shareholders. However, if there are no funds remaining, not even bondholders will be paid.

When the global economy entered into recession in 2007/08, the risk of corporate default increased significantly, and the prices of corporate bonds tended to fall, often significantly. As more companies defaulted, this had a domino effect on the bond prices of other companies, as investors offloaded their holdings of even investment-grade bonds, where there was only a small chance of default. These bonds could be bought in the secondary market at bargain prices, and a situation arose where corporate bonds with good yields, but with prices considerably below par value, provided alert and less risk-averse investors with some excellent opportunities. These investors reaped their rewards as they earned not only a very decent return but also good capital growth.

The price of a corporate bond depends on the bond's credit rating combined with various market factors, and it must be noted that the price in the market is rarely the same as its par value, unless the bond is close to its redemption date.

At any particular time, a company may have a range of bonds in issue to raise funds for different purposes and with varying maturities.

4.4 Buying and selling corporate bonds

Corporate bonds are available to both the personal investor and the institutional investor, but trying to obtain information may sometimes be rather complicated. The bonds may be bought and sold before maturity in the secondary market at either a premium or a discount. If bought in the secondary market, the bond's yield to maturity should always be considered.

The majority of bonds are not traded on exchanges, although in the USA some corporate bonds are listed on an exchange, while in the UK both buying and selling prices for corporate bonds are available through the LSE.

The important point to observe concerning bond trading is that there is no one central trading place or exchange, as there is for equities. In this respect, corporate bonds are over-the-counter (OTC) instruments, and can be traded anywhere in the world. However, they tend to be traded over the telephone and through computer links.

Specialised bond dealers will make a market in the bonds, quoting both buying and selling prices. Within each bond-dealing firm there will be any number of traders who buy and sell to both the institutional and retail markets. The dealers, therefore, provide the liquidity in the market. Both dealers and brokers make their profits on their spreads, which can be wide, especially on corporate irredeemable bonds.

Settlement of corporate bonds takes place through CREST, Euroclear and Clearstream.

Test yourself 8.4

a) Why are corporate bonds attractive to investors?

b) What are the two main types of corporate bond?

5. Eurobonds

Eurobonds are debt instruments intended for the global market and, although they are issued within European countries, they are also issued in many other countries. They may be denominated in Euros, but also in many other marketable currencies including the United States dollar, UK sterling, Japanese yen and Swiss Franc.

The Eurobond market is now a vital source of finance for large national corporations, multinational corporations, supranational organisations, and sovereign states, particularly those of emerging markets and developing countries. The Eurobond market provides such borrowers with access to a vast pool of medium to long-term international debt capital.

Eurobonds are unsecured bonds, both issued and traded internationally. They have bearer-like characteristics and are issued in countries other than those of the currencies in which the Eurobonds are denominated. This means a country's central bank will not have any jurisdiction over Eurobonds issued in its own currency. For example, US dollar-denominated Eurobonds may be issued or may originate in any country other than the USA, while Japanese yen-denominated Eurobonds may be issued in any country other than Japan.

5.1 Naming conventions

US dollar-denominated Eurobonds are referred to as Eurodollar bonds, Japanese yen-denominated Eurobonds are referred to as Euroyen bonds, and UK sterling-denominated Eurobonds are referred to as Eurosterling bonds. A US dollar-denominated bond, although originating outside of the USA, may be issued by a US corporate in another country, for example, the Ford Motor Company may issue a US dollar-denominated Eurobond in London.

5.2 Characteristics of Eurobonds

- Eurobonds may be issued with either fixed or floating rate coupons.
- They provide anonymity to purchasers as there are no public registers. Therefore an issuer does not know who holds its eurobonds.
- They are OTC products, having no central exchanges. Dealing is done by telephone and computer terminals using brokers.
- They may be tailored to a particular country's regulatory regime.
- They are redeemed at maturity upon presentation to the issuer by a holder or a third party acting on behalf of the holder.

- They are listed on recognised exchanges but, as they are bearer-like bonds, there is no central register; holdings are recorded by the clearers.
- It is possible that the principal is redeemed in one currency whereas coupons are paid in another currency.
- The country in whose currency the Eurobond issue is denominated will have no jurisdiction over that bond issue. For example, Japan will have no jurisdiction over Euroyen bonds issued in Sweden.

Eurobonds are specialist medium to long-term (5 to 10 years), unsecured and highly rated debt securities, used as a means of raising capital in international rather than domestic markets, and are fully negotiable. They are intended for institutional investors and indeed are only offered to institutional investors in the primary market. However, they may be purchased by individual investors in the secondary market. In practice, most purchasers of Eurobonds tend to be investment funds. They are only issued by governments and institutional investors.

Historically, Eurobonds were only issued in bearer form and as such were unregistered by the issuer. It is still true to say that there is no central register maintained by the issuer; however, holdings must be recorded somewhere. This function is carried out by clearing agents rather than the issuer, but access is not open to governments or tax authorities.

Eurobond accounts are maintained with clearers and stockbrokers, so it would be possible to say that an institutional investor has perhaps a holding of US$50 million of another company's Eurobonds. There is no public register available for scrutiny and the issuer does not know who holds its bonds. Holdings are recorded rather than registered, and there are no certificates issued. Credits and debits will be passed over these accounts. Redemptions and coupon payments will be claimed on behalf of the current holder and credited to a client's account, while additional Eurobond purchases will be debited to the client's account. This is all completed electronically.

5.3 The rationale for issuing Eurobonds

The prime function of Eurobonds is to raise medium to long-term debt capital in international markets rather than domestic markets. Some of the other reasons for their use include the following.

- Issuers may not be able to obtain finance from their domestic banks or issue bonds in their domestic market.
- Issuers may wish to select countries with favourable tax regimes or with less tough regulatory requirements compared to those of the home country.
- The selection of a currency in which the Eurobond is denominated is more stable than the currency of the country of the issuing party, and consequently the Eurobonds will be far more marketable.
- They may be used to finance the development of emerging market economies.

- Eurobonds are held anonymously; there is therefore no requirement for the issuer to maintain a central register of holders. This results in a reduction of the administrative burden for the issuer.
- They are often used by parent companies to finance overseas subsidiaries.

5.4 Eurobond issuance

Eurobonds are OTC products, driven by telephone and computer-based systems; as such there is no formal marketplace, as there is with equities. However, they must be listed on RIEs (recognised investment exchanges).

A need to raise finance will have already been identified, with the issuer having a requirement to raise medium to long-term debt capital. If the method decided upon is by way of a Eurobond issue, the following process will occur. This will initially be in the primary market, as a new issue of securities, and will be executed by means of a placing. This may be a relatively short process, depending on whether or not the issuer has made previous Eurobond issues. Advisors will determine the process and calculate the various timescales.

There are two requirements before trading in a new issue of Eurobonds can begin:

1. Eurobond issues must be admitted to listing. In the UK this role is undertaken by the United Kingdom Listing Authority (UKLA), a division of the FCA.
2. Admitted to trading on a recognised investment exchange.

As is the case with straight bonds, Eurobonds have a nominal amount, face value, maturity date, and coupon. Coupons tend to be fixed, but may be variable, according to the terms and conditions of the particular issue. They are paid gross, without deduction of taxes. Any tax liabilities are the responsibility of the holder. The minimum investment is usually in the region of US$500,000, which tends to exclude individual investors.

5.5 Regulation

Eurobonds are regulated by the International Capital Market Association (ICMA), which is a self-regulatory organisation providing rules and regulations on issuance and trading. In the UK, the FCA is not able to regulate Eurosterling bonds, as these are issued outside the UK's jurisdiction. However, any UK financial entities involved in Eurobond issuance will be regulated by the FCA.

5.6 Considerations

When a party executes a Eurodollar issue then, at maturity, proceeds will have to be paid in US$ to the bondholder, with annual coupons having to be serviced throughout the life of the bond. Also, due consideration must be given by the issuer as to how this will be achieved. If the currency of the country where the bond is issued depreciates significantly against the currency of denomination of the Eurobonds, this may prove to be very serious indeed, as the issuer may incur significant exchange rate losses.

Making it work 8.2: Kenya and Eurobonds

In January 2018, the Kenyan government issued $3 billion in Eurobonds. This was its first issue since 2014, and was listed on the London Stock exchange.

The $3 billion was split into two separate issues:

- 10 year bond paying a coupon of 7.25%
- 30 year bond paying a coupon of 8.25%

The Kenyan treasury specified that the purpose of this issue was:

- usage in infrastructure development
- to retire existing debt

Kenya chose to issue its eurobonds in US dollars rather than the Kenyan shilling, as the shilling is not as marketable as the dollar, rather than obtain finance from its own financial institutions.

The annual coupons for these bonds appear rather high. However, this reflects the fact that many authorities, including the credit rating agencies, are sceptical of their affordability. The country's official rating agencies, S&P and Fitch Ratings, have both retained Kenya's credit score at B+, which implies possibility of a default, however, with some margin of safety.

Making it work 8.3: Israel and Eurobonds

In January 2018, Israel listed its first ever eurobond issue on the London Stock Exchange. The issue was Euro 2.25 billion. This is, in fact, Israel's largest ever euro denominated bond offering, and its first euro denominated bond since 2015. Israel was the first non-European state to issue a euro denominated bond with a 20-year tenor.

This issue comprised:

- Euro 1.5 billion 10-year debt with a 1.5% annual coupon – medium to long-term debt.
- Euro 0.75 billion 20-year debt with a 2.375% annual coupon – long-term debt.

One of the stated purposes was to lengthen the country's debt profile. This offering was oversubscribed nearly four times, with the order book closing at over Euro 9.5 billion. Israel selected the Euro for this bond issue, rather than its own currency, the Shekel, which is not as marketable.

Moody's currently rates Israel as A1 stable.

5.7 The participants in the Eurobond market

Issuer

This is the party that has a need to obtain medium or long-term finance for a specific purpose or purposes, such as a major capital project or refinancing. Issuers may not wish or be able to raise finance in their own country, and so may look to the international debt markets. Issuers tend to be sovereign governments (including those of emerging markets), large national and multinational corporations with high credit ratings, and international banks and large international organisations, such as the European Bank for Reconstruction and Development.

Purchasers (investors)

Purchasers are those participants who buy the Eurobonds from the issuers through an intermediary in the primary market, or OTC in the secondary market. Eurobonds are intended for purchase by institutional investors who seek medium to long-term secure products.

Intermediaries

The potential Eurobond issuer will approach an investment bank in order to handle the issue, and this party will be referred to as the lead manager, to which the issuer will then award the mandate. The lead manager may request other banks to join in order to form a management group, which will not only manage the issue but also negotiate all the relevant terms and conditions. The Eurobonds will be issued through a placing with many clients, or possibly just a single client.

The lead manager has the power and responsibility to make the bond issue, and they can also act as an authorised advisor. Although this function may be delegated, the authorised advisor may appoint experienced agents, who may include law firms to oversee the necessary listing requirements. The lead manager may form a syndication team, or may underwrite the issue alone. The various roles of the participants may overlap or even become blurred; nonetheless, there are a number of functions that must be carried out.

Advisors will determine the process and calculate the various timescales. However, trading cannot begin until both admission to listing and admission to trading have occurred. Pivotal to this process of listing Eurobonds is the preparation of the listing documents, referred to as listing particulars (or LPs). If these are completed carefully and in a timely manner, the listing process can be significantly reduced.

Other banks will be responsible for ensuring payment at redemption, and coupon payments throughout the course of the Eurobond's life.

5.8 Additional points

- Over 75% of Eurobond deals are originated and executed by dealers based in London.
- Eurobond prices change in relation to interest rate and currency movements.

- As Eurobonds are only offered to institutional investors, the listing requirements are less rigid than for other debt securities such as corporate bonds.
- Settlement in the Eurobond market is T+3.
- Settlement is done through two separate and independent clearing houses, Euroclear and Clearstream, which will record holdings.

Test yourself 8.5

a) What are US dollar-denominated Eurobonds called?

b) Who regulates Eurobonds?

c) Why are Eurobonds issued?

6. Methods of eliminating or reducing bond-related risks

Bonds are generally considered to be reasonably safe investments. However, as with other classes of investments, they are still exposed to a number of specific risks, which we shall now consider. Any investor in bonds ought to give due thought to risks relating to the bonds they are purchasing, and consider the most appropriate ways to mitigate them.

6.1 Default risk

Of all the risks, default risk has to be of paramount consideration. After all, investors buy bonds because they want a return of capital at maturity, together with the regular payment of coupons, up to and including at maturity. If bond issuers either fail to repay capital in full at maturity, or fail to make coupon payments as and when they fall due, or perhaps try to reach an arrangement to pay a lower amount, they will be in default.

For UK gilts and US Treasury securities, the risk of default is assumed to be nil. Corporate bonds generally have greater risk of default in comparison to gilts; however, with the bonds of most blue-chip companies, the risk is still deemed to be minimal. If a company does go into liquidation, the bondholder may receive absolutely nothing if the company has no assets and only huge liabilities. Consider the Greek debt crisis when the Greek government was potentially going to default on its debt obligations.

Risk-averse investors should purchase gilts or investment-grade bonds rather than junk bonds. All investors should ensure that they are aware of the credit reference agencies' rating, relating to specific bond issues, in order to assess credit and default risk.

6.2 Issue-specific risks

Before purchasing any bond, an investor should read and understand the relevant bond prospectus thoroughly, including full terms and conditions.

Some corporate bond issues have call facilities, allowing the issuer to repay the bond early, which may not be what the investor wants. This could be problematic for the investor who is expecting a specific return of capital at maturity and payment of coupons up to maturity. The bondholder might not even receive the original coupon rate for the duration of the bond. It should also be noted that when the call date has been reached, there is no certainty in relation to the coupon payments and the market price of the bond may equate to the call price. Issuers will tend to call in the bonds when market rates fall, because they can borrow more cheaply, as they will no longer have to pay the current bondholder more than these lower rates.

As the callable date approaches, care needs to be taken not to buy such a bond OTC or in the secondary market. This is because an investor might mistakenly believe they have a bargain, as the issuer is likely to call the bond. If nothing else, there may be the cost of commission, and the investor may have to buy a lower-rated bond to obtain a similar coupon, or alternatively accept a lower coupon from the same issuer in the event that the bond is called.

Purchases of such bonds should ensure that they have a contingency plan in the event that the bonds are called by the issuer. The prices of callable bonds tend to fall when interest rates fall (a situation referred to as 'price compression').

6.3 Market risk

An investor will buy bonds, either directly in the primary market or in the secondary market, at a specific price and yield. However, prices will fluctuate from day to day, and in the event that an investor has to sell early because of unforeseen circumstances, they will have to accept the prevailing market price, possibly incurring a capital loss and loss of coupons. If the market goes into turmoil then panic selling may ensue, as happened in 2008.

Investors should try to ensure they have enough liquidity to avoid having to sell their bonds early.

6.4 Inflation

Essentially, this is the risk that the bond will not keep pace with purchasing power.

Inflation is always an important consideration. The longer the term of the bond, the greater the risk that inflation may erode the real value of both the coupon and redemption proceeds. If there were to be hyperinflation, this could reduce significantly the value of these components. By contrast if there is deflation, this will increase the value of the coupon payments and final redemption proceeds. This is not the same as interest rate risk (discussed next).

6.5 Interest rate risk – also referred to as market risk

Interest rate risk will tend to increase the longer the bond is held.

When external market interest rates rise, bond prices fall, because investors will switch to alternative products. Conversely, if market rates fall, bond prices will rise, and investors will tend to switch to bonds. Generally, the higher the level of interest rates, the greater the perceived risk. If, for instance, the rates in the market rise above the bond rate, the corporate bond rates become less competitive and thus the market price of the bonds will fall; whereas if the external market interest rate falls, the corporate bonds become more competitive and, therefore, more attractive to investors, and so the bond price will tend to rise. This will generally only apply to those bonds with interest rates lower than the external rates, as there would be no reason to switch. Generally, when external market interest rates rise, the price of the bond will go down. As the price goes down the yield will rise; this, hopefully, will make the bonds competitive with those bonds offering higher interest rates. If it is necessary to sell a bond before its maturity date, there is a possibility that money could be lost if, when the bond is sold, the price is less than when purchased. Ensure you have enough spare money to avoid having to sell the bond.

6.6 Maturity risk

A bond that has a redemption date many years into the future will have a higher coupon than a shorter-dated bond issued by the same party. This reflects the great deal of uncertainty in the financial world. The other risks mentioned here increase with time and therefore the coupon offered for longer-dated issues will tend to be higher.

6.7 Event risk

Typically, the risk of a capital restructuring of the issuer affects the value of a bond. An example of event risk is where the corporate issuer of the bond becomes the target of a **leveraged buy-out,** thus increasing the risk of lending any money to that company.

leveraged buy-out
This happens when the existing management of a company acquires a controlling interest in that company using external capital.

Other negative events which may cause bond prices to fall include:

- mergers and acquisitions;
- investigations by regulators;
- negative profit figures;
- the leaving of a key executive; and
- product recall.

6.8 Fiscal and currency risks

Fiscal risks include the setting of punitive (extremely high) taxes, either in the domestic market or overseas market, such as the introduction of, or increase in, withholding taxes.

Overseas investors purchasing UK sterling-denominated bonds will expect to receive sterling coupon payments throughout the life of the bond, and sterling proceeds at maturity. If sterling depreciates (goes down) against their home currency, this will have a negative effect. Although the overseas investor receives the expected (sterling) capital amount at maturity, the sterling amount received may be insufficient to match a foreign currency liability when converted back into the domestic currency.

In relation to international investment, the risk of exchange controls being introduced should also be considered.

6.9 Commissions and spreads

Although not a risk, care always needs to be exercised regarding commission and other costs. Wide spreads can impact on profitability.

6.10 Earning potential

Although not a risk, there is a downside to bonds. If the company does particularly well, the holder only receives their fixed rate of interest; whereas with equities, an investor may do extremely well, as returns are not restricted to a single fixed coupon rate.

6.11 Opportunity cost

This is particularly pertinent to longer-term bonds, as an investor's capital is committed for a considerable period of time. There is a possibility that a better opportunity could arise where far better returns could be achieved; however, the investor is unable to take advantage of this opportunity because the money is already tied up in the corporate bond. This may also be referred to as holding-period risk.

6.12 Liquidity risk

This is a situation which arises when bond holders are unable to sell their bonds due to lack of demand.

6.13 Risk mitigation

In order to mitigate risk potential bond holders can check bond activity which will be an indicator of its liquidity. In the USA investors can use FINRA's Market Data Centre.

6.14 Diversification

If funds allow, investors should try to buy a range of bonds with different maturity dates and coupon rates, ensuring a diversified bond portfolio that include gilts, corporate bonds may bonds.

Buying bonds in a relatively new company (start-up) carries a far higher risk than investing in an established company.

In the USA the Securities and Exchange Commission SEC has designated 10 rating agencies as Nationally Recognised Statistical Rating Organisations (NRSROs). These organisations review a considerable amount of data, notably financial, in relation to bond issuers. They assign ratings from AAA (Aaa) to D, or no rating at all. Not all agencies will rate all bonds and there might different ratings applied to the same bond by the different agencies.

6.15 Rating downgrades

Where either the bond itself, or the issuer, receives a rating downgrade, this will negatively affect the price of that bond. This could be good for new buyers, as the yield will increase, however, this would be bad for existing bond holders.

Chapter summary

- Fixed-interest or fixed-income securities are those that pay an annual fixed rate of interest (known as coupons), which do not vary with any external factor (interest rates such as LIBOR).
- These coupons are known from the outset, are usually for the same amount, and are paid at regular intervals, generally semi-annually.
- The most common and most significant of fixed-interest security products are bonds, whether gilts, corporate bonds or eurobonds.
- Gilts are fully marketable UK government sterling-denominated bonds issued by the DMO, on behalf of HM Treasury, as part of its debt management responsibilities.
- Companies may raise capital by the issuance of bonds.
- When investors purchase corporate bonds, they are in effect making a long-term loan to a company.
- Companies from any business sector may issue bonds.
- Eurobonds are unsecured bonds, issued and traded internationally, with bearer-like characteristics. They originate in a country other than the country of the currency in which the Eurobond is denominated, and are not regulated by the country in whose currency the bond is denominated.

Test yourself answers

Test yourself 8.1

a) The main parties to a bond are:

- bond issuer (also referred to as the borrower or debtor);
- initial purchaser (also referred to as the lender, creditor or investor); and
- bondholder (or current owner).

b) A straight bond is a long-term, negotiable fixed-interest debt security, containing absolute contractual obligations, whereby the issuer borrows a fixed amount of capital (referred to as the principal amount or face value) from another party, referred to as the purchaser, for a specific period.

c) Redeemable bonds are bonds that have a specific maturity date and will be redeemed, whereas irredeemable bonds do not have a maturity date and there is no obligation for issuers to redeem them.

d) Callable bonds contain an embedded call facility, where the bond issuer has the right, but not the obligation, to redeem the bond before its specified maturity date under certain criteria, which will obviously be advantageous. The issuer will call in the bond and repay at least the face value to the current holder.

The decision to call rests with the bond issuer, not the holder. This must be contrasted with puttable bonds. Coupons on callable bonds tend to be higher than for straight bonds in order to compensate the holder for the risk of the bond being called by the issuer.

Puttable bonds are those containing an embedded put facility, giving the holder a right without any obligation to force the issuer to redeem the bond before the official maturity date. In other words, the holder can 'put' their bond back to the issuer for repayment before the bond's maturity date. The put price that the issuer must pay to the holder is usually 100% of the face value. The decision to redeem rests with the bondholder and not the issuer.

e) An issuer of a straight bond has two distinct and absolute contractual obligations (the specific details being contained within the bond's original offering notice), as follows:

1. To repay the principal amount to the bondholder on a specific future date (redemption date or maturity date).
2. To make regular fixed-interest rate payments (coupons) to the holder at predetermined intervals throughout the bond's life, up to and including the redemption date.

Test yourself 8.2

a) Gilts are issued in order to finance the:

1. Central Government Net Cash Requirement (CGNCR), which is the difference between the government's expenditure and income;
2. annual repayment of maturing gilts; and
3. servicing semi-annual gilt coupon payments.

b) The UK gilts market is composed of two main types of securities: conventional gilts and index-linked gilts.

c) GEMMs are primary dealers in the UK gilt market, trading in conventional gilts, indexed gilts or both. They are competing market makers providing liquidity in the primary market and are comprised of banks or securities firms that have been endorsed by the DMO as primary dealers in UK government bonds. Wholesale GEMMs specialise in market making to institutional investors, whereas retail GEMMs service clients dealing in smaller amounts.

Additionally, they will provide the DMO with market intelligence and make possible gilt transfers from the DMO to other investors; they will also provide the figures for the overall daily turnover to the DMO.

d) The DMO is an executive agency of HM Treasury and, as its name suggests, it has responsibility for the management of government debt through its participation in the gilt market. It has as its main objective the reduction, over the longer term, of the cost of meeting the government's financing needs, while also considering the risks involved in achieving this.

The DMO is the issuer of gilts, operating in both the primary and the secondary markets. It not only controls the issue of gilts but also ensures that the market remains solvent. Its functions include maintaining an orderly and regulated environment, and ensuring investor protection. It also confers or revokes primary dealer status and controls the entry and exit of GEMMs, and indeed holds gilts itself in order to help manage the market.

Test yourself 8.3

a) Index-linked gilts (IGs) are second only to conventional gilts as part of the government's overall gilt portfolio and were first issued to institutional investors in 1981. The coupons on IGs, as with those of conventional gilts, reflect market rates at the time of issue. In contrast to conventional gilts, both the principal and the coupons are altered in line with the RPI. Coupons, and the principal paid on redemption, are adjusted to take into account accrued (built-up) inflation since the first issue of the IG.

b) The clean price is the price that is quoted in the press and does not include any accrued interest. If an investor were to purchase a gilt some days, weeks or even months after the last coupon payment date, there would obviously be an element of accrued interest. An investor would, therefore, pay the 'dirty price' – the clean price plus accrued interest. The dirty price is thus equal to the clean price plus interest accrued since the payment of the last coupon.

c) Gilt coupon payments are (in most cases) made semi-annually to the registered holder (this is also the case with equities.). There must, however, be a cut-off date when gilts become ex-dividend and are as such denoted 'XD'. Gilts become 'XD' seven working days prior to the due date of the next coupon payment.

If an investor purchases a gilt on or after the XD date, the coupon will be paid to the previous holder (the registered holder on the XD date). As a result, the price paid for the gilt in the secondary market will be lower. An ex-dividend period must exist in order to allow the registrar to ensure that coupon payments are made to the entitled party.

Interest on gilts accrues on a daily basis and so a purchaser is entitled to any accrued interest for the previous six-month period. Hence, the gilt is referred to as being cum dividend. However, the XD date is the last day on which transfers will be accepted. This means an investor who buys gilts prior to the XD date is entitled to accrued interest for the six-month period. On or after this date, the investor would not be entitled to the interest payments.

If an investor buys a gilt between the XD date and the coupon payment date, they are still rewarded in lieu of interest for the intervening period. This is reflected in a lower selling price.

Test yourself 8.4

a) For investors, corporate bonds are attractive, as they provide fixed coupons. There is less risk than with ordinary shares in the same company. However, investors receive no equity in the company, but coupon rates tend to be higher than for gilts because of the perception of increased risk. The rewards to the investor are the periodic payments of coupons, usually biannually, until the bond's maturity date, and the promise of the repayment of capital at maturity.

b) There are two main grades of corporate bond: investment-grade bonds and high-yield bonds (often referred to as 'junk bonds').

Test yourself 8.5

a) Eurodollar bonds.

b) Eurobonds are regulated by the International Capital Market Association (ICMA).

c) The prime function of Eurobonds is to raise capital medium to long-term debt capital in international markets. Some of the reasons for their use include the following:

- Issuers may not be able to obtain finance from their domestic banks or issue bonds in their domestic market.
- Issuers may wish to select countries with favourable tax regimes or with less tough regulatory requirements compared to those of the home country.
- The selection of a currency in which the Eurobond is denominated is more stable than the currency of the country of the issuing party, and consequently the Eurobonds will be far more marketable.
- They may be used to finance the development of emerging market economies.
- Eurobonds are held anonymously; there is therefore no requirement for the issuer to maintain a central register of holders. This results in a reduction of the administrative burden for the issuer.
- They are sometimes used by parent companies to finance overseas subsidiaries.

Chapter nine
Collective investment schemes

List of topics

1. Retail Distribution Review (RDR)
2. Collective investment schemes
3. Open-ended investments
4. Closed-ended collective investments
5. Fund supermarkets
6. Investment trust companies (ITCs)
7. Split capital trusts (SCTs)
8. Assessing ITCs and SCTs
9. Real estate investment trusts (REITs)
10. Exchange-traded funds (ETFs)
11. Venture capital trusts (VCTs)
12. Hedge funds
13. Private equity (PE)
14. Assessing a collective investment
15. Comparison of open-ended and closed-ended funds

Introduction

This chapter looks at the more important types of collective investments available to investors. It includes an explanation of open-ended investments including unit trusts, OEICs and UCITS funds, and a description of closed-ended investments in their various forms. The chapter also explains ETFs, venture capital trusts, hedge funds and private equity investments. It concludes with sections on how to assess a collective investment and a look at the differences between open-ended and close-ended investments.

1. Retail Distribution Review (RDR)

In June 2009, the Retail Distribution Review (RDR) was introduced by the FSA (now the FCA) and introduced a set of requirements which became effective from 31 December 2012.

The RDR is effectively a set of rules intended to introduce more transparency and fairness in the investment industry. The most significant aspect was that financial advisers are no longer permitted to earn commissions from fund companies in return for either selling or recommending their investment products.

Instead, investors have to agree fees with an adviser from the outset. Investors should receive a simple document setting out both the advice charges, as well as those for managing their money. Financial advisers would offer either 'independent' or 'restricted' advice and would have to explain the difference between these two types to their client:

- Independent advice will be given by an independent financial adviser (IFA), who will be able to advise on all investment and pension products and will also be able to recommend products from across the entire market.
- Restricted advice will offer a more limited service.

These changes will bring the rest of the investment industry in line with common practice in the exchange-traded fund industry – one of the reasons why ETF providers have been able to keep costs low is by not paying commissions to advisers. This change should also enhance standards across the board, with all advisers, whether selling one company's products or qualified independent financial advisers (IFAs), who are required to gain additional qualifications and complete continuing personal development (CPD) training every year. Investors should be able to receive an enhanced return on their investment.

However, there are a number of key issues, including the following:

- There are concerns that this attempt to improve standards may see some potential investors excluded from financial advice altogether. Those on lower incomes will not be able to afford the costs of the better and more qualified independent financial advisers. This situation has been exacerbated because many of the main UK banks will no longer provide any investment advice.
- As a result, consumers will have to decide themselves what product they require.
- There may also be confusion as to what type of advice the consumer is receiving – is it independent or restricted?

When the RDR was introduced, the former Chairman of the Financial Services Authority, Sir Callum McCarthy, outlined six objectives:

1. an industry that engages with consumers in a way that delivers more clarity for them on products and services;

2. a market which allows more consumers to have their needs and wants addressed;
3. remuneration arrangements that allow competitive forces to work in favour of consumers;
4. standards of professionalism that inspire consumer confidence and build trust;
5. an industry where firms are sufficiently viable to deliver on their long-term commitments and where they treat their customers fairly; and
6. a regulatory framework that can support delivery of all these aspirations and which does not inhibit future innovation where this benefits consumers.

2. Collective investment schemes

Collective investment schemes (CISs), which may also be referred to as 'pooled' investments or mutual funds, are schemes or arrangements where many investors collectively invest their monies into a single fund rather than make any single investment by themselves. Collective schemes provide investors as a group or collective the opportunity to invest easily and at relatively low cost, pooling their money into a professionally managed and diversified portfolio. They would be unable to achieve this diversification by themselves. The investor should aim to find a scheme that reflects their investment aims and objectives.

Such collective schemes' funds hold a variety of diversified underlying assets including equities, property and bonds. It is likely that any single fund will have a very diversified portfolio which may hold many hundreds of different stocks in order to mitigate the investment risk of the underlying portfolio. CISs will also remove the burden from an investor of having to monitor the underlying portfolio assets; this exercise will be performed by the fund manager, who will also will makes any decisions concerning investments in the underlying assets but within the scope of the agreed mandate. Their objective is to provide returns for the fund's investors, in the form of either capital growth (an increase in the price per unit) or income as dividends paid to the unit holders or shareholders in direct proportion to the number of units they own.

Generally, there is considered to be far less risk involved in holding a basket of shares when compared to the risks associated with investing in a single company share or a handful of assets, or indeed a single asset class, as the likelihood of failure is reduced.

Collective investment schemes may also be used to gain exposure to specialised markets where direct investment would be too risky or expensive to undertake as a single investor. A UK investor may find it much easier and safer to buy into a collective scheme investing in Japan rather than to try to buy shares in individual companies listed on the Tokyo Stock Exchange. Holding investments in more than one geographical region can also form part of a diversified investment strategy.

CIS managers themselves benefit from the support of multiple teams including both researchers and analysts who help in making investment decisions. This expertise would then be used to achieve returns for the investors. A private investor would find it very time consuming trying to match a similar level of research.

Collective investment schemes may or may not be regulated. By contrast to an individual investor, who would make his or her own investment decisions. As collective investment schemes are professionally managed, the investment manager will take any decisions in relation to the portfolio rather than the individual themselves.

There are many different types of collective investment scheme available designed to meet the investment requirements of various types of investor whether individual, professional or institutional. Examples are provided throughout this chapter. Each of the collective schemes will invest in a sector or sectors that match the investors' needs. They will all benefit from the manager's skill and knowledge of particular markets.

In the United Kingdom, the creation of a collective investment scheme is deemed to be a regulated activity and must be authorised by the FCA and a legal definition is provided in section 235(1) of the Financial Services and Markets Act 2000 (FSMA):

> A collective investment scheme is any arrangement with respect to property of any description, including money, the purpose or effect of which is to enable persons taking part in the arrangements (whether by becoming owners of the property or any part of it or otherwise) to participate in or receive profits or income arising from the acquisition, holding, management or disposal of the property or sums paid out of such profits or income and (b) which are not excluded by the Financial Services and Markets Act (Collective Investment Schemes) Order 2001 (SI 2001/1062).

The salient points that should be elicited from this definition are that collective investment schemes are as follows:

- Financial structures in which profits either in terms of capital gains and /or income earned are shared through collective investment.
- The collective investors do not have any day-to day control over the management of the schemes assets or property and do not make any investment decisions in relation to a scheme's underlying assets.
- Specifically, if any investor does exert any form of control it will not be considered to be a collective investment scheme for the purpose of this definition.

2.1 Reasons for using collective investment schemes

Collective investments are professionally managed diversified funds. This element of diversification helps to reduce the level risk of rather than investing in a just a handful of securities. Some funds have a range of diversified assets including bonds, equities, property and near-cash assets while others will be more specialised funds in terms of geographical area (Japan), sector (financial) or equities (UK smaller companies). They:

- provide investors who may only have a relatively small amount of capital with the opportunity to obtain exposure to areas in which they would not ordinarily be able to do by themselves;
- afford exposure to a diversified portfolio, which they would not be able to do by themselves;
- offer a spread of risk because they diversify and thus naturally spread the risks;
- reduce the administrative burden for investors;
- allow losses in some areas to be counterbalanced with profit in others – provided that there is sound management;
- allow access to professional expertise in dealing with the specified asset classes;
- offer portfolio administration at a relatively low cost;
- are suitable for investors without financial acumen or limited time to invest;
- reduce the cost of having to employ an investment manager directly; and
- eliminate day-to-day monitoring as is the case for some derivative instruments such as CFDs.

A fund manager will makes decisions concerning investments in underlying assets within the scope of the agreed investment mandate. The objective is to provide returns to the fund's investors, either in the form of capital growth (an increase in the price per unit) or income (dividends paid to the unit holders in proportion to the number of units they hold).

One purpose of investing in collective investment scheme is if an investor believes a fund manager will be able to make better investment decisions than they can.

2.2 Additional considerations

The scheme manager will use the fund to invest in various asset classes through a variety of securities, with not all having the same risk level. Therefore, investors should be mindful of the underlying assets comprising a particular fund and ensure that they are happy with the level of associated risk. Profits will be made by selling units or shares at a higher price than the price paid.

2.3 Types of collective investment scheme (open-ended or closed-ended)

Collective investment schemes are either 'open-ended' or 'closed-ended'. When deciding whether or not to invest in a collective (pooled) investment scheme, this is one the most important considerations and is particularly pertinent in times of market turmoil, which will be discussed more thoroughly later in this chapter. Each of these terms will be explained in the following sections.

3. Open-ended investments

Open-ended collective investment schemes are so-called because they are always open to new investors and have a variable asset pool unlike closed-ended schemes where there is a fixed asset pool represented by a fixed number of shares. In theory, open-ended schemes could issue an unlimited amount of units to investors. The managers of these schemes will make the market for the units and will always sell or buy units at or very near to their net asset value (NAV). Indeed, the scheme managers are obliged to buy units back from unit holders should the unit holder wish to cash-in their investment. Whenever a new investor chooses to invest money or an existing investor chooses to withdraw money in the open-ended fund, this net asset value is equal to the price and weight of the securities in the fund.

Open-ended scheme units are bought and sold on demand at their net asset value (NAV), which itself is based on the value of the fund's underlying assets less all liabilities. This is calculated as the total value of the underlying assets divided by the number of units in issue and is usually calculated each trading day at a specific time (and shown on a per unit basis). This is not the case with closed-ended schemes, the shares of which trade at either a discount or premium to NAV rather than at NAV.

Open-ended funds could in theory issue an unlimited number of units and when an investor wishes to purchase units, the fund-manager will create new and additional units. By contrast, if another investor wishes to sell units, the fund manager will buy back the units and cancel them and there is an obligation for the fund manager to redeem units/shares from a holder should he or she wish to sell them. As open-ended funds create and redeem shares on demand, investors may buy or sell shares at any time irrespective of whether or not other investors (unit holders/shareholders) of the scheme wish to buy or sell their shares.

The units/ shares of an open-ended company are always directly purchased from and sold to the fund manager, and never on the secondary market. The fund management company is always prepared to sell units to new investors, thus increasing the overall pool of assets. The funds received from investors are added to the existing portfolio and will be used to buy more assets and thus will create more units.

In an open-ended investment fund, the number of units in existence will change daily, and the size of the fund will expand or contract as new investments into the fund are made and thus new units created. Similarly, the number of units in existence will decrease as investors sell their units.

Worked Example 9.1

Assuming that an open-ended fund, perhaps a unit trust, has a total fund value of £100 million and there are 40 million issued units:

Open-ended fund value £100,000,000

Units in issue: 40,000,000

Net asset value = $\frac{£100,000,000}{40,000,000}$ = £2.50 per unit

An existing investor (unit holder) decides it is now advantageous to sell his investment currently 1,000,000 units value £2.50 = £2,500,000.

As a result of this investor's withdrawal, the fund value will diminish to a value of £97,500,000; consequently the number of issued units will reduce to 39,000,000.

There will now be $\frac{£97,500,000}{39,000,000}$ = £2.50 per unit

It can now be seen that there is a decrease in the value of the fund by £2,500,000.

- The number of units has decreased to 39,000,000.
- The unit price remains constant at £2.50.
- Other investors units holdings and the value remains unchanged at £2.50 per unit.
- Unit value can only increase as a result of an appreciation in the value of the underlying assets, not directly as a result of a cash investment.

Worked Example 9.2

If an open-ended fund currently has a total value of £500,000,000:

Number of units in issue 250,000,000

Therefore: $\frac{£500,000,000}{250,000,000}$ = £2.00 per unit

A HNWI (high net worth individual) has decided to invest exactly £1,000,000 capital in a unit trust. At the current price, the investor will be able to acquire 500,000 units.

The fund value will increase to £ 501,000,000 and the number of issued units will increase to 250,500,000.

$\frac{£501,000,000}{£2}$ = 250,500,000 units

$\frac{£501,000,000}{250,500,000}$ = £2.00 per unit

- There is an increase in the value of the fund by £1,000,000.
- The number of units has increased by 500,000.
- The unit price remains constant.

- Other investors units and value remain unchanged.
- There is always a direct correlation between the unit price and the value of the underlying assets.
- Unit prices will change on a daily basis according to the value of the underlying assets.
- The underlying assets will be revalued every day at a specific time, often 12:00 noon.

In an open-ended scheme, the total value of the fund changes not only as a result of incoming or outgoing funds but also due to any appreciation or depreciation in the value of the individual's underlying assets which comprise the portfolio, as these will change on a daily basis. However, the value of each unit only changes as a result of a change in the value of underlying assets and not because of incoming or outgoing funds.

3.1 Forward pricing

All open-ended schemes are subject to what is referred to as forward-pricing, which means that when investors either buy or sell units, they will not know at the time when they place their order the actual price they will have to pay or the amount they will receive for their units. The cost or proceeds will not actually be known until the deal is actually completed. The fund is revalued each business day – for example, at 12:00 noon. Therefore, if an order had been placed at perhaps 9:00 a.m. the same day, investors will not know the execution price until after 12:00 noon. If an order is placed after 4:30 p.m., the price will not be known until after noon on the next business day. The rationale underpinning forward pricing is to act as a deterrent to short-term trading, which would adversely affect the fund manager's investment strategies. After all, open-ended funds are for the longer-term.

4. Closed-ended collective investments

It has been stated already that with open-ended collective investment schemes the pool of assets is subject to constant change as new investors add funds while others withdraw funds. Similarly, as the assets of the fund increase or decrease by extra contributions or withdrawals, so too the number of units (shares) in issue will change. This is not the case with closed-ended schemes, where there is a fixed amount of share capital usually raised by an IPO. This means that the asset pool and number of shares (amount of share capital) will not increase. Instead, the issued shares will be traded on the secondary market and subject to the usual forces of supply and demand. Additional funds may be raised by those methods employed by companies – for example, a rights issue.

It should be emphasised that:

- closed-ended funds are not open to new investors and their share capital is limited – neither expanding nor contracting in response to investor demand; and
- as the number of shares is set from the outset and shares are bought or sold in the secondary market, the share price itself may trade at either a premium or discount to the NAV but not at NAV.

4.1 Undertakings for Collective Investment in Transferable Securities (UCITS)

In the EU, open-ended CISs are governed by the EC directive that introduced the law for Undertakings for Collective Investment in Transferable Securities (UCITS). This important European enactment, initially adopted in 1985 and updated as UCITS III in 2001, continues to be successful, and is being considered by countries outside the EU as a blueprint for introduction of similar laws. In the UK, UCITS resulted in the creation of open-ended investment companies (OEICs) as a new type of collective investment scheme structure.

derivative funds
A fund of financial instruments. A financial instrument is an asset having a monetary value or recording a monetary transaction (such as an option or futures contract).

index-tracking/tracker funds
A collective investment scheme in the form of a mutual fund or exchange-traded fund that aims to replicate the movements of an index of a specific financial market regardless of market conditions.

funds of funds (FOF)
An investment strategy of holding a portfolio of other investment funds rather than investing directly in shares, bonds or other securities. This type of investing is referred to as multi-manager investment.

UCITS III consists of two directives: the Management Directive and the Product Directive.

The Management Directive aims to give management companies (company or group) that manage collective investments a 'European Passport', which enables them to operate throughout the EU. A simplified prospective concept was also introduced to provide full and understandable product information, to assist marketing throughout EU (see developments below).

The Product Directive allows funds to invest in a wide range of financial instruments including money funds, **derivative funds**, **index-tracking funds** and **funds of funds**.

With EU-wide marketing, the objective is to reduce costs for the consumer through economies of scale.

UCITS IV was approved in January 2009 for introduction in 2011. This aims to introduce further simplification through:

- Key Investor Information (KII);
- a notification procedure;
- cooperation between member states; and
- a range of other smaller changes.

Test yourself 9.1

a) **Why do investors use collective investment schemes?**

b) **What funds are covered under the Product Directive?**

4.2 Types of open-ended investments

In the UK there are two main types of open-ended schemes: unit trusts and OEICs (open-ended investment companies). Each of these will now be explained while making reference to others. The important matter is to understand how the schemes operate and how they differ from closed-ended schemes.

4.2 Unit trusts

The Financial Conduct Authority (FCA) regulates the sales and marketing of unit trusts. The first unit trust for British investors was created in 1931 by M&G. Today, there are many differing types of unit trust ranging from very general to those which specialise in different areas with different aims and objectives. Some will have active strategies while others passive. Investors will need to decide which unit trust is most appropriate to their needs by matching with their overall investment objectives and thus will select one based on this. Investors may make such decision by themselves, or with the assistance of their own independent financial adviser. Some unit trusts may focus on achieving high income while others may focus on capital growth. There are balanced unit trusts that endeavour to achieve a combination of both capital growth and income growth.

First and foremost, unit trusts are open-ended collective investment schemes intended to spread investment over a wide range of assets to in order to reduce risks. This diversification enables an individual investor together with many other individual investors to have access to a large and diversified portfolio of underlying assets for a relatively small amount through a single investment which they would probably not be able to achieve by themselves. Unit trusts will have a wide range of underlying assets, which may include fixed interest securities, money market instruments. There are also specialist unit trusts focusing perhaps on the equities of UK smaller companies; however, even within such a specialised portfolio there will still be many different equities – perhaps 50–100. Unit trusts may also be specialised in terms of sector, perhaps the financial sector or even by geographic area, such as Japan, Europe or the USA. As units may be bought or redeemed at any time, it is less common for open-ended funds to invest in physical property. This is because if a significant number of investors were suddenly to decide to sell their units, it might prove more difficult to realise property investments rather than other forms of investment. Unit trust managers also may not be able to meet immediate demand.

All unit trusts will have a trust deed, the parties to which will be a manager (a limited company) and the trustees in which the legal title is vested (a financial institution such as a bank). The trustees will hold the assets of the unit trust comprising a varied range of underlying assets on behalf of the beneficiaries – the unit holders. These will be held by the trustees on trust for the beneficiaries.

The underlying assets will be valued and be divided over a number of units. At launch, the fund may have a value of, say, £10,000,000 which will be divided into small but equal units – for example, there may be 2,000,000 issued units. This would ostensibly give rise to a net asset value of £5.00 per unit. However, this would not be the price a new investor would pay for units, nor would an existing unit holder receive this should they wish to cash in their units subsequently. There may be a spread of £4.95–£5.05 between the bid/offer prices. Therefore, an investor would pay £5.05 for a unit while receiving only £4.95 per unit should they wish to cash in their units.

The price at which the fund manager sells units (the offer price) is the creation price. The price at which the fund manager buys units (the bid price) is the liquidation price.

Unit trust charges

In addition to the spread differential, there may be other charges including:

- an initial charge covering set-up costs, typically 2–3% of the value of the units purchased;
- an annual management charge of 1–2% of the value of an individual total unit holding; and/or
- an exit charge, where there is not an initial charge.

4.3 Open-ended investment companies (OEICs)

Open-ended investment companies are open-ended collective investment schemes that are professionally managed. They were introduced in the UK in 1997 following legislation and are run as companies with a board of directors issuing shares rather than units. In a similar manner to unit trusts, investors' money is pooled. Although there is a board of directors, it is the shareholders who own a fund's underlying assets. In the UK, OEICs are regulated by the FCA.

Contributions are combined with other shareholders funds and are invested in a selection of stocks, shares and other assets by the fund manager. This is known as the fund's investment portfolio.

This pooling of money with that of other investors provides the fund manager with more buying power to make additional and more diverse investments than could be effected by any individual investor. This reduces risk by spreading the fund across a number of different investments.

Again, like unit trusts, the value of an OEIC fund is linked to the performance of its portfolio. When the value of the underlying portfolio increases, the value of investors shares will grow too. The same applies if the value of the portfolio falls, meaning that so will the value of each share.

As collective investment funds, the principles of OEICs are broadly similar to those of unit trusts. However, there is one significant difference. The shares of OEICs are subject to what is known as 'single pricing', meaning that there is neither a bid nor offer price, and notably there is a single price for both buying and selling shares. Consequently, any initial charge is taken as a separate commission rather than as a spread.

As with unit trusts, OEICs do have 'variable capital', thus fund managers will create new shares as money is invested and cancel existing shares when funds are withdrawn. In a similar vein to unit trusts, OEIC funds' underlying assets are divided into equally priced shares, subject to daily revaluation. The price of OEIC shares varies directly with the underlying net asset value of each fund.

Test yourself 9.2

Why do UK investors choose open-ended funds?

4.4 European variants of OEICs

Investment company with variable capital (ICVC)
An ICVC is another name for an OEIC and is used in mainland Europe.

The names ICVC and OEIC are often used interchangeably. They again are open-ended and created in such a manner that they can be offered on a Pan-European basis and are structured as companies and controlled by an authorised corporate director (ACD) who fulfils the role of fund manager. The assets of the ICVC are owned by the depository whose role is similar to that of a unit trust trustee.

Sociétés d'investissement à Capital Variable (SICAVs)
A SICAV (Société d'Investissement à Capital Variable) is an open-ended collective investment scheme constituted as an investment company and similar to a UK OEIC. It is a corporate entity issuing shares rather than units. They are offshore funds domiciled outside of the UK and are mostly prevalent in Western Europe especially Luxembourg, Switzerland and France but may still be marketed throughout Europe including to UK investors.

Investors are shareholders and are allowed to express their views on the management of the company at the annual general meetings. The other difference is the administrative constraints of which the SICAV is subject to, but in practice have no real consequences.

SICAVs often have many sub-funds that invest in many different global markets, including:

- equity funds;
- bond funds;
- property funds; and
- smaller companies sector.

Investment can be in one or more of the sub-funds, and can then easily be switched into other funds.

The differences between OEICs and SICAVs
- OEICs are open-ended investment companies based in the UK, whereas SICAVS tend to be operated from Luxembourg, Switzerland and France.

- SICAVs are taxed differently to OEICs in the UK as they operate under the jurisdiction of the country where they are located.
- A main consideration for UK investors is whether these funds have 'distributor' or 'non-distributor' status, as this affects how they are taxed. If the former, they are taxed as per a UK unit trust. If the latter, then all returns are taxed as income, which is less attractive for many UK investors as they cannot use their capital gains tax allowance to avoid tax on gains. The boards of SICAVs must apply for 'distributor' status each year and in order to qualify for this status, it is a requirement that 85% of yearly profits have to be distributed to investors by way of dividends.
- SICAVs are 'UCITS III' funds, which means their managers have the ability to use derivatives to generate higher returns, rather than simply to reduce risk.
- SICAVs tend to have higher fees than unit trusts and OEICs. Their total expense ratios – a measure of their management and performance fees – tend to be higher than those of an OEIC.
- Time zone differences mean that SICAVs are valued at 3 p.m. while most funds in the UK are valued at noon. Because of this, many fund supermarkets have yet to offer SICAVs to retail customers.

Fonds communs de Placement (FCPs)

FCP (Fonds Communs de Placement) are open-ended mutual funds, constituted as a contractual common ownership entity without legal personality. The FCP is a co-ownership entity that issues units of a fund; the investor is a member of the co-ownership but has no rights related to a shareholder. Like unit trusts, they are professionally managed open-ended collective investment schemes.

The Irish Common Contractual Fund (CCF)

A CCF is an Irish regulated asset pooling fund structure, first introduced in 2003, which enables only institutional investors, to pool assets into a single fund vehicle with the aim of achieving cost savings, enhanced returns and operational efficiency through economies of scale. It is an unincorporated body established under a deed where investors are 'co-owners' of underlying assets held pro rata with their investment. There are now over 70 such funds in existence.

A CCF is established by a management company and only institutional investors are permitted in this structure. The CCF is authorised and regulated by the Central Bank of Ireland, and can be structured as a UCITS or an AIF.

Taxation of CCFs

A CCF is transparent for Irish legal and tax purposes. Investors are treated as if they directly own a proportionate share of the underlying investments in the CCF and therefore profits are treated as accruing or arising to the investors as if they had not passed through the CCF. The availability of double tax treaties reliefs are between the investor and investment jurisdiction. Therefore, in a situation where you have a UK pension fund investor, it is the UK treaty with the country of investment that one would look to in order to determine the withholding tax rate on the equities held.

A key policy goal of the Irish Tax authorities is to enshrine the tax transparency of the CCF into any new double tax agreements, with a number of Irish treaties already confirming CCF transparency.

Key tax benefits of the CCF include the following:

- The CCF benefits from Ireland's competitive tax regime providing certainty, stability and transparency.
- A CCF can avail of tax transparency in over 20 markets of investment; examples of such markets include Australia, Canada, Germany, Italy, the UK and the USA.
- Similar to all Irish regulated funds, the CCF benefits from a tax neutral regime.

The CCF – the non-tax benefits

- CCFs can be used as an efficient pooling master vehicle under UCITS IV allowing direct investment for institutional/pension funds seeking tax transparency.
- CCFs have a flexible structure to meet the demands of asset owners such as multinationals and can be established as a single or multi-fund vehicle with single or multiple managers.

5. Fund supermarkets

Fund supermarkets were established in the late 1990s to enable investors who wished to choose their own open-ended fund to invest without paying the full initial fees.

As their name implies, they are financial supermarkets specialising in the provision of funds and other investment products. They are in effect online 'platforms', although instructions may be taken by telephone, allowing investors to buy and hold a wide range of funds including unit trusts, OEICs, investment trusts and other investment products from a host of fund management companies together in one portfolio. One of the most important facets of fund supermarkets is that an investor is able to select one or many funds from different fund providers such as Fidelity or JP Morgan. They also afford investors the ability to monitor their portfolio and to invest in a tax-efficient manner. By going through a fund supermarket rather than buying a fund directly from a fund management company itself, it could be cheaper as they offer discounts to the initial charge levied by the fund management company. All investments from different fund managers can be viewed in a single portal.

They usually provide extensive research and information including which companies, sectors and country each fund manager is invested in, historical and recent performance figures and analysis of the investment styles adopted by fund managers. Funds supermarkets try to match needs of an investor with the funds they provide, thus encouraging self-investment.

The crucial point is that fund supermarkets are designed for those who are making their own investment decisions execution only. They are especially intended for those investors who will make their own decisions in terms of both selecting and buying investments. Brokers will only invest based on instructions provided by the investor and will not provide advice. This does not, however, preclude investors seeking advice from an IFA.

Fund supermarkets offer investors access to a wide range of investment products, the ability to monitor their portfolio, invest tax efficiently and reduce administration all via a single portal. This means investors are entirely responsible for selecting and buying their own investment products, and that an investment broker will only place their funds into the products selected, rather than advising them which investments to select.

Some fund supermarkets will only offer unit trusts and OEICs (open-ended investment companies) while others will specialise in investment trust companies and others provide access to stock-exchange listed investments, such as shares and exchange traded funds (ETFs).

Fees are always a major consideration for investors. A skilled fund manager may help to smooth market turmoil or achieve market-beating returns, but with annual fees traditionally around 1.5% or more.

Following the FCA's ban on commission, fund charges have fallen, with 0.75% becoming the norm. Additionally, fund supermarkets, as is the case with financial advisers, will add a separate charge for their service, either as a fixed annual fee or a percentage of assets. In addition to offering access to funds and other investments, they allow investments to be placed within a tax-efficient wrapper – normally a stocks and shares ISA or a self-invested personal pension (SIPP). Within these tax-efficient wrappers, dividend income is untaxed, even if it exceeds the annual dividend allowance. Interest from corporate bonds and gilts, and from funds that invest in these assets, is also tax free. There is no capital gains tax on any investment profits within either ISAs or SIPPs.

Test yourself 9.3

a) **What are the main European equivalents of an OEIC?**

b) **What are the advantages of using a fund supermarket?**

5.1 The Alternative Investment Fund Managers Directive (AIFMD)

This is a regulatory framework for alternative investment fund managers (AIFMs), including managers of hedge funds, private equity firms and investment trusts.

The AIFMD was implemented in the UK on 22 July 2013. It has a wide scope and with a few exceptions, covers the management, administration and marketing of alternative investment funds (AIFs). Its focus is on regulating the AIFM (fund manager) rather than the AIF (the fund). It is directed at those firms offering asset management services to professional investors.

An AIF is a 'collective investment undertaking' that is not subject to the UCITS regime, and includes hedge funds, private equity funds, retail investment funds, investment companies and real estate funds. The AIFMD establishes an EU-wide harmonised framework for monitoring and supervising risks posed by AIFMs and the AIFs they manage, and for strengthening the internal market in alternative funds. It also includes new requirements for firms acting as a depositary for an AIF.

Aims of the AIFMD

- To enhance supervisory practices among EEA competent authorities to support timely and pre-emptive action to prevent market instability and the build-up of systemic risk in the European financial system.
- To improve investor protection for retail, professional and institutional investors by imposing new depositary standards and enhanced transparency through new investor disclosure rules and mandatory reporting to competent authorities
- To encourage efficiency and cross-border competition by deregulating national barriers and creating level playing fields by means of harmonised rules on an EEA-wide passport for full-scope EEA AIFMs to market and manage AIFs.

5.2 Closed-ended collective investment schemes

Unlike the units and shares of open-ended collective investment schemes, closed-ended schemes shares tend to trade at either a premium or discount to Net Asset Value (NAV) rather than specifically at NAV. This reflects supply and demand for the shares per se than the value of underlying assets portfolio.

6. Investment trust companies (ITCs)

In the UK, the investment trust sector is one of the largest sectors of the LSE. Investment trusts companies (also investment trusts or investment companies), like open-ended funds such as unit trusts and OEICs, are collective investment schemes in that they pool investors' money and use it to manage a portfolio of selected assets that should pay dividends and/or grow in value over the long term. However, although the purposes of open-ended funds and closed-ended schemes are similar, there are some significant differences.

The most important matter to consider is that the inclusion of the word 'trust' is rather misleading, as investment trusts or investment trust companies (ITCs) are not trusts at all. They are actually quoted limited companies that issue shares (not units) on recognised stock exchanges. In the UK they are governed by the Companies Act, the AIFMD in the EU and similar legislation across the world that support collective investment schemes. There will be a board of directors rather than trustees who are answerable to its shareholders.

ITCs are closed-ended companies, meaning that the number of shares (share capital) is fixed from the outset – when the ITC is first launched by means of an IPO. This is in contrast to the number of units or shares open-ended funds, which increase or decrease in direct response to investor demand (or lack of it). The fact that the share capital is fixed means that investors cannot withdraw funds, thus enabling directors to plan ahead. This is not the case with open-ended funds, where investors can withdraw funds whenever they wish by redeeming their shares.

The managers of the ITC will invest the funds raised into equities, gilts, corporate bonds and other assets including property. However, this is the maximum amount of capital the fund manager has to work with from shareholders together with borrowings discussed subsequently. Investors who did not buy shares at launch may buy and sell shares on the secondary market through brokers rather than directly through the fund manager.

The value of an ITC's asset pool can increase based on asset appreciation or perhaps sound investment decisions. However, any appreciation in asset value is not distributed to the shareholders, who will only receive their returns in terms of dividends and increases in the value of their shares.

As is the case with all limited companies, ITCs will have a memorandum, articles of association and a prospectus which will outline the specific purpose of the ITC and which specifies the asset classes and geographical areas in which it will invest. The directors cannot deviate from this investment strategy without the approval of shareholders. The business of the ITC is ultimately to increase shareholder value.

As the number of shares is fixed, the share price is dependent on the difference between the supply of shares and the demand for the same shares in the secondary market, rather than directly on the value of the underlying investments held in the fund.

6.1 Capital structure and Net Asset Value

An ITC has a fixed capital structure meaning that the fund manager is not concerned with the size of the underlying fund as is the case with open-ended funds where the fund manager may have to sell their most valuable assets in order to satisfy unit holder withdrawals. This allows the manager of an ITC to take a longer-term view without having to sell assets. This will also allow the fund manager to achieve better long-term performance. The return to ITC investors is composed of two elements:

1. capital growth – increase in the ITCs share price; and
2. income – in the form of dividend payments.

Investors may purchase their shares either through an IPO or alternatively through a stockbroker with the share price being dependant as with many other quoted shares by the forces of supply and demand. The market price may be dependent on a number of factors including:

- the value of the underlying assets held by the ITC;
- the availability of the shares in the market-supply and demand; and
- level of demand for the ITC shares.

There are, therefore, two figures which must be considered when deciding whether or not to commit funds into investment trust shares:

1. the net asset value (NAV) per share (which is the value of the underlying portfolio after any liabilities have been accounted for, divided by the number of shares in issue); and
2. the quoted share price at which the trust is trading.

The value of an ITC's investments is calculated as the net asset value (NAV) and expressed on a per share value. This is calculated as the value of an ITC company's assets less the total value of its liabilities and usually expressed on a per share basis. The NAV is usually calculated at 12:00 daily for most ITCs; for more specialised ITCs, this may be weekly.

The relationship between the quoted share price and NAV gives rise to the terms discount and premium. If the quoted share price is less than the NAV, the share price is said to be trading at a discount to NAV. Conversely, if the share price is trading above NAV, the share price is said to be trading at a premium to NAV. It is more common for ITC shares to trade at a discount than a premium.

ITCs shares trade at a premium to NAV for the following reasons:

- Investors are bullish and believe that the price of the ITCs share will rise.
- Where an ITC is paying a high and growing dividend.
- The fund manager or management team have a good reputation and investors have confidence in them.
- If an investment trust has been in the news or is one of the only trusts operating in a specific area.
- Perceived undervaluation in reported ITCs' NAVs. This may include unquoted investments, such as property or private equity, and thus investors may believe that the NAV of a trust has risen beyond its officially reported value.
- Where its assets are rising quickly in value causing high demand for its shares.
- Where the ITC is the subject of a potential takeover or reorganisation.

ITCs shares trade at a discount to NAV for the following reasons:

- Investor have concerns of the management performance and have been selling. This can mean the trust's share price falls faster than its NAV, increasing the discount.
- Investors may be sceptical and believe that the trust's NAV is far less than quoted.
- A lack of faith. Investors may believe bad management is going to reduce the investment trust's NAV instead of growing it. This is often seen with ITCs with a poor track record.

- ITC trading at a discount may not be the bargain it first appears – or at least the discount may not be set to narrow in the near future.
- Perceived overvaluation in reported ITCs' NAVs. This may include unquoted investments, such as property or private equity, and thus investors may believe that the NAV of a trust has fallen beyond its officially reported value.

6.2 Gearing advantage

Investment trusts are considered to have a higher risk profile than open-ended schemes because they have the ability to borrow, which open-ended schemes do not. This borrowing of money is often referred to as gearing or leverage. The fund manager will then use the borrowed money to make additional investments and potentially produce a better return on the capital employed in order to enhance fund performance and hence shareholder value. Borrowing to invest may be advantageous when markets are rising as profits are magnified, however, when markets are falling losses can also be magnified. If incorrect decisions are made, such gearing can lead to significant losses, especially if the cost of borrowing increases dramatically. Potential investors should be aware that some ITCs use more gearing than others and the range varies from no gearing (0%) to as much as 20% under normal market conditions. An investment trust's gearing policy may be found in its prospectus and annual reports. Potential investors should refer to these documents before making any financial commitment.

There are times when it is better to hold cash especially in a falling market. As ITCs do not have any restriction on the amount of cash it may hold, it can hold 100% of its funds in cash and invest when there are signs of a recovery.

6.3 Dividend advantage

ITCs enjoy a unique selling point for income investors which open-ended schemes do not – the ability to smooth annual dividend payments, where the fund managers can set aside up to 15% of the dividend payment it has generated. They can use this money to supplement dividend payments in future years if the income yield in those years fails to meet expectations. This could be the case if the underlying companies that form the ITC's underlying portfolio cut their own dividends or fail to make dividend payments at all.

6.4 New share issues

ITCs are able to increase their capital structure by issuing new shares. The procedure follows normal market practice, as explained in Chapter 3.

formula asset value
In this context, the calculation used for the merger of an ITC's ordinary and 'C' shares, based on the net asset values of the separate portfolios within the fund at the agreed merger date.

A prospectus is issued, and shareholder approval has to be obtained at a general meeting of the company. New shares known as 'C' shares are issued, and the money raised is invested through a separate fund, but remains part of the ITC. When all the money raised by the issue of new shares has been invested, usually by a predetermined date, the new fund and the existing fund will join together using a formula agreed by shareholders in the prospectus. This conversion calculation is known as the **formula asset value** (FAV).

6.5 Warrants

When new issues are undertaken by ITCs, it is usual to issue warrants at the same time. A warrant is an equity instrument that allows the holder to convert the warrant into an ordinary share at a predetermined price fixed at issue on a specific date or dates in the future.

Warrants have an expiry date after which they become valueless, and are therefore classed as 'wasting assets' for accounting and investment purposes. They are quoted on a stock market and can trade at a premium or discount to the share price of the ITC.

Shortly before the date of conversion, an investor should calculate whether to convert to the underlying share or sell the warrant and buy shares in the market. If an instruction has not been received at the time of the final conversion date and the warrant has a value, an ITC will usually sell these outstanding warrants on behalf of their holders in the market and hold the proceeds in a separate account until claimed.

6.6 Share buy-backs

The number of shares an ITC has in issue can be reduced by buying back its own shares in the market. Shareholders normally give the directors permission, for a set period (for example, until the next AGM), to buy back shares at a price determined by the level of discount. Such an operation has become popular in recent years as a method of reducing the share price discount to the NAV, allowing the ITC to avoid winding up due to the action of corporate raiders. The shares bought back can either be cancelled or held in reserve to reissue at a future date under particular conditions approved by shareholders.

Test yourself 9.4

a) **What are ITCs and how are they governed?**

b) **What is meant by total return?**

c) **With reference to ITCs, what are warrants? When are they issued, and why?**

Stop and think 9.1

Describe the relationship between the quoted share price and the net asset value of an investment trust company (ITC).

7. Split capital trusts

Split capital trusts (SCTs) were first introduced in the 1960s. They were and still are a variant on investment trust companies, and are closed-ended. SCTs had a similar objective to ITCs: managing a portfolio of underlying investments in order to enhance shareholder value. They were created in order to meet the needs of more than one type of investor. However, SCTs differed from ITCs in a number of significant ways:

- SCTs had a limited duration, typically 10 years. After which they were wound up and the proceeds distributed to the different share classes. This is not the case with ITCs.
- Offered two classes of share in order to cater for the investment needs of different types of investor – those seeking income and those seeking capital growth. However, this did not preclude an investor from buying different classes of share.
- After the conclusion of the specified lifespan, the SCT was wound up, all of the assets were sold, liabilities settled and the proceeds distributed according to the prospectus.

Income shareholders receive the returns generated from the company's investments during its lifetime. Capital shares shareholders will receive a proportion of the lump sum when the assets are realised after the expiry. Investors could therefore concentrate on either capital growth or income by buying selecting the class of share that is most appropriate to their investment needs and tax status.

7.1 Reasons for investing in a split capital trust

Today, split capital trusts have evolved into far more complex investments and investors should not make any financial commitment unless they understand the potential risks and rewards fully. Prior to making any investment, it would be prudent to seek advice from an IFA. There are now more often than not more than two share classes, and the reasons for investing in SCTs include the following:

- SCTs like ITCs still invest in other companies and they will issue all classes of share simultaneously.
- There is a specific date when the SCT will be wound up. Investors know that at this date they should receive some form of distribution, or the opportunity to roll over into a new SCT with a new life span.
- Different classes of share are provided to meet the needs of different investors.
- Some share classes have no income associated with them, consequently there is no income tax liability. They can also be useful if there is an unused capital gains tax allowances or to offset capital losses.

7.2 Procedure on winding-up

As SCTs have evolved, it may be that all share classes do not have a limited life but at least one will. This means that on a set date, it will be necessary to sell some or all of the assets and distribute the proceeds to those particular shareholders. In the event that the whole company has a finite life, this will activate a winding-up procedure as set out in the SCT's own articles – regulations that would typically use the following protocol:

- All assets (the company's own investments) will be realised.
- All liabilities will be paid, including bank loans.
- Any remaining funds will be distributed to the shareholders in harmony with the agreements.

At the conclusion of the SCT, there is a strong likelihood that the provider will offer another opportunity for shareholders to reinvest their money in a new split capital trust which is effectively a roll-over and which will be executed in order to reduce tax liabilities particularly for higher-rate taxpayers. However, there will not be any obligation to commit to the new offering. Share retention until the official winding-up date is not essential, as the shares may be sold on the secondary market.

7.3 SCT Share classes and distribution on winding-up

Annuity income shares
They are similar in nature to retirement annuities with investors making lump sum investments in return for a regular high yield. They are most appropriate for investors requiring security of income while inappropriate for those requiring the return of capital.

Income shares
These are suitable for those investors requiring income rather than capital returns. The returns available on these shares are generally considerably higher than those available on bank deposit accounts, however, without capital growth. In theory, shareholders ought to receive all of their capital back at winding-up, but more often than not they do not as it should be understood that shareholders are committing to a limited company which could become insolvent before the official winding-up date. Even income is not guaranteed and may fluctuate from year to year. The amount of money an income shareholder will receive at winding-up depends on how well the SCT performs. Income received is generated from the underlying assets, notably dividends derived from the underlying equities themselves.

Zero dividend preference shares
As their name implies, this class of share provides absolutely no dividend payment throughout the duration of the SCT; however, SCTs do provide a predetermined amount at redemption. This does not mean that a return is guaranteed. In the event that the SCT is unsuccessful, there may be absolutely no return of capital. However, the word 'preference' in the title does mean that

ZDPs involve less risk than capital and income shares, as they are paid out before either of these share classes but after bank borrowings and debentures when the trust winds up, meaning investors are more likely to realise capital growth than with capital shares. In highly geared SCTs where money has been borrowed in order to increase capital growth and income, they can be very high risk, especially if borrowing cannot be repaid.

Capital shares

Capital shareholders will receive all or most of the capital appreciation at winding-up – they will receive the remaining assets after liabilities have been settled and all other shareholders (income and ZDP) have been paid. They are most appropriate for investors seeking capital appreciation, and are not suitable for those who are less risk averse. As with ZDPs they provide absolutely no income, however, they may yield very high capital returns should the SCT perform well. Unlike ZDPs, there is no predetermined return. This is potentially very good as investors in such shares may receive considerable returns in contrast to ZDPs, which will receive as a maximum the predetermined amount or less. The potential downside is that after the payment of all other share classes, there could be nothing remaining.

Income and capital growth shares

They are a type of hybrid share in that they provide income and capital growth. However, that are at the bottom of the ranking at wind up. They tend to pay a lower return than ordinary income shares as there is a possibility of capital growth when the SCT is wound up.

When deciding whether or not to invest in an SCT, it is important remember that it is a company that is being invested in and the performance is dependent upon the performance of the underlying assets combined with the investment skills of the fund managers. Having selected the most appropriate SCT for their needs, investors should then decide on the most appropriate share class. It is also important to be mindful that all SCTs will not provide all classes of shares discussed within the chapter; there may be other classes not discussed here. Investors should also look at the level of gearing within an SCT; this should not be more than 20% of the overall funding.

Making it work 9.1: SCTs – a risky business?

Some UK SCTs had substantial bank borrowings and cross holdings (investments in other high-income STCs) to enhance income receipts, enabling them to pay high dividends, for which there was a strong demand. When asset prices fell, initially due to the technology bust, some trusts found that the value of their assets, which were falling, did not cover the bank borrowing covenants. The banks then put them into liquidation to recover their loans.

Fortunately, many (but not all) SCTs eventually recovered, and regulations have now been implemented by the FCA to prevent this situation from arising again.

8. Assessing ITCs and SCTs

In order to assess ITCs and SCTs properly, an investor has to be able to determine the level of gearing and work out from this the asset cover: the number of times that the value of investments held covers the total amount of borrowings.

Both ITCs and SCTs are able to borrow money from a bank, and invest this money in further assets, with the expectation that the return will outweigh the cost of borrowings. If this happens, then the return to investors will be enhanced. In contrast, underperformance plus borrowing costs will result in a lower return to investors. Borrowing for this type of investment is known as financial gearing.

SCTs are, by their capital structure, geared as to their different share classes. This arises from the predetermined entitlement to the assets of the company at the **winding-up date** (see section 6).

winding-up date
The date, often predetermined, when a company or class of share is liquidated and shareholders receive the net proceeds.

Test yourself 9.5

a) **What is a simple SCT share structure?**

b) **What are the two main reasons for the popularity of SCTs?**

Stop and think 9.2

How does risk arise with SCT investments?

9. Real estate investment trusts (REITs)

Real estate investment trusts (REITs) were first introduced in the UK in 2007. Since then, many of the UK's largest property companies have converted to REIT status and in addition to this a number of start-up UK REITs have been established. They are actually closed-ended investment companies and not trusts. A REIT may be a single company REIT or alternatively a group REIT owning and managing property on behalf of its shareholders.

They are companies solely dedicated to property investment meaning that, unlike many other property investments, they can hold commercial and/or residential property, but not owner-occupied buildings.

They are traded on the LSE or AIM, as are other company shares. They provide a relatively easy method for retail investors to access property investments indirectly for minimum outlay while providing shareholders with exposure to the risks and rewards of owning property without actually having to make a property purchase.

For a company to qualify for REIT status, there are a number of specific criteria that must be satisfied. These are determined by HMRC and include the following:

- Company conditions – a potential UK-REIT has to carry out a property rental business, which may be a UK property investment business or alternatively an overseas property investment business.
- Property rental business conditions – at least 75% of the company's profits must derive from that property rental business.
- Balance of business conditions – at least 75% of the company's gross assets must comprise assets or cash involved in the property rental business.

If REIT status is granted and the REIT adheres to these criteria, it will pay neither corporation nor capital gains tax on their property investments. This also serves to attract investment in UK real estate.

REITs are most appropriate for income investors rather than those seeking capital growth, as they have to pay out 90% of their income derived from property to shareholders as dividends. The fact that there is no capital gains tax or corporation tax will also mean that investors will only be subject to personal income tax at their marginal rate – the dividends will not be taxed twice.

9.1 Benefits of REITs

UK REITs provide a wide range of benefits to companies and investors alike. They are listed on the main market or AIM, and as such enjoy many of the benefits associated with London's equity markets.

The benefits for REIT companies include:

- if a company or group of companies is granted REIT status, this will grant exemption from corporation tax on profits and gains from their UK qualifying property rental businesses;
- the provision of a tax-efficient structure;
- access to new investor capital; and
- potentially closer performance to Net Asset Value (NAV).

The benefits for REIT investors include:

- provision of tax transparency;
- provision of potentially high-yield returns, as REITs must distribute at least 90% but maybe more of their taxable income derived from property rental income to shareholders; and

- the income being treated as property rental income rather than dividends – the taxation from property is transferred from the corporate level to investor level.

9.2 Appraising REITs

- REITs must distribute at least 90% of their taxable income derived from property rental income to shareholders.
- There will also be changes, possibly capital appreciation, of the REIT shares and changes in Net Asset Value (NAV) which represents the value of all the underlying assets owned by a REIT (for example, if the assets are owned by the REIT), less any debt. If the value of the properties increases, either through market movements or development activity, the REIT's NAV will increase.
- If a REIT, or the sector in which it invests, is particularly popular, demand might cause the share price to move to a premium over the NAV. The same process in reverse might cause the REIT to a discount. However, as a general rule, REIT share prices will tend to move in harmony with the NAV.
- Since REITs are required to pay out 90% of their income to investors, it can be difficult for them to accumulate sufficient capital to reinvest in new properties from their own earnings. For companies looking to expand, there will be two main methods of funding growth – selling new shares, perhaps by a rights issue or alternatively increasing debt/gearing.
- Such gearing will prevents investors' shareholdings from being diluted, as they would be if the REIT chose to raise more equity, but the level of debt in a REIT is something investors should monitor.
- REIT debt is usually measured in relation to the NAV through what is called loan-to-value (LTV), the proportion of the property portfolio that is funded by borrowings.
- As property values can change quickly, it could means that a REIT with a high level of debt/gearing can quickly find itself in difficulty as its LTV increases dramatically – especially if a downturn also impacts rental income, reducing the ability to service or repay debt.
- REITs are different – there are specialised REITs focusing on specific segments of the property market such as health care or retail. Investors should consider these differences and see if they will match their own investment aims and objectives.

10. Exchange-traded funds (ETFs)

Exchange-traded funds are open-ended collective schemes, and are in some respects similar to unit trusts or OEICs, but are actually set up as listed companies issuing shares. They allow investors to gain exposure to many companies or underlying assets with a single purchase, although similar to index-tracker funds, they allow greater flexibility.

The shares of the ETF company are issued by way of an IPO. The proceeds raised are then used to buy a portfolio which more or less (but not exactly) mirrors a particular index – for example, S&P 500 or sector (financial) – and will then track that particular index or sector.

The created shares and issued are given to a market maker in exchange for an entire portfolio of shares with the ETF fund manager. There is no cash exchange between the ETF manager and the market maker. The creation and cancellation of units is strictly between them. Thus the fund manager will create or redeem shares in exchange for securities which are then traded to other investors by the market maker at a bid and offer price – supply and demand.

Share prices will vary throughout the course of each business day which is in contrast to unit trusts which are only valued once daily. The prices of the shares will more or less reflect the index on which the ETF is based, but not exactly, and indeed more or less at NAV. However, this may not always be the case, for instance if the ETF were based on the FTSE 100 but only had 95 of the FTSE 100 company shares included within the fund. If five of the FTSE company shares not included in the portfolio rose substantially, the rise in the FTSE might not be reflected in the ETF share price.

A key issue to consider is in respect of the issuance and redemption (cancellation of ETF shares) which is between the ETF manager and a market maker. The principal and relationship is similar to that of a unit trust manager and unit holder, in that the manager will issue new units and cancel existing ones.

The ETF manager will issue new shares and cancel existing shares in exchange for an entire portfolio of securities based on a specific index or sector. Thus ETF shares are created by receiving underlying shares from market marker and redeemed by returning underlying shares to the market maker. There is absolutely no exchange of money and therefore no stamp duty has to be paid.

ETFs are suitable for private investors; however, they may only be traded on the secondary market and may be purchased through brokers. The prices of the shares will reflect the supply of and demand for the ETF shares per se which tend to trade at or near NAV – for example, the value of the shares in the S&P 500 index. Unlike traditional unit trusts or OEICs, shares are not sold to investors or bought from investors at NAV. Dividends paid are based on the underlying portfolio.

Advantages and disadvantages of ETFs

Advantages include the following:

- They trade at or very close to net asset value and track the respective index closely but not exactly.
- Live prices are available in contrast to other open-ended funds, which are only valued once a day.
- Charges are relatively low. There is no initial charge with ETFs and there are no brokerage charges between ETF managers and market makers, which keeps charges down.
- No stamp duty is payable on purchase.

- They can be held in an ISA or SIPP with the related tax advantages.
- They allow investor exposure to foreign markets, including S&P 500.
- They are regarded as a particularly good way of investing in international markets because an investor is buying that market's index.
- ETFs are shares quoted on a stock market, but they are not affected like ITCs by premiums and discounts, as the dealing price reflects the market index, minus fund fees and a small tracking error.

The disadvantage is that as no commissions are paid to IFAs, they tend not to recommend them.

European ETFs are covered by UCITS legislation, with assets held by a custodian. There is no counterparty exposure for ETFs investing in securities under UCITS, but a commodity-based ETF is likely to require one. Investors should check if there is a counterparty before investing, and should also check if an ETF holds 'real' investments – for example, an index – as ETFs described as synthetic are very high risk.

More complicated ETFs are becoming available as the product develops and demand grows. They are popular with private investors in the USA and Europe because:

- the cost of investing is low; and
- the buying or selling price is near to the value of the underlying assets.

Test yourself 9.6

a) Why invest in REITs?

b) Why are ETFs popular with investors?

11. Venture capital trusts (VCTs)

First introduced in the UK in 1995, venture capital trusts (VCTs) are limited companies whose shares are traded on the London Stock Exchange just like Barclays or BP. However, rather than banking or oil, they aim to achieve returns for their shareholders by investing in other companies, typically smaller companies looking for further investment to expand their own business. The purpose of VCTs is to encourage individuals to invest in companies not yet listed on any recognised stock exchange. In return for such investment, the VCT shareholders will receive a number of tax benefits.

VCT investment is an extremely significant yet high-risk area of the UK economy, as smaller companies may struggle or fail completely. However, without funding from venture capitalists many now famous companies would never have been able to establish themselves and thus would not be able to have expanded their businesses. VCTs are therefore aimed at wealthier, sophisticated investors who can afford to take a long-term view. The Financial Conduct Authority (FCA) suggests that a sophisticated investor is somebody with an annual income in excess of £100,000 or investable assets of more than £250,000. Investors in VCTs must be over 18 years of age. VCT investment should account for no more than 10% of a well-diversified portfolio.

VCTs afford their shareholders the opportunity of indirect investment into a portfolio comprising, for example, 20–30 start-up companies which they might not ordinarily be able to access. Such diversification will also help mitigate the risk of direct investment in only one or two start-up companies.

VCTs will raise money from investors by selling their shares and the funds raised together with any loan capital (they are allowed to borrow), and then use the money to invest in a portfolio of unquoted and thus higher-risk start-up companies, which may include companies listed on AIM. The VCT's percentage holdings of these companies will form the portfolio of underlying assets, which will help the shareholders achieve their income and capital returns.

In order to encourage investment in this area, the UK government currently offers generous tax benefits to VCT shareholders in terms of both income and capital returns, including tax relief of up to 30%. The tax rules and related benefits are subject to change; therefore, it is strongly recommended that students consult HMRC's website for the current information.

It is important to be aware that VCTs must be approved by HMRC and must invest in or lend money to unlisted companies which themselves must also be qualifying companies.

Shareholders may invest in many different companies through different VCTs and ostensibly obtain exposure to maybe 100 different unlisted companies by investing perhaps in four VCTs, but there are maximum amounts of tax benefits. At the time of writing, the maximum annual investment relief can be claimed is on £200,000 and the percentage on which relief can be claimed is 30%. There is no income tax payable on dividend income.

Shareholders are only able to claim tax relief in the tax year they invest and there is no need to pay any income tax on any dividends whether new issues or in the secondary market. There are also exemptions from capital gains tax when shares are sold; however, there is no relief for capital losses against income. In order to qualify for tax relief, the entire VCT trust investment must be kept for five years. If any of the shares stop qualifying in this time, income tax relief on those shares only will cease; however, it will be retained if there is a connection with the VCT or a company in which it is invested. Income tax relief against your investment in the VCT must be newly issued shares.

A VCT will typically invest in perhaps 20–30 such businesses selected by the fund manager and who is skilled in identifying opportunities among new companies. The fund manager will target and negotiate attractive deals for investors, and will provide expertise to the start-up companies in order that they themselves can expand and thus provide greater returns for shareholders.

Investors should always be mindful that the VCT company will be looking to sell their share of any particular business between three and seven years after their initial investment and will subsequently use the proceeds of the sale to invest in other start-ups.

A maximum of 15% of the total fund may be invested into any single start-up company. The primary source of income is the receipt of tax-free dividend payments. VCTs are particularly attractive to those seeking to reduce their tax bill and generate income from their capital. 30% income tax relief for subscriptions in new VCT fund raisings. There is no capital gains tax (CGT) to pay on disposal.

Risks for investors

- VCTs are unlikely to be suitable for those investors with limited capital who may need access to their money in the short term, or for whom loss of the investment could cause financial hardship.
- VCTs are inherently higher risk, as smaller companies can be prone to failure. They may struggle or fail completely.
- VCT shares are relatively illiquid and consequently they are difficult trade and it may be especially difficult to sell on the secondary market.
- The market price of the shares may not reflect the value of the underlying portfolio of interests in the companies.
- Dividend income is not guaranteed.
- Shareholders may receive less than they invest, when they sell shares, if the company becomes bankrupt or if there is a fall in the value of underlying assets.
- Investors should also be aware of risks affecting specific VCTs For instance, a further issue arises from smaller VCT funds that fail to raise sufficient money at launch. The resulting portfolio of investments may be more concentrated and it could increase the risks and charges.
- All VCTs tend to have higher charges than other types of fund and usually have performance fees.
- It is possible that HMRC could withdraw the tax status of the VCT if it fails to meet the qualifying requirements. If this happens, any tax rebate may have to be repaid. Each VCT will issue a prospectus at launch which gives details of specific risks and it should be read thoroughly before considering an investment

Although some VCTs may be viewed as less speculative than other closed-ended investment schemes, shareholders should remember that as a whole, they are exposed to substantially higher risks than standard equities.

VCT charges

There is an annual management charge. Total fees are around 3.5% and will be charged to the fund. A shareholder can invest up to a maximum £200,000 in VCTs in any one tax year, and spread this across a number of VCTs in order to benefit from this tax relief. However, the maximum tax rebate is the amount of income tax that the investor has actually paid.

In order to keep the rebate, the shares must be held for five years and the rebate is only available when investing in a new issue of shares in a VCT or a top-up, not on any VCTs shares bought on the open market. However, VCTs bought on the secondary market count towards the £200,000 allowance for the tax year in which they were purchased, despite the fact there will not be an income tax break.

All tax treatments are subject to change and any benefits depend on personal circumstances. If the VCT manager fails to meet the relevant investment rules, the tax benefits could be withdrawn retrospectively.

12. Hedge funds

Alfred W. Jones described a hedge fund as being one which is hedged or protected from risk. In 1949, his company A.W. Jones & Co. launched the first hedge fund. The name is derived from the fact that the hedge-fund manager uses a variety of strategies in order to increase gains and offset any losses by hedging their investments. They are definitively collective investment schemes and are considered alternative investment vehicles.

They are open-ended funds like unit trusts and OEICs; however, there are significant differences and not designed for and marketed to ordinary retail investors. Instead they are appropriate for and tailored to institutional investors and sophisticated investors, as explained within the venture capital trusts section.

They would typically be UHNWI or HNWI individuals with significant assets and income who would have a very good understanding of the strategies employed by the hedge fund manager and the inherent risks and rewards. All investors must fully understand that the fund manager's focus is to achieve absolute returns despite market conditions, and that because the manager employs higher risk strategies in trying to achieve these returns, they could also incur significant losses. Hedge funds offer investors an alternative to traditional investments such as equities, indices and bonds; however, they come with significantly increased risk.

In common with mutual fund managers, hedge fund managers will invest in traditional assets such as bonds, equities and so on. However, there are many significant differences between standard open-ended funds and hedge funds, including:

- a lack of regulation in relation to the hedge fund per se, however, the hedge fund managers themselves will be subject to regulation; and
- as hedge funds are not regulated, fund managers can use a range of securities and strategies in pursuit of absolute returns-strategies which mutual funds are unable to employ.

In their documentation, hedge fund managers will provide potential investors with an indication of the strategies they will employ and the level of gearing the fund will use.

The use of derivative instruments including futures and options which are used not only for hedging but also are used speculatively in order to increase profits. When used speculatively there is often increased risk.

Hedge fund managers leverage (investing with borrowed funds), which may significantly increase returns if the money borrowed is used to buy quality assets. However, if poor assets are purchased instead and interest rates on the borrowed funds increase, this may have an adverse impact on the fund.

Hedge funds are relatively illiquid when contrasted with mutual funds, although shares can be sold back to the fund manager. There is what is referred to as a lock-up period when investors cannot sell their shares at all. However, to reiterate, hedge funds are absolutely open-ended funds as investors are not allowed to sell their shares on the secondary market to other investors; instead they are obliged to sell them back to the fund manager exclusively.

Short selling

Short-selling stock is a very popular strategy employed by hedge fund managers who are willing to take on a potentially substantial risk of capital loss. Short-selling involves the sale of stock that the fund does not own or shares that fund manager borrows.

Fund managers will execute these transactions because they believe a particular share is considerably overvalued and thus the price will fall, usually substantially, and that if the stock were sold today it could be bought back at a lower price at some point in the future. If this is achieved, a profit will be made comprising of the difference between their selling and buying prices. If, however, the share price rises rather than falls, the fund will lose – often substantially.

When fund managers short-sell shares, they are exposing the fund to a potentially large financial risk. In some instances, when other investors and traders become aware that a particular share has a large short interest, meaning a significant percentage of its available shares have been short-sold by speculators, they attempt to force up the share price. This may then force the hedge fund managers with short positions to 'cover' or buy back the shares before the price goes too high, before a large amount of speculation causes massive losses.

Charges

Hedge fund managers are remunerated in a different way from unit trust managers, as the latter receive their remuneration irrespective of how well they perform. By contrast, hedge fund managers are paid based on performance. There is an annual management fee in the region of 2% of the underlying fund assets; additionally there is a performance fee, which may be as much as 20% of the fund's returns. This can be both advantageous and disadvantageous, as the fund manager has to earn his or her money, but may be tempted to take excessive risks in pursuit of maximum returns. This may be good for investors who do not want to pay fees to a poorly performing fund manager.

Summary

Hedge funds are considered to be very high-risk investments. The funds raised from the investors, whether institutional or HNWI together with any borrowed funds, are used to invest into a wide range of underlying assets generally not available to retail investors. The fund managers employ riskier strategies than ordinary mutual fund managers in pursuit of absolute returns, even when markets are falling. They are collective investment schemes that operate without regulation, allowing managers to run a portfolio that other mutual fund managers cannot do because they use leverage, derivative instruments and short-selling. They also use currencies interest rates and borrow multiples of the amount contributed by investors. They are able to borrow up to ten times of the fund to speculate on currency movements. A number of criticisms have been levied at hedge funds in addition to the fee structure, regarding both the lack of regulation and transparency and also the use of short-selling, which many believe is used to manipulate markets. There is also no easy way to determine the level of portfolio risk.

Making it work 9.2: Selling short – nothing new?

Going short of a share is nothing new. Hedge funds that operate in such a manner are trading in a similar way to the jobbers who existed in the LSE before the 'big bang' in 1986, when the LSE still operated a 'two-tier' market.

Under this old system, the LSE was split into brokers and jobbers. Brokers were agents who bought shares from, and sold shares to, jobbers on behalf of their clients. Jobbers were principals who held shares in companies in which they traded and dealt only with brokers.

Jobbers kept a 'book' on each company in which they traded, recording the balance of shares held. They bought and sold shares from and to brokers, and it was not unusual for them to sell shares not held to a broker (for example, to allow the broker to complete an order), taking the view that the shares could be bought back, preferably at a lower price, thereby balancing the 'book'. Jobbers therefore had a short position on their 'book', which they closed when they bought shares in the company they had gone 'short'.

Making it work 9.3: The dangers of short-selling

The dangers of short-selling were proved when, in October 2008, Porsche announced they had increased their stake in Volkswagen to 42.6% of the voting shares, as well as holding cash-settled options on a further 31.5%, giving Porsche a total controlling position of 74.1%.

At the time, it was believed that many hedge fund managers had taken short positions in Volkswagen because they thought the share price would fall. However, when Porsche made their announcement, the share price rose.

The state of Lower Saxony, in Germany where Volkswagen is located, owned a further 20.1%, which left very few free shares in the market for the large number of short-sellers to close their positions by buying shares in the market to balance their books. The result was a further rapid rise in Volkswagen's share price, as demand for shares increased dramatically.

Stop and think 9.3

Do you think hedge funds are suitable investments for all investors?

13. Private equity (PE)

Private equity (PE) investment may be explained as medium to long-term finance (typically four to ten years), provided in return for an equity stake in potentially high growth but importantly unquoted companies. It must be emphasised that while venture capital trusts focus on the provision of finance for start-up and early stage unquoted companies, PE focuses on the provision of funding for mature, already established companies that require funding which will support business growth or restructuring. After their investment period, the PE company will look to sell its stake, either on the stock market, or to another corporate buyer or another investor.

Private equity companies typically support management buyouts and management buy-ins in these unquoted companies. The support is provided through management expertise and a close working relationship between the private equity backer and the company management team.

In contrast with publicly listed companies, which can often have many thousands of shareholders, private equity managers work with a management team to enhance the running of the business. This governance structure leads to much shorter lines of communication between manager and investor, ensuring constant engagement between the two parties.

Active engagement means the private equity manager will work alongside the company management team to enhance the value in the business. This may involve all areas of operation, including procurement marketing and sales. This will also ensure that the business remains committed to providing value and increasing growth even after the PE company has sold its stake.

Private equity firms are often referred to as general partners (GPs) and usually raise money from institutional investors such as pension funds or insurance companies. This money is then invested into a fund structured as a limited partnership (LP) which is managed by the GPs. The capital raised then is used to invest in companies, either to purchase a minority or majority equity stake. GPs will also invest their own money into the funds they manage. This ensures that their own interests are aligned with those of the LP.

Private equity funds typically have a fixed life-span of four to ten years. By the end of a ten-year investment, they will have had to return the investors' original money, plus any additional returns made. This generally requires the investments to be sold, or to be in the form of quoted shares, before the end of the fund.

It is the institutional investors in the funds (limited partners) who first receive any returns generated by a fund. When these returns pass a certain point, known as the 'hurdle rate', the GPs receive a return. In order for GPs to be able to raise funds from LPs successfully, they must demonstrate a track record of delivering good returns from their previous funds.

Making it work 9.4: An example of Private Equity

Sir Richard Branson announced that he was going to move into the private equity world. He was aiming to raise a $500 million fund which would be co-managed with Metric Capital based in London. Metric Capital provides funding for small- to medium-sized European businesses.

Sir Richard will become a partner in the fund which will follow investments in consumer businesses in Europe and the USA, valued at € 2 billion. It will focus on businesses addressing the digitalisation of consumer businesses and those selling experiences rather than physical products. The idea is that the targeted companies would be able to expand more quickly than with an alternative backer. Sir Richard will not only provide advice but also act as a partner.

It is said that when the PE fund eventually sells its assets (stakes in the companies), the fund will donate 10% of its profits to charitable causes.

Test yourself 9.7

a) **What was the purpose behind introducing VCTs?**

b) **What is short-selling?**

c) **What are the two types of private equity structures?**

14. Assessing a collective investment

There are several points an investor should consider before making an investment in a collective product.

14.1 The total expense ratio (TER)

The **total expense ratio (TER)** is a very important figure for investors to know, and it should be the first thing an investor finds out when analysing a fund. The ratio is calculated by adding up all the costs of running a fund including management charges, auditor's fees, custodian fees and dealing charges incurred over a year divided by its asset value at the end of the year. All funds should quote this figure. In the USA, the figure has to be clearly stated. The larger the TER, the more impact it will have on a fund's performance, especially if the investment is held for a long period.

total expense ratio (TER)
The measure of the total cost of managing and operating an investment fund to the investor. It is calculated by dividing the fund's total annual costs by the fund's total asset value for the year and is expressed as a percentage.

The TER does not include costs such as bid/offer spreads, commissions or market impact costs. Open-ended funds usually have a TER of around 1%. This compares with a figure of between 0.5% and 1% for closed-ended funds. Special situations or overseas funds usually have a higher TER due to additional charges like currency, difficulty of obtaining accurate valuations and higher dealing charges. For larger funds, the TER will be lower than smaller, more specialised funds as many of the costs of running funds are fixed costs, which do not depend on size.

Since the RDR, the cost of investing in collective funds has reduced, which means TERs will fall to the benefit of investors. It should be noted that with increased transparency of costs under MiFID II, charges will become lower.

14.2 Fund performance

The performance of a fund is usually the next thing an investor will examine. Taking a long-term view will show how the fund has coped with market fluctuations, and will give an indication of the likely future performance. Three- and five-year performance figures are often given, but 10 and 15 years would be even better. A longer period is often available for closed-ended funds. A number of indicators can be used to assess fund performance.

The share price and NAV movements for closed-ended funds and mid-price movements for open-ended funds can be compared, usually on a graph, against the fund's chosen benchmark index. Other indices such as the FTSE All-Share in the UK can also be used. The dates used in marketing material will be carefully chosen to indicate the best possible performance for a fund, so other time periods against market movements should also to be considered – for example, discrete (individual) year-by-year performance.

Annual reports issued by funds will give plenty of information, much of which is required by law and regulation, including a complete list of the investments held. The annual report will also contain a fairly detailed report by the manager, and, in the case of a company, a view of the likely future performance from the chairman.

For closed-ended funds, an investor can analyse discount/premium and the gearing over a chosen period. Dividend and interest payments can be analysed for yield funds. Total costs under forthcoming legislation of MiFID II will be available for comparison of funds.

14.3 Investment risk

The investment risk associated with investing in a collective investment is normally much lower than investing directly in shares or other investments, because the spread of underlying investments is considered to reduce risk.

The level of risk will increase for investments made in specialist funds or funds with more complicated structures. For example, PE and hedge funds are high-risk funds, but the returns can be very rewarding for the investor who understands them and is prepared and able to take such risks. Venture capital funds are in the same risk category as PE and hedge funds, and likewise returns can be rewarding. Other collective investment products are of lower risk, with closed-ended funds being slightly more risky than open-ended due to the fact that investors are allowed to borrow with the object of enhancing returns.

The use of funds-of-funds investments does reduce the level of risk, especially if an investment is made into the PE or hedge fund sector. Funds of funds with an absolute return objective can be worth the higher charges levied if the fund is successful. Such funds invest in equities, bonds and alternative asset classes, moving the level of exposure between these asset classes depending on market conditions to obtain a positive return.

Whatever investment is made, an investor must understand the risk being taken and be comfortable with it.

14.4 Assessing a fund manager

The performance of a fund often depends on the fund manager. There are four important characteristics that a fund manager should possess:

1. integrity: they do what they say they will do;
2. technical competence;
3. ability to communicate competence and integrity through numbers: that is, good performance compared to the market conditions; and
4. permanence: the length of time a manager has run a fund is important as frequent changes of manager may result in a fund underperforming.

Test yourself 9.8

a) **What ratio is used for the cost comparison of funds?**

b) **How risky is it to invest in a collective investment compared to investing directly in shares or other investments?**

Stop and think 9.4

When considering fund performance, why are marketing dates important?

15. Comparison of open-ended and closed-ended funds

The investment objective of both of these types of products is the same: to spread the risk for an investor across a market or sector using a professional manager. However, these products have built-in difficulties of which the investor should be aware.

Open-ended funds tend to be more expensive to invest into (apart from in the USA), which can have an impact on the investor's return if the fund is held for many years. There is pressure to reduce these costs from new entrants to the market, especially in Europe. Mutual funds, which are numerous in the USA, have a much lower cost structure, and they are starting to appear in Europe. This should be good for investors.

Open-ended funds can only hold a small amount of the fund's total assets in cash as set out in their trust deeds. This is understandable, given that an investor expects their money to be invested and not held in cash. However, this can become a problem in volatile markets when a fund manager is required to invest the money received, even if they believe that market conditions will change and prefer to remain in cash.

Another important point arises with open-ended structures as a result of selling the fund's shareholdings: as a market falls, only the shares that can be sold easily (that is, the more liquid shares) are sold. The manager is then left with a portfolio of shares difficult to deal in, and when markets recover, they will require a lot of skill to start the fund performing again. This situation arose following the 1987 stock market crash and has been a feature of the recovery from the crisis that started in 2007.

Another example of this effect is open-ended property funds, where the underlying investments (buildings) can be difficult to sell because of prevailing conditions in the property market; investors wishing to withdraw from their investment may have to wait several months or years. An investor waiting for an asset sale in such circumstances may very well sell at the bottom of the market and not only suffer a loss but also then watch the fund recover as confidence returns to the property market. This happened in the early 1990s.

Closed-ended funds can also have their problems during a recession, often due to their level of borrowing. However, many closed-ended funds like ITCs held a high percentage of cash during 2008, having sold some of their more vulnerable assets early in the credit crisis. For example, one fund (the Personal Assets Trust) was 100% cash at the start of the credit crisis. This flexibility allows ITCs to survive over difficult periods, which explains why some in the UK are over 50 or even 100 years old.

Another problem for ITCs in a recession is discount to net asset value. As markets fall and the asset value drops, investors sell, and prices fall quite dramatically, resulting in an increase in the discount. However, even shares in specialised ITCs can still be sold even if the price obtained is low. The size may be small and the price may not be great, but at least an investor is not locked in, as would be the case for open-ended property investors. Fund managers of ITCs do not need to sell good investments at a depressed level in a recession. Investors benefit when recovery comes and the fund performs because it has kept its quality investments.

Despite these difficulties, collective investments remain a positive investment choice for:

- smalls investor saving monthly through a saving scheme linked to either an open-ended or closed-ended product;
- high net worth individuals (HNWIs) investing through the stock market into a closed-ended product with exposure to specialised markets;
- long-term investors in ITCs; and
- ETFs.

HNWIs are also major investors in PE and hedge funds.

Test yourself 9.9

a) Outline the built-in difficulties in open-ended and closed-ended funds.

b) What problems do open-ended funds suffer from in a recession?

Chapter summary

- There are two main types of collective investment schemes (CISs): open-ended and closed-ended.
- By using a CIS, the investor pays for a manager's investment knowledge and skill through charges associated with a product.
- In the EU, open-ended CISs are governed by the EC directive that introduced the law for Undertakings for Collective Investment in Transferable Securities (UCITS). In the UK they are governed by the Retail Distribution Review (RDR).
- The two most common open-ended investment structures in the UK are unit trusts (similar to mutual funds in the USA) and open-ended investment companies (OEICs). Non-UCITS/OEICs/UT investment are governed by the AIFMD.
- Investment trust companies (ITCs) are closed-ended investment funds. They are quoted companies that invest in a range of shares in other quoted companies. Because ITCs generally have a fixed capital structure, managers can take a long-term view as to the types of assets that the fund will hold.
- Split capital trusts (SCTs) are a type of ITC that normally have a specified life and a share structure that is 'split' between income and capital shares.

- Real estate investment trusts (REITs) enable investors to have exposure to property without having to purchase property directly.
- Exchange-traded funds (ETFs) are a collective investment of shares where the underlying portfolio mirrors a specific index or sector.
- Venture capital trusts (VCTs) are closed-ended companies that are listed on the LSE. They allow investors to spread their investment across a portfolio of small companies, and thereby reduce the risk of investing directly into start-up companies.
- A hedge fund is a fund that invests in a range of investments with the objective of obtaining an absolute return for its investors. Hedge funds are often accused of manipulating markets by the practice of short-selling.
- PE is focused on the provision of funding for mature, already established companies that require funding which will support business growth or restructuring. After their investment period, the PE company will look to sell its stake, either on the stock market, or to another corporate buyer or another investor. Private equity companies typically support management buyouts and managing buy-ins in unquoted companies.
- When assessing CISs, investors should take into account costs calculated under MiFID II rules or the total expense ratio (TER), fund performance and their own feelings about risk.

Test yourself answers

Test yourself 9.1

a) Investors may have different reasons for investing in such products, but there are several points on which they will tend to agree. In particular, they wish to have a spread of investments:

- in a particular sector of markets (for example, small companies or geographical locations);
- to reduce risk through exposure to a spread of companies or sectors; or
- to benefit from the manager's research of particular markets.

b) The Product Directive allows funds to invest in a wide range of financial instruments including money funds, derivative funds, index-tracking funds and funds of funds.

Test yourself 9.2

UK investors are more aware of open-ended investment structures as these funds run regular advertising campaigns through their management house, making investors more likely to choose to invest in them.

Test yourself 9.3

a) European equivalents of OEICs are:

- an investment company with variable capital (ICVC);
- Sociétés d'Investissement à Capital Variable (SICAVs);
- Fonds Commun de Placement (FCPs); and
- The Irish Common Contractual Fund (CCF).

b) Fund supermarkets were established towards the end of 1990s to enable investors who wished to choose their own open-ended fund to invest without paying the full initial fees. Investing in this way has several other advantages.

- Less paperwork is involved if investments are made in different managers' funds.
- The investor is able to obtain an overview of their funds held in their portfolio easily.
- Most fund supermarkets have online dealing facilities, so the investor can change their portfolio holdings easily.

Test yourself 9.4

a) Investment trust companies (ITCs), sometimes known as investment trusts or investment companies, are closed-ended investment funds and not trusts at all. They are in fact quoted companies that invest in a range of shares and other securities in other quoted companies. They are governed by the Companies Act in the UK, the AIFMD in the EU and similar company legislation in countries around the world that support closed-ended quoted collective investment companies.

b) A total return is the growth in value of an ITC over the years, plus the amount of dividends paid.

c) When new C share issues are undertaken by ITCs, it is usual to issue warrants at the same time. A warrant is an equity instrument that allows the holder to convert the warrant into an ordinary share at a predetermined price fixed at issue on a specific date or dates in the future.

Test yourself 9.5

a) The simplest SCT capital structure is made up of:

- ordinary income shares;
- capital shares; and
- zero dividend preference shares (ZDPs, also called 'zeros') which, as the name implies, pay no income.

b) There are two reasons for the popularity of SCTs over the years.

- *1. Taxation of income:* Most countries levy a higher rate of tax on income compared to capital gains, and some also increase that level if the income is unearned. If a high-rate taxpayer invests in shares that pay no income – zero dividend preference (ZDP) shares – they are likely to receive a larger overall return on their investment as this class of share is normally subject to capital gains tax (CGT) rather than income tax. Well-covered ZDP shares are potentially a very attractive investment to high-rate taxpaying investors, whether they are resident in the UK or overseas.

- *2. Distribution of income:* Both ITCs and SCTs are required to distribute 85% of income to shareholders. An ITC pays a dividend to all its shareholders, whereas an SCT only pays a dividend to the income shareholders and not to the capital or ZDP shareholders. If an ITC and an SCT of the same size (market capitalisation) received the same amount of income from their investments, then income shareholders in the SCT would share a greater amount than the ordinary shareholders of the ITC (ZDPs and capital shareholders do not receive any income). This makes income shares in a SCT more attractive to investors, like pension funds, which require an income.

Test yourself 9.6

a) REITs enable investors to have exposure to property without having to purchase property directly. It is also far easier to buy or sell shares in a REIT than physical property, making REITs an attractive investment within a portfolio.

b) ETFs are popular with private investors in the USA and Europe because the cost of investing is low, and the buying or selling price is near to the value of the underlying assets.

Test yourself 9.7

a) Venture capital trusts (VCTs) were launched in the UK in 1995 to attract investment into small high-risk unquoted UK companies. The government believed that introducing VCTs would help raise money for start-up and early stage investment in companies. As well as unquoted companies, AIM-traded companies are also available for investment through a VCT.

b) Short selling is the sale of a security that is not owned by the seller or that the seller has borrowed.

c) The two types of private equity structure are limited partnerships and PE (private equity) investment companies.

Test yourself 9.8

a) The total expense ratio (TER) is the ratio used for the cost comparison of funds.

b) The investment risk associated with investing in a collective investment is normally much lower than investing directly in shares or other investments, because the spread of underlying investments is considered to reduce risk. However, the level of risk will increase for investments made in specialist funds or funds with more complicated structures such as PE (private equity), hedge and venture-capital funds. Other collective investment products are of lower risk with closed-ended funds being slightly more risky than open-ended, due to the fact that they are allowed to borrow with the object of enhancing returns.

Test yourself 9.9

a) Open-ended funds tend to be more expensive to invest into (apart from in the USA), which can have an impact on the investor's return if the fund is held for many years. There is pressure to reduce these costs from new entrants to the market, especially in Europe. Mutual funds, which are numerous in the USA, have a much lower cost structure, and they are starting to appear in Europe. This should be good for investors.

Open-ended funds can only hold a small amount of the fund's total assets in cash as set out in their Trust Deeds. This is understandable given that an investor expects their money to be invested and not held in cash. However, this can become a problem in volatile markets when a fund manager is required to invest the money received even if they believe that market conditions will change and prefer to remain in cash.

Closed-ended funds can also have their problems during a recession, often due to their level of borrowing. However, many closed-ended funds like ITCs held a high percentage of cash during 2008, having sold some of their more vulnerable assets early in the credit crisis. For example, one fund (the Personal Assets Trust) was 100% cash at the start of the credit crisis. This flexibility allows ITCs to survive over difficult periods, which explains why some in the UK are over 50 or even 100 years old.

Another problem for ITCs in a recession is discount to net asset value. As markets fall and the asset value drops, investors sell, and prices fall quite dramatically, resulting in an increase in the discount. However, even shares in specialised ITCs can still be sold even if the price obtained is low. The size may be small and the price may not be great, but at least an investor is not locked in, as would be the case for open-ended property investors (see above). Fund managers of ITCs do not need to sell good investments at a depressed level in a recession. Investors benefit when recovery comes and the fund performs because it has kept its quality investments.

b) Another important point arises with open-ended structures as a result of selling the fund's shareholdings: as a market falls, only the shares that can be sold easily (that is, the more liquid shares) are sold. The manager is then left with a portfolio of shares difficult to deal in, and when markets recover, they will require a lot of skill to start the fund performing again. This situation arose following the 1987 stock market crash and has been a feature of the recovery from the crisis that started in 2007.

Another example of this effect is open-ended property funds, where the underlying investments (buildings) can be difficult to sell because of prevailing conditions in the property market; investors wishing to withdraw from their investment may have to wait several months or years. An investor waiting for an asset sale in such circumstances may very well sell at the bottom of the market and not only suffer a loss, but also then watch the fund recover as confidence returns to the property market. This happened in the early 1990s.

Glossary

Accrued interest Interest accumulated since the payment of the last coupon.

Acid-test ratio The ratio of current assets (minus inventory) to current liabilities.

Actuary A statistician who computes insurance risks and premiums.

Algorithmic trading A type of trading based on the use of mathematical formulae which are designed to replicate and speed up the human decision processes that would normally be used to decide trading strategies.

Arbitrage The simultaneous buying and selling of investments in different markets in order to take advantage of differing prices for the same asset.

Articles of association The internal rules of a company covering what has to be done, the roles and responsibilities of the company directors, and the positions required to perform their relevant duties.

Asset Something of value (to its owner). However, if sold, the price obtained will only be the amount a buyer is willing to pay for the asset.

Balance of trade Part of a country's balance of payments that relates to the value of goods and services imported and exported.

Bank basis A convention where interest rates are based on a 365-day year in the case of sterling and Japanese yen, whereas a 360-day year is used for US dollars and many other currencies.

Best execution Occurs when a trade of a particular size is transacted at the best available price and cost in the market at the time of the trade.

Bid price (bonds) The same as the buying price, which will be paid to a bondholder in exchange for a bond.

Bond A contract to repay borrowed money and interest at regular intervals during the life of the bond (similar to a loan).

Building societies Mutual associations largely dedicated to home-mortgage finance. They are broadly similar to savings and loans associations in the US. Since the Building Societies Act 1986, various (but not all) societies converted to banks, and offer services such as current accounts.

Business cycle Also known as the economic cycle. The period of time over which an economy moves from an expansion phase to a contraction phase and back again.

Call options Provide the holder with the right (without obligation) to buy an underlying asset.

Call protection A period of time after a callable bond has been issued during which it will not be 'called'. This is to afford the investor a certain degree of protection.

Callable bond A bond which has the potential to be 'called' by its issuer under certain circumstances which are advantageous to that issuer (contrast with 'puttable' bonds).

Capital return What is returned to the investor at the end of the predetermined investment period or when the asset is sold.

Capital structure The manner by which a company is financed, by using share capital, debt capital or both.

Carry trade An FX strategy where investors hope to profit from interest rate differentials (IRD) between currencies.

Central counterparty (CCP) A dealing system used in stock markets where deals are settled with a single party rather than between investors, thereby reducing settlement risk.

Central Government Net Cash Requirement (CGNCR) This is the measurement of the annual cash requirements of central government. It is essentially the difference between central government's income and expenditure in cash terms.

Certificates of deposit (CDs) Fully negotiable short-term MMIs which are, in effect, acknowledgements of indebtedness issued by banks and other financial organisations to other institutional investors. Unlike T-bills and CP, CDs are not issued at a discount but rather have coupons.

Clean price In relation to bonds, this is the price without taking into account the accrued interest since the last coupon payment.

Clearing houses Places or institutions where mutual claims and accounts are settled, as between banks.

Closed-ended fund A collective investment scheme with a limited number of shares quoted on a stock market.

Collective investment scheme (CIS) An arrangement that enables a number of investors to 'pool' their assets and have these professionally managed by an independent manager.

Commercial paper (CP) Often nicknamed 'corporate IOUs' and used by large companies as a cheaper alternative method to bank borrowing. It is issued as a method of raising short-term unsecured finance. CP has fixed maturities between 1 and 270 days.

Companies House The UK registrar of those companies incorporated in the United Kingdom. It is an executive agency of the Department for Business, Innovation and Skills.

Computershare A privately owned plc having the responsibility for both maintaining the register of gilt holdings and for the administration of the

DMO's gilt purchase and sale service. It also performs this service for a considerable number of equities. There are a small number of bearer gilts that are not registered.

Constitutional document Documents required for the foundation of a business.

Conventional gilts Gilts where both the principal repayments and coupons are fixed in nominal terms.

Corporate bond A fixed-term contractual agreement between a company and a bond holder. The capital will be returned after a specified period with the company making regular interest or coupon payments to the bond holder.

Counterparty A party to a contract.

Coupon The total amount of annual interest (which is usually split into two equal semi-annual payments). This coupon will be expressed as a fixed percentage of the nominal amount.

Covered option (*see also* **naked options**) An option is written by a writer who already owns the underlying asset on which the option is based. Thus the writer protects himself from adverse price movements.

Covered warrants Similar derivative instruments to 'ordinary' warrants. However, they differ in that they are issued by third parties rather than the original share-issuing company.

CREST The electronic settlement system for gilts, equities and other corporate securities in the United Kingdom.

Cum dividend The purchaser of a bond or gilt 'cum dividend' is entitled to receive interest accrued since the payment of the previous coupon.

Currency futures contracts Exchange-traded derivative products traded in exactly the same manner as ordinary futures contracts. However, they are based on foreign currencies rather than commodities or indices.

Currency swaps Financial instruments sometimes referred to as cross-currency swaps. They are contractual agreements between two parties swapping principal and fixed interest in one currency for principal and fixed interest in another currency. They are not derivative instruments.

Current ratio The ratio of current assets (including inventory) to current liabilities.

Dark pool A type of electronic trading venue that allows big institutions to execute large trades away from an exchange's normal public, or 'displayed', order book.

Debenture Fixed-term borrowings of a company carrying a fixed rate of interest which must be paid to the debenture holders. Debentures may or may not be made under seal.

Debt capital The percentage of debt contained within a company's capital structure. This may include debentures and long-term bank borrowings.

Defined benefit (DB) pension A pension plan that commits to paying a specified amount to each employee on retirement, depending on the number of years of work and salary level. The commitment to pay the specified amount rests with the employer.

Defined contribution (DC) pension A pension plan for which contribution amounts are specified. On retirement the amount received by the employee depends on how much has been invested and how the fund has performed. The liability for ensuring the amount generated will meet with the requirements of the employee in retirement rests with the employee.

Deflation A sustained fall in the prices of goods and services.

Derivative funds A fund of financial instruments. A financial instrument is an asset having a monetary value or recording a monetary transaction (for example, an option or futures contract).

Derivatives Financial instruments, the prices of which are based on (derived from) the prices of different classes of underlying asset. Derivatives may be traded on exchanges, as in the cases of futures, or alternatively may be OTC products, as is the case with interest rate swaps.

Directors' report A report provided by the directors of a company which is intended to provide all stakeholders with explanations and interpretations of the figures contained within the statement of comprehensive income and other matters of significance.

Dirty price This is the clean price of a gilt plus accrued interest since the last coupon payment.

Dividend A distribution made by a company to its shareholders, normally paid twice a year.

Dividend cover A shareholder ratio which shows how many times the ordinary share dividend is covered by the net profits after tax.

Dividend payments These are usually made in twice-yearly instalments (the interim dividend and the final dividend) to the ordinary shareholders of a company and are usually made out of profits.

Dividend yield (DY) A shareholder ratio which indicates the percentage of its earnings a company's directors are prepared to pay out to shareholders from excess revenue. Most significantly it represents the current year's return on the shareholders' investment.

Double-dated gilts Gilts having two redemption dates. The UK government has the option to redeem the gilts anywhere between the two specified dates. It is assumed that gilts will be redeemed on the earlier date if not specified.

Earnings per share (EPS) The amount of net profit attributable to each single issued ordinary share after deductions including interest, tax, preference share dividends and any minority interests.

Endowment policy A life insurance contract also known as an assurance contract which pays a lump sum on maturity (after a specific term of years) or death.

Equities Shares in a quoted company.

Equity capital This is the percentage of a company's capital structure which is financed by share capital. This would include both ordinary and preference shares.

Eurobond A bond which is issued and traded outside the jurisdiction of the country whose currency the bond is denominated.

Euroclear A multi-currency settlement system for European securities where securities are held in dematerialised (non-paper) form.

Exchange-traded funds Listed funds that usually track an index comprising of the underlying stock which make up the index or use derivatives to achieve the same returns as the index. They are used to track the value of assets generally, including commodities such as gold.

Ex-dividend period This is a period of seven business days prior to coupon payment date. A seller of a bond within the ex-dividend period will receive the entire future interest payment but effectively pays back a portion to the purchaser by receiving a lower amount for the bond. A purchaser of a bond will not have entitlement to the forthcoming coupon payment.

Financial instrument A document that has a monetary value.

Fixed charge This means that identifiable assets are used to secure the bond and can be sold to repay the debenture bondholders in the event of a default.

Fixed-interest securities Invested products that usually have a fixed rate of return. There are some exceptions.

Flat yield The gross annual coupon expressed as a percentage of the nominal amount.

Floating charge This is secured against a range of assets determined by the company which crystallises in the event of a default.

Flotation The selling of some or all of the shares in a company which is being brought to market for the first time on a recognised investment exchange.

Formula asset value In this context, the calculation used for the merger of an ITC's ordinary and 'C' shares, based on the net asset values of the separate portfolios within the fund at the agreed merger date.

Fund supermarket Often a website or brokerage firm which aims to provide an alternative and more convenient way of investing in collective investment schemes.

Funds of funds (FOF) An investment strategy of holding a portfolio of other investment funds rather than investing directly in shares, bonds or other securities. This type of investing is referred to as multi-manager investment.

Fungible Interchangeable and not able to be told apart (such as £10 notes). Fungible securities of the same class are therefore interchangeable and indistinguishable.

Futures Legally binding, standardised forward contracts between two parties (a buyer and a seller) to either buy or sell a predetermined quantity of a specified asset (commodity or financial asset) of a specific quality requiring the delivery of that specified asset on a fixed future date, the price of which will be agreed today by both the buyer and seller.

Gearing or leverage The use of a resource, often borrowed funds or debt, in a way that the potential positive or negative outcome is enhanced. The objective is to increase a return substantially.

Gilt-edged market makers (GEMMs) These are firms that have been recognised by the DMO as primary dealers in conventional gilts. There are also IL GEMMs specialising in index-linked gilts. They are prepared to make prices (at all times the market is open) to investors.

Gilts UK government bonds.

Gross redemption yield (GRY) The interest yield adjusted to take in to account gains or losses to redemption.

Hedgers Investors who attempt to reduce or eliminate risks within their existing portfolio by taking counterbalancing action.

High net worth individual (HNWI) A classification used by the financial services industry to denote an individual or a family with high net worth. The figure associated with high net worth of liquid financial assets (after property assets) is $1m.

Hybrid company A cross between a company with a share capital and a company limited by guarantee.

Hyperinflation Very rapid inflation that leads to a complete loss of confidence in the sustainable purchasing power of a country's currency. It can lead to economic collapse.

Index-linked bonds These are government-issued bonds which ensure that an investor receives a return greater than the rate of inflation for the life of the bond.

Index-linked gilts Gilts where both coupons and the final redemption payment are related to movements in the retail prices index. IGs should extinguish the impact of inflation.

Index-tracking/tracker funds A collective investment scheme in the form of a mutual fund or exchange-traded fund that aims to replicate the movements of an index of a specific financial market regardless of market conditions.

Inflation A rise in the general price level of goods and services. Often measured over a 12-month period.

Interbank deposits The simplest and most liquid of all MMIs which are available for varying maturities. The majority of interbank deposits are for three months or less. They are unsecured and are usually for a minimum amount of £500,000.

Inter-dealer brokers (IDBs) Firms authorised by the DMO and LSE providing facilities for dealing in gilts exclusively between GEMMs.

Interest The cost of borrowing money. Also, the sum of money earned from lending or putting it on deposit.

Interest rate swap A contractual agreement between two counterparties where one agrees to swap with the other a stream of fixed-interest payments (cash flows) in return for a stream of floating-rate interest payments. Both interest streams are based on the same notional (hypothetical) amount over a specific period.

Interest rates An interest rate is the charge made for a loan/paid on a deposit; interest rates are usually expressed in terms of percentage per year.

Interest yield The yield based on the actual price paid by the purchaser rather than the nominal amount.

Intermediation The process of moving funds between savers and borrowers in return for interest paid by a borrower to an intermediary, such as a bank, who in turn pays interest at a lower level to the saver.

Interoperability The ability of different (trading) systems to work together.

Intrinsic value An inner value, a value contained within.

Introduction A method whereby an unlisted company can obtain a stock exchange listing without raising any capital or issuing shares. It would be used where the shares of a company are already widely held in the public domain. It is a marketing operation and would be used where there will be a guaranteed secondary market.

Investment Forgoing the use of money now to receive more money later.

Investment company A company whose main business is holding securities of other companies purely for investment purposes.

Irredeemable bonds Bonds which may be redeemed at the discretion of the issuer but for which no redemption date has actually been specified.

Leveraged buy-out This happens when the existing management of a company acquires a controlling interest in that company using external capital.

Liquidation The process whereby a company is 'liquidated' (where its assets are turned into cash). Liquidation may be voluntary or involuntary (as in the case of bankruptcy). Assets will be sold, liabilities paid and any balance returned to the equity holders. There is a statutory order of pay out.

Liquidity The flow of cash from depositors to banks and from banks to borrowers.

Market makers Organisations, usually investment banks or stockbrokers, that stand ready to make markets in particular securities. They buy and sell the securities on their own behalf and will always have a bid and offer price available.

Markets in Financial Instruments Directive (MiFID) A European Union law that provides harmonised regulation for investment services across the 30 member states of the European Economic Area.

Maturity date The same as the redemption date. The date when the bond is redeemed and cancelled. The bond holder will receive the principal amount from the issuer.

Maturity mismatch When a bank or institution has substantial long-term assets like fixed-rate mortgages but short-term liabilities such as deposits. This can be measured by a duration gap which calculates risk due to changes in interest rates.

Maturity transformation An acceptance by an institution of short-term deposits which are lent out on a different basis, usually long term.

Money supply The total amount of cash (notes and coins) in circulation, bank deposits and other forms of near money savings. There are various measures of money supply which include varying degrees of the above.

Money-market instruments Short-term low-risk financial instruments such as commercial paper, Treasury Bills and certificates of deposit (CDs).

Mortgage loan A loan provided by a financial institution such as a bank secured against a property or other real estate.

Multilateral trading facility (MTF) An alternative trading venue to existing exchanges which does not have a listing process. MTFs require a rule book, trade transparency and an accessible notice of prices and charges. The legal status of MTFs was defined by MiFID.

Multiplier effect A tool used by governments to stimulate aggregate demand by using money to create jobs.

Mutual fund An investment vehicle that is made up of a pool of funds collected from many investors for the purpose of investing in securities on their behalf by a manager and structured to match the investment objectives as stated in the prospectus.

Naked (uncovered) option Where a call option is written without the writer actually owning the underlying assets upon which the option is derived.

Net asset value The total value of an investment trust company's assets minus the total value of its liabilities. Usually expressed on a per share basis.

New issues The issuing of new securities, either for a company coming to the market for the first time or as a rights issue for an already-listed company in order to raise additional capital.

Nil paid Under a rights issue, existing shareholders are given rights to subscribe for new shares at a specific price. The rights themselves become fully tradable securities. As the existing shareholders have paid nothing for these rights, they are referred to as nil paid.

Nominal amount An amount similar to par value or principal amount. The amount which must be returned at maturity or on which coupon or interest payments are based.

Nominal value A stated unit amount. In the UK bonds are issue in multiples of £100 nominal.

Offer for sale A method by which a company can raise capital via a new issue. This method usually involves an issuing house who will buy the securities and then sell them at a slightly higher price to the general public.

Offer for subscription An offer of shares to the general public and institutional investors alike. Shares are offered directly to the public without using an issuing house. The public may apply for shares, offered by the company, at a fixed price or alternatively will be invited to tender.

Open-ended fund A collective investment scheme which can issue and redeem shares at any time (unless stock market conditions prevent this happening). An investor will generally purchase or sell shares (redeem) in the fund directly from the fund itself rather than existing shareholders.

Options Standardised derivative contracts purchased by a holder (the purchaser) from a writer (the seller) or third parties which give the holder the right (without any obligation) either to buy or to sell standard quantities of an underlying asset on or before a specified fixed future date.

Passporting The practice where collective investment funds may be marketed by their management house across European Economic Area (EEA) states without having to separately 'set up' the fund in each state. It also allows investment firms to set up offices in other EEA member states and conduct cross-border business without the need for separate licensing in each jurisdiction.

Price/earnings ratio (PER) An indicator of how many years' earnings (at the current level) can be purchased with one ordinary share purchased at the current market price of that same share.

Primary market Where bonds are issued for the first time. In the gilts market this would be the issuance by the DMO through its auctions.

Prospectus A document which sets out in accordance with legislation the terms and constitution of a company which is applying for its shares to be issued on a recognised stock exchange.

Put options Provide the holder with the right (without obligation) to sell an underlying asset.

Quantitative easing (QE) An instrument a central bank uses to bring down interest rates for companies and households by creating money in the economy.

Ratio The quantitative relationship between two numbers which indicates the number of times one number either contains or alternatively is contained by the other number.

Recapitalisation Occurs when a company changes its capital structure.

Recognised investment exchange An investment exchange that has been approved by the UK's FCA.

Redemption date The same as the maturity date, the date when the bond is redeemed.

Reserve account An account or accounts comprising funds set aside for specific purposes such as the purchase of capital equipment.

Reverse yield gap The difference when the yield on government bonds is greater that the yield on equities.

Right of pre-emption The legal right of existing shareholders to subscribe, prior to general release, for new equity capital of the same class or any class of security (warrants and convertible loan stock), which may potentially have a diluting effect on their percentage shareholding. This would include rights issues.

Rights issue A method by which a company can obtain additional capital (cash) by selling new shares. Rights issues give the right to existing shareholders to subscribe for new shares in a company in direct proportion to their existing holding. Allocations are made in the form of a rights letter.

Rump gilts Gilts where there is a relatively small amount outstanding in terms of nominal value. GEMMs are not required to make a market in rumps but the DMO will make a bid price if it is requested to by a GEMM.

Savings Money that is not spent.

Scrip issues These increase the number of shares in circulation by reducing the price of the shares in direct proportion. There is no dilution of a shareholder's current percentage holding. This is a process to make shares which appear expensive more marketable.

Secondary market The market for second-hand securities. Securities are bought and sold between investors rather than the original issuer. The securities must have been issued in the primary market first.

Securitise Make a package of loans into a tradable investment.

Separate Trading of Registered Interest and Principal Securities (STRIPS) This is where the gilts are 'strippable', allowing the coupons and principal to be traded separately.

Share A unit of ownership of a company, also known as stock.

Shareholders The owners of a company.

Speculators Investors who make profits from price volatility (frequent changes).

Spot FX contract A binding obligation between two parties where one party agrees to sell a currency to another party in exchange for another currency. The deal is immediate with the exchange of the currencies taking place on T+2 (transaction day plus two working days).

Spread A range of selling and buying prices. The selling price will be shown on the left-hand side of the range and the buying price on the right-hand side.

Standardised options 'Standardised' refers to a situation where the specifications contained within any one contract will not vary from those specifications contained within any other contract in relation to the same underlying asset.

Statement of comprehensive income The account which indicates whether a business made a profit or loss in a given period.

Statement of financial position A snapshot of a company's account balances – both assets and liabilities – shown at a given date.

Stock split (or share split) A corporate action where a company issues additional shares to existing shareholders. There is a reduction in the nominal value of each share in direct proportion to the increase in number of additional shares issued.

Sub-prime Residential mortgages issued to high-risk borrowers.

Swap bank A bank which is either directly or indirectly involved in a currency swap. If directly involved, it will be the counterparty to the swap. If indirectly involved, it will facilitate the relevant aspects of the currency swaps between corporate counterparties.

Systematic internalisers These are investment firms which 'match', 'buy' and 'sell' orders they receive from clients in house, rather than placing orders with a central exchange.

Time value The option premium price less intrinsic value

Total expense ratio (TER) The measure of the total cost of managing and operating an investment fund to the investor. It is calculated by dividing the fund's total annual costs by the fund's total asset value for the year and is expressed as a percentage.

Transferable securities Classes of investments which are negotiable on share exchanges or other dealing platforms. Shares and bonds fall into this category.

Treasury Bills (T-Bills) Registered, redeemable and unconditional short-term (less than one year) obligations of a government issued by a central bank at a discount to face value. They are used to finance a government's short-term funding requirements.

Trust A structure whereby the legal title of assets is transferred by an individual (settlor) to trustees for the benefit of third-party beneficiaries. The trustees will look after the assets for the benefit of the third-party beneficiaries with the settlor sacrificing all control of the assets. Trusts are mainly used as tax-planning tools and for succession planning.

UCITS A set of European Union directives for collective investment funds available throughout the European Economic Area on the basis of a single authorisation in the fund manager's state.

Undated gilts Gilts that do not have a redemption date. They are sometimes referred to as 'irredeemables' or perpetual gilts. However, should the government wish to do so, it may redeem them.

Underlying (asset) Assets upon which derivative instruments are based.

Unit trusts This is a collective form of investment constituted under a trust deed. It is an open-ended investment fund. Open-ended means that the size of the fund is dependent on the number of units in issue as well as their value. In the UK, most unit trusts have converted to OECIS. In the US, they are known as mutual funds.

Unquoted company A company whose shares are not quoted on a stock exchange. The trading of shares in a unquoted company is normally covered by the company's formation documents as governed by company law.

Warrant A security that entitles the holder to buy shares in the issuing company at a specified time and price.

Wind-up date The date, often predetermined, when a company or class of share is liquidated and shareholders receive the net proceeds.

Writer This is the original seller of an options contract providing the purchaser with a right without any obligation to buy or sell an underlying asset.

Yield The income generated on an annual basis expressed as a percentage of the purchase price.

Yield gap The difference between the yield on long-term government bonds and the dividend yield on equities.

Zero dividend preference shares (ZDPs) Also known as zeros, ZDPs are preference shares that do not pay any dividend.

Directory of web resources

General

Association of Investment Companies
www.theaic.co.uk

BATS
www.batstrading.com

Bloomberg
www.bloomberg.com

Chartered Institute for Securities and Investment
www.cisi.org

Companies House
www.companieshouse.gov.uk

Deutsche Börse Group
www.deutsche-boerse.com

Euroclear
www.euroclear.com

Euronext
www.euronext.com

European Commission
ec.europa.eu/index_en.htm

FE InvestEgate
www.investegate.co.uk

FE Trustnet
www.trustnet.com

Financial Conduct Authority (FCA)
www.fca.org.uk

Financial Stability Board
www.financialstabilityboard.org

Financial Times
www.ft.com

Information Commissioner's Office
www.ico.gov.uk

Institute of Chartered Secretaries and Administrators (ICSA)
www.icsa.org.uk

Intercontinental Exchange
www.theice.com

International Organization of Securities Commissions
www.iosco.org

Investment Management Association
www.investmentuk.org

Investor Chronicle
www.investorschronicle.co.uk

Legislation.gov.uk (The National Archives)
www.legislation.gov.uk

London Stock Exchange
www.londonstockexchange.com

MarketWatch (Wall Street Journal)
www.marketwatch.com

Money Week
www.moneyweek.com

Motley Fool (online investment community)
www.fool.co.uk

NASDAQ OMX
www.nasdaqomx.com

National Crime Agency (NCA)
www.nationalcrimeagency.gov.uk

New York Stock Exchange
www.nyse.com

New York Times
www.nytimes.com

Reuters
www.reuters.com

Selftrade
www.selftrade.co.uk

Serious Fraud Office
www.sfo.gov.uk

The City UK
www.thecityuk.com

The Economist
www.economist.com

Tokyo Stock Exchange
www.tse.or.jp/english/about

UK Debt Management Office
www.dmo.gov.uk

US Federal Reserve Board
www.federalreserve.gov

US Securities and Exchange Commission
www.sec.gov

Wall Street Journal Europe
www.online.wsj.com/europe

GEMMs

Barclays Capital
www.barcap.com

Citigroup Global Markets Ltd
www.citigroup.com

Goldman Sachs International Ltd
www.gs.com

Santander Global Banking and Markets
www.santandergbm.com

Winterflood Securities
www.winterflood.co.uk

Inter-dealer brokers

BGC Brokers LP
www.bgcpartners.com

Dowgate
www.dowgatecapitalstockbrokers.co.uk

ICAP Electronic Broking Ltd
www.icap.com

Tullet Prebon Gilts
www.tullettprebon.com

Credit ratings agencies

Moody's
www.moodys.com

Standard and Poor's (S&P)
www.standardandpoors.com

Index

www.ingramcontent.com/pod-product-compliance
Ingram Content Group UK Ltd.
Pitfield, Milton Keynes, MK11 3LW, UK
UKHW051928100926
8556IPUK00022B/1438

9 781860 72735